CU00941773

Forensic Intelligence

To Roger

from Robert Milne

with best wishes

12/9/2014 on the QM2.

Forensic Intelligence

Robert Milne

CRC Press
Taylor & Francis Group
Boca Raton   London   New York

CRC Press is an imprint of the
Taylor & Francis Group, an **informa** business

CRC Press
Taylor & Francis Group
6000 Broken Sound Parkway NW, Suite 300
Boca Raton, FL 33487-2742

© 2013 by Taylor & Francis Group, LLC
CRC Press is an imprint of Taylor & Francis Group, an Informa business

No claim to original U.S. Government works

Printed in the United States of America on acid-free paper
Version Date: 20120409

International Standard Book Number: 978-1-4398-6038-0 (Hardback)

This book contains information obtained from authentic and highly regarded sources. Reasonable efforts have been made to publish reliable data and information, but the author and publisher cannot assume responsibility for the validity of all materials or the consequences of their use. The authors and publishers have attempted to trace the copyright holders of all material reproduced in this publication and apologize to copyright holders if permission to publish in this form has not been obtained. If any copyright material has not been acknowledged please write and let us know so we may rectify in any future reprint.

Except as permitted under U.S. Copyright Law, no part of this book may be reprinted, reproduced, transmitted, or utilized in any form by any electronic, mechanical, or other means, now known or hereafter invented, including photocopying, microfilming, and recording, or in any information storage or retrieval system, without written permission from the publishers.

For permission to photocopy or use material electronically from this work, please access www.copyright. com (http://www.copyright.com/) or contact the Copyright Clearance Center, Inc. (CCC), 222 Rosewood Drive, Danvers, MA 01923, 978-750-8400. CCC is a not-for-profit organization that provides licenses and registration for a variety of users. For organizations that have been granted a photocopy license by the CCC, a separate system of payment has been arranged.

Trademark Notice: Product or corporate names may be trademarks or registered trademarks, and are used only for identification and explanation without intent to infringe.

Library of Congress Cataloging-in-Publication Data

Milne, Robert.
    Forensic intelligence / Robert Milne.
        p. cm.
    Includes bibliographical references and index.
    ISBN 978-1-4398-6038-0 (alk. paper)
    1. Criminal investigations. 2. Forensic sciences. I. Title.

HV8073.M563 2012
363.25--dc23   2012009749

Visit the Taylor & Francis Web site at
http://www.taylorandfrancis.com

and the CRC Press Web site at
http://www.crcpress.com

I wish to dedicate this book with love to my wife, Lesley. Without her help and support, I would not have been able to complete this work.

Contents

**2   The Value of Forensics in Crime Analysis and
      Intelligence   43**

3   Research and Analytical Processes   63

**5 Best Practice in Recovery of Forensic Evidence
from Crime Scenes   121**

Forensic Intelligence
CD ROM Contents

Treadmark Express

A fully working version with a 30-day free licence for stand-alone computers giving access online to a ~20,000 footwear coding database, which is routinely updated. Treadmark Express can export files for loading into other Treadmark Express installations, although for larger organizations there is a fully networked version.

Treadmark

Macromedia demonstration of Treadmark in operation.

Please note Treadmark Express is being upgraded in 2012 to PathfinderXpress and its full network version for larger organizations is now branded as IFIIS (Integrated Forensic Intelligence & Information System). This is because IFIIS is expandable with modules designed to cover other forensic evidence types. However, PathfinderXpress software is in essence similar to Treadmark Express and any upgrade to a full licence version will include the provision of the latest version of PathfinderXpress. The Treadmark software is fully operational and will connect to the NFRC reference footwear database on line to facilitate pattern identification and coding.

Operation Bigfoot footwear pattern distribution graphs (London, 2005)

Footwear pattern spreadsheet covering only the most commonly found patterns for all of Metropolitan London during the first half of 2005. Note that every borough has a different distribution of patterns caused by their local criminal populations. In 2012, using the National Footwear Reference Collection database, there are fewer uncoded marks because the NFRC has 20,000 patterns, whereas Bigfoot had only some 700 patterns as a reference at the time.

UK National Footwear Reference Collection (NFRC)

Coding descriptors with exemplar images. Note that users of Treadmark must use these descriptors to enable accurate searching of the NFRC.

Example CSI forensic intelligence template
This template covers the most common fields required for input to police intelligence systems, with examples.

Functions of the Forensic Intelligence Unit document (R Milne)
Shoe and tool marks coding document
Suggested codes for entry into forensic features files (if provided) in crime report systems.

The vision of forensic intelligence and strategic thinking
Report during the development project by R Milne.

A unified format spreadsheet for merging drug legacy data from different forensic science laboratories
This spreadsheet was created for merging LGC forensics data with UK Forensic Science Service legacy data to assist in working on 'upstreaming' forensic drug-linked cases. Readers wishing to work with other organisations would have to cross reference the different terminology from the forensic science providers.

Forensic Intelligence Report (FIR) template

Role description example: Forensic intelligence manager

Footwear intelligence process map

Treadmark Express user manual pdf file

Ballistics intelligence process map—inputs and outputs
In the text, there is a full explanation of all of the abbreviations in this diagram. It is included for reproduction in A3 format.

Preface

This textbook is the first practical guide to the use of forensics in crime and intelligence analysis aimed at police, crime scene investigators (CSIs), and crime analysts. It is not intended as a primary source in crime analysis and intelligence techniques, but rather as a reference source explicating the value and significance of forensic recoveries. If these are properly processed and recorded, they can be used as a major intelligence source for use by crime investigators and analysts. Indeed, forensic expertise can be used to generate intelligence products either individually or in support of other crime analysis and intelligence products, the likes of which can be useful to police action.

The CD ROM included with this book has a fully working copy of Treadmark Express footwear evidence software, which will connect on the Internet to the UK National Police Improvement Agency's (NPIA), National Footwear Reference Collection (NFRC) of approximately 20,000 footwear sole patterns. This software will enable the storage, search, and comparison of footwear scene marks and offenders' footwear, enabling users to screen marks for further comparison by footwear examiners. Included is a copy of the Treadmark users' manual.

In addition to Treadmark, the CD contains exemplar templates for the input of forensics, behaviours, and method data into intelligence systems for readers to adapt in developing their own approach to forensic intelligence. The NPIA footwear coding descriptor guide is included, plus exemplar spreadsheets for marrying disparate legacy data from different forensic science providers to enable the use of the data by analysts. The process map for ballistics intelligence integrated into the Metropolitan Police intelligence system is included so that readers can enlarge the diagram intended to be viewed in A3 format. The full descriptions of the terms in the ballistics intelligence processes diagram are included in the text, showing the inputs to and outputs from the UK National Ballistics Intelligence Service (NaBIS).

The book draws on the author's 40 years of experience as a crime scene examiner, latent print examiner, and the head of Forensic Intelligence, New Scotland Yard, in the London Metropolitan Police Intelligence Bureau (MIB). The mission of Metropolitan Police Forensic Services was and is to maximise crime scene examinations and results; this means finding ways to lower the cost of investigations and make more efficient the collection and analysis of pertinent crime scene information necessary to solve cases in real time.

In comparative terms, the Metropolitan Police (Met) is one of the largest and best resourced police services worldwide, and it was one of the first law enforcement organisations from the 1960s onward to modernise and civilianise forensic services in order to provide a stable forensic support service. Likewise, the adoption of the UK National Intelligence Model (NIM) led the Met into changing its business model to make it an intelligence-led organisation. Civilian crime analysts were also recruited to provide intelligence and analytical services at the NIM's three levels of crime analysis: level 1 in local community policing, level 2 in more serious and cross-divisional crime, and level 3 covering serious crime. Serious crime is encountered at NIM levels 2 and 3, but level 3 is considered to be the level of very serious crime.

It is through the practical applications of forensics in our modern intelligence-led environment that the contents of this book have been created. Forensic intelligence techniques are used in countries where all police staff happen also to be sworn officers. As such, civilianisation in forensic and intelligence roles, though not a prerequisite to setting up a capability, is becoming the rule rather than the exception. It is an unfortunate fact that sworn officers, regardless of their intellectual prowess, progress through periodic promotion, yet, often as they move up, positions for newly promoted officers at higher ranks are sparse within forensics or intelligence analysis units. Intelligence expertise essentially is lost on promotion, creating a trickle-down effect to other areas in policing. Many long-term experts in technical posts are created by civilianisation, as well as the ability directly to recruit personnel with the right academic backgrounds.

Processes from the world of academia in police and crime science are also called upon for covering crime mapping, geographical profiling, investigative psychology, and the processes inherent in generic police intelligence models, which are often akin to the UK NIM, having their roots in problem-solving work, originally researched in the problem-solving laboratory in Washington, DC. These processes, combined with forensics, provide powerful tools in the areas of crime scene linking, linking offenders to crimes, and to improving crime detection rates. Where possible, the UK NIM is compared with the Comparable Statistics Model (COMPSTAT) used by police services in the United States to show the convergence of aims and how the basic generic techniques in both models are used broadly to achieve similar objectives.

It should not be assumed that forensic intelligence is only for large, well resourced police organisations because nothing could be further from the truth. In pioneering the uses of forensics in intelligence from the 1980s onward, its roots were in volume crime on police divisions when only limited resources of information technology were available. Indeed, in dealing with crime intelligence and forensics, small is beautiful. It is the smaller police services, as described Chapter 3, that have the luxury to concentrate the force of intelligence analysts alongside forensic services management on a smaller number of cases based within their jurisdiction. In the same tight working environment, colleagues can easily share information and develop intelligence from the analysis of crimes, source intelligence, and forensics. Some of the smaller police services using forensic intelligence achieve best results for this very reason.

The main purpose of the book is to offer a forensic intelligence resource for police services of all sizes and capabilities, from the large organisations with thousands of staff with big budgets down to the small service with few officers, who, by making use of basic crime recording and intelligence processes, can make best use of all of their forensic recoveries.

All that is known of evidentiary procedures relative to each of the main crime types is covered in this text, outlining also the processes involved in the production of intelligence products from the police data and forensic links. All that is required of a professional wanting to move into creating intelligence for the police is a business model that ensures that crime scenes are adequately examined forensically combined with basic police information technology resources in criminal records, crime reporting, intelligence records and systems recording, police stops, etc. and Microsoft Office.

Within this text, scene linking and the significance of crime clusters with forensic recoveries will be of particular interest to crime analysts, whereas those investigators dealing with suspects will be interested in chapters covering assessments of the potential numbers of detections, which can be accrued by understanding the significance of the forensic links leading to an arrest. The techniques of taking reactive forensic results and turning those reactive results into intelligence products for proactive upstreaming of casework will be of significance to drug squad detectives.

The majority of publications about forensic science cover best practice and basic advice about evidence recovery and storage. This book takes the subject of forensics further by covering the issues about what is done with all the evidence recovered at crime scenes, as only a small percentage makes it into a laboratory or fingerprint bureaus. Ultimately, it is this information that lends itself to further analysis and the dissemination of new forensic intelligence.

I am confident that the enthusiastic reader will find information and advice to enable best use of forensics in the modern police intelligence-led environments of the twenty-first century. That enthusiasm and the results that may accrue from gaining the practical guidance that, thus far, only this book has strived to provide will help to improve policing business models of those interested in breaking through to this exciting field. The goal is to elicit progress within the forensic intelligence system—a goal of mine for decades and the main reason why this book has been published.

Working in an intelligence-led environment starts at the lower level with the rank-and-file officers and support professionals and moves up through the chain of command. It should not just be driven by the few at the top of the intelligence business inside organizations, who often have too distant a view, offering grand strategies around few objectives, which leads to the neglect of "smaller" issues until they flare up into large strategic problems by default. If *everyone* thinks along the lines of conceptualizing their strategies and tactics to deal with their own remits and prepares problem assessments around the work in hand (or even life goals), the prospects of a highly efficient intelligence-led system of criminal investigation would be within grasp. It would not be beyond the wit of man to arrange the knowledge and system assets inside modern policing so that an intelligence-led due process is set out for all to follow in the course of daily work, with forensics being an integral part of the process.

At least by this process it is expected that an intelligence gathering procedure can be followed by all to provide explanation and proof of the accounts of actions taken. This can be achieved without entombing the organization in a bureaucratic straightjacket, which can be so slow to respond that problems have moved on before action is taken, as is often the case today. A major factor in the whole business of dealing with crime is securing evidence to provide proof and truth, for without it we just think or know something is going on and can only disrupt it without taking out the causes.

Robert Milne

Acknowledgements

Over the past 40 years, I have had the privilege of working with forensic practitioners in virtually all disciplines of forensic science and police officers from many specialisations and other national (UK) and international police services. From the ranks of sworn police officers, I would like to single out the following friends and colleagues.

The late Detective Sergeant Charlie Collins was an old time copper who taught me so much in the early 1970s in my early years as the first ever scenes of crime officer to be employed at Harlesden 'Q' District Northwest London. Charlie was an extraordinary man who, in his military career with the 6th British Airborne, was dropped in a glider on D-Day and drove out of it in a light aluminium tank, surviving the experience through the end of WW II. In his police service, serving as a detective up to the 1980s, he stayed true to the principles of using forensics in crime detection, embracing the opportunities in the creation of a first-class developing business model, or what is now called a CSI capability. I had the privilege of working on some extraordinary cases with him, including my first experiences of installing covert radio alarms in premises subject to seasonal attacks by burglars.

At the other end of my service with the Metropolitan Police, I wish to thank Detective Superintendent Barry Nicholson, a model officer in implementing modern applications of academic and logistical thinking in policing. Barry was the former operational manager of the Met Intelligence Bureau (MIB) up to 2009, and I thank him for his co-operation, understanding, and patience during the time I developed the MIB Forensic Intelligence Desk. The motto for the MIB is 'Seeing the Whole Picture' and Barry made sure that the MIB did exactly that.

From the area of Met Forensic Services, my thanks must go to Roger Shearn, the former head of Forensic Services in Territorial Policing of the Metropolitan Police. It was Roger who developed our business group from a point where it had no proper budget and no information technology to an efficient organisation pioneering cutting-edge, efficient forensic support to the Metropolitan Police and providing the modern facilities to develop forensic intelligence. Gary Pugh, OBE, still the director of Forensic Services at Scotland Yard, was later pivotal in securing the funding to enable Forensic Services to modernise and face the challenges of the twenty-first century.

Without Gary's assistance and support, progress would have been so much slower and undoubtedly more difficult.

Support from forensic scientists (especially our Met Lab scientists) must be mentioned, particularly Roger Davis, John Birkett, and Dave Baldwin (forensic marks specialists); Dean Ames (drug and toxicology specialist); Mary Newton (DNA and sexual offences specialist); and Rachel Green's team (Forensic Science Service, customer services, and accounts management). The help offered by these scientists in improving forensic data products and securing legacy data from casework was invaluable.

Others outside the police service who were partners and stakeholders in forensic intelligence development are Peter Mansi, head of Fire investigation, London Fire Brigade, and from the world of academia, Professor David Canter and Dr. Donna Youngs from the International Academy for Investigative Psychology for their work with the Metropolitan Police in developing the Interactive Offender Profiling System (IOPs) and for improving my awareness of modern techniques to take forensic intelligence forward. Thanks to Professor Gloria Laycock for her team's work in crime science development at the Jill Dando Crime Science Institute, London University, and for hosting the UK crime mapping conferences.

Thanks must go to my scenes of crime colleagues and forensic intelligence staff with whom I had the pleasure of working

Tony Phillips, former Met senior scenes of crime officer and a pioneer in forensic scene linking; Jacob Maselino, Met senior forensic practitioner for his keenness and professionalism; Bob Furse, Met senior forensic practitioner, a master of forensic crime scene linking; Marie Doran, head of the Met's Fugitive Unit, for her insight into police working practices and valuable work as a forensic intelligence crime analyst; and Bob Green, formerly from the Police Standards Unit at the UK Home Office, who provided valuable budgetary support for so many vital developments in scenes of crime forensics in the UK, especially the work on forensic intelligence in a number of UK police forces.

I thank Meredith Gafford, MA in forensic psychology, for her time and patience proofreading and editing the first few chapters of this manuscript and to Derek Manning for his assistance in proofreading all of the rest of the manuscript. Derek wrote the Ford Motor Company quality manual and his insight into working models and practices in organisations was immensely useful. Academics such as Meredith are part of the future of criminal investigation and true pioneers in the developing of investigative psychology. I also thank Mike Jones, a forensic scientist, for his insight into the problems in forensic science presented by the uses of Bayesian probability methods by scientists and a discussion of the concepts around truth and probability.

Thanks are extended to Foster & Freeman Ltd for their assistance and SAS, a progressive information technology company that produce the Memex crime intelligence and police casework systems.

Finally, from the world of industry, thanks go to Mike and Grahame Sandling, directors of Crime Scene Investigation Equipment Ltd and Crime Scene Products (Florida) Inc., for their unending enthusiasm in developing new ideas to bring to market the equipment to enable forensic professionals to bring criminals to justice.

The Author

Bob Milne has completed over 39 years service with the Metropolitan Police Forensic Services Directorate, New Scotland Yard, as a forensic practitioner in the roles of ACPO registered fingerprint expert, crime scene examiner, and manager.

He was trained by the Metropolitan Police Detective Training School and Crime Academy but also has the London University Kings College diploma in fingerprint expertise and crime scene examination. He is a fellow of the Fingerprint Society, member of the Forensic Science Society, the London regional representative of the International Association of Arson Investigators, member of the International Association for Identification, and a full associate of the International Academy for Investigative Psychology. He has written articles and made presentations on electrostatic mark lifting, the mathematics of scene linking, the crime mapping of forensic evidence, forensic intelligence in arson investigation, the design of self-contained sequential treatment fingerprint laboratories, and on the subject of forensics in intelligence-led policing.

He started his service in 1969 in the Fingerprint Bureau, New Scotland Yard, and in 1971 became one of the first scenes of crime officers (CSIs). He worked mainly in London's East End, London's main crime hot spot. In his service, he has examined virtually all types of crime scenes, including many homicide cases.

In 1975, he met his wife, Lesley, at an armed robbery scene and married her in 1976. He still has the scenes of crime photo album from the day they met. He progressed through forensic services management and was in the early 1980s the head of scenes of crime Whitechapel, Tower Hamlets Borough. In the 1990s, he was a crime scene coordinator dealing with mainly homicide and serious crime cases.

He is the inventor of the Pathfinder three-electrode wireless electrostatic dust mark lifter system used by CSIs worldwide.

Between 2001 and his retirement in 2008, Bob worked on the development of forensic intelligence. This involved the requirement to train as a police intelligence unit manager and manage the Metropolitan Police Forensic Intelligence Unit as part of the Met Police forensic services developments team in the Met Intelligence Bureau. The MIB dealt with the production of forensic intelligence products for police tasking and coordination.

Since retiring from the Met Police in 2008, Bob has worked in the role of technical consultant with Crime Scene Investigation Equipment Ltd, developing and improving crime scene examination equipment and forensics software applications. In 2011 he became an associate fire investigator with Fire Investigations (UK) LLP and Fire Investigations Global LLP, a role that is ongoing.

Introducing Forensic Intelligence

1

Introduction

Intelligence, in the context of the investigation of criminal activity, should give those who practise it improved results and fresh leads into new areas of investigation. When planning a business model, even in crime intelligence, it pays to look at the basic definitions in relation to the field because only then can the question be asked, 'Does my model actually deliver intelligence to deal with forensic findings and results, or is it a performance analysis and review model tasking staff to deal with that which is already known and often already being implemented?'

In fact, most of the textbooks useful to problem-solving crime analysts or intelligence-led problem-oriented policing do not so much as mention the word 'forensic' in the text or indices. This happens to be a serious omission, for forensics can deliver many of the truths required to accurately unearth offenders' identities and link crimes to serial offenders. Other analysis outside casework, which is surveillance or informant led, is based merely on opinion or probability and can have a higher percentage of false links, misses, or errors, leading inevitably to investigative failures.

Semantics: 'Forensics' and 'Intelligence'

In dissecting the term 'forensic intelligence', the word 'forensic' means two things in classical and modern times:

- To bring evidence before the forum or a court of law in classical times
- Scientific evidence in the form of comparisons and scientific findings applied to the law in modern times[1,2]

The word 'intelligence' in the online 2011 *Oxford Dictionary* is a person or being with the ability to acquire and apply knowledge and skills. From my own experience, I believe it to be an ability to produce solutions or resolve problems in new and novel situations.

The terms 'forensic' and 'intelligence', when combined in practice and applied to criminal intelligence, give more strength and ability to the intelligence-led effort on problem-oriented policing.

Forensic intelligence provides information necessary to provide solutions and bring the issues before those who spearhead, task, and coordinate the effort against crime and disorder.

Forensic Intelligence: Professor Olivier Ribaux's Definition

Professor Olivier Ribaux[3] defines forensic intelligence in the following way:

> By definition forensic science already plays an intermediate role between the specialized field of science and law enforcement. Forensic intelligence is the accurate, timely and useful product of logically processing forensic case data. Of importance is the implication of an additional level of consideration, where collectively (across numerous investigations or various disciplines), the outcomes of forensic analyses become the source of intelligence.

In order to highlight the concept of forensic intelligence, a working definition is required. The following definition was derived from practical working experience and is based on already established and commonly used techniques. The point of the definition is that the concept of forensic intelligence is mainly about what is done with forensic evidence to make progress in casework in relation to other information and intelligence. Most texts on the topics of forensics and crime analysis thus far have not covered these aspects in any detail. There is a need for basic definitions and terminology in order to make progress on the issues raised. To support the definition, a general statement of the methods employed in forensic intelligence is given next and the methods listed are general generic techniques used in forensic science and crime.

Forensic Intelligence: A Working Definition

> The application of forensic science to crime intelligence, in order to determine the facts at issue, to enable the production of intelligence products for action in the areas of the linking of crimes and the matching of offenders to crimes.

Forensic intelligence methods include

> The matching of fingerprints, DNA profiling, chemical, biological analysis, matching of physical marks, the coding and categorisation of forensic data into databases, digital image analysis, telephone communication, computer network data and the mapping of forensic recoveries, enabling forensic data

to reveal patterns of criminal activity and the production of intelligence products for action.[4]

To those involved in criminal investigation, there is nothing unusual about the methods used to enable a forensic intelligence capability; however, in most police services, forensics is generally used on a case-by-case basis. Forensics is often viewed by crime intelligence analysts as the domain of the crime scene investigators. This compartmentalisation of thinking can and has led to disastrous failures in major investigations.

The Concept of 'Entities' in Police Recording Systems

The main purposes of crime intelligence and crime analysis are to detect offenders and/or disrupt their activities, thus moving toward the ultimate goal of crime reduction. In this context, the offender must be viewed as an 'entity' that has a living space, journey to crime, methods, behaviours, description, and unique biometric features and that, through actions, generates intelligence information from sources and leaves forensic evidence whilst engaged in criminal activity. **Indeed, all people, real locations, forensic exhibits, latent marks, DNA profiles, etc. are real entities.**

The concept of entities applies to all real things, for each real item can be the focus of a record. For example, a burglary is reported at 2 West Street; a crime report record is created for the address, but inside the report are many fields covering details of the investigation, the alleged victim(s), suspects, etc. To find details in the fields across many crime reports and information in other systems, users have to seek the information relevant to the 'entities' they seek by proxy. In other words, the entity itself is not the focus of the search or enquiry. If the address at West Street was the focus, then all records in relevant systems (not just the crime report system) would respond with the address as the location entity with all records relating to that entity.

At this time, police systems are based on records rather than on entities. To achieve an entity-based approach, most police systems have to be data warehoused, usually by extracting copies of all records in different systems daily into data warehouse servers, enabling entity-based searching to be carried out in the data warehouse servers. Such an example is the Metropolitan Police Service Integrated Information Platform (IIP), which enables entity searches across crime reports, crime intelligence, and custody and stops databases. Without such an approach, most searches are made by proxy or are looking for entities within records-based systems. Entities are found in subsets of data, usually in headed fields where they may be recorded. The consequence of using records-based systems at this time is that analysts' time is consumed in the creation of spreadsheets from different systems and then having to compare or merge the spreadsheets to seek common factors relating to the entity or real item, which is the real focus of the research.

It is therefore wise to view the process of intelligence and crime analysis holistically across all the available disciplines ranging from recorded facts, intelligence information, and recovered forensic evidence.

The primary objectives of this book are to raise awareness of forensics as intelligence sources for those involved in investigations, crime analysis, and forensic examinations. When considering forensics, service providers involved in forensic examinations, crime intelligence, and analysis should consider these key issues by asking the following questions:

Do crime analysts within our organisation have any meaningful awareness or training in the significance of forensic recoveries?

How many fingerprint identifications and DNA matches against crime scene forensic recoveries did our service achieve in the past year? Has this number increased or decreased from the prior year?

With respect to the fingerprint and DNA (hard evidence) recoveries, did the matches result in arrests and prosecutions? Are there useful hard evidence forensic hits that are not making their way to analysis or being turned into detections? Also, what is the trend relative to follow-up analysis performed on the bulk of these fingerprint or DNA identifications and matches?

What is our service's track record in expanding fingerprint and DNA hits by the use of intelligence and crime analysis research?

What additional achievements has our organisation made using other, 'softer' forms of forensics such as shoe marks or tool marks apart from fingerprints and DNA? What results can be achieved from using the softer forms of evidence?

As 80% to 90% of forensic materials recovered never make their way into a forensic laboratory, what are the ways that we can utilise this material to solve cases? Is my organisation keeping track of forensic matches against offenders, particularly prolific offenders?

How can forensic intelligence enhance the nine standard crime analysis techniques listed in Chapter 3 to be used to drive police intelligence-led models?

What are the implications of not investing in a proper digital evidence imaging, measuring, and comparison system (e.g., Treadmark or Shoeprint Image Capture and Retrieval [SICAR]) as a knowledge and system asset to deal with footwear and tool mark evidence?

Has our service negatively experienced what is defined as the 'CSI effect' derived from the television series, which has increased the expectations of juries and courts in the capabilities of forensic examinations and services?

If the answers to these questions are mainly 'no' or 'I do not know', then your service is missing big tricks in improving its results and is not using a major set of tools to enable real intelligence links and forensic matching techniques to improve your business. If you have answered 'yes', then the following chapters will be your go-to reference for continuing success in forensic intelligence management. Regardless of your current position, it is important to read this book carefully as it will help to clarify some of the preceding issues as well as offer solutions to day-to-day problems in forensic intelligence.

If the volume crime work stream seems daunting and your organisation is having difficulty in recovering or dealing with forensics effectively, then major problems can arise in major investigations. In these conditions, there will not be any forensic context in which to relate recoveries, even for petty crime. Further development of forensic recoveries can quickly lead to the identifications of single offenders, crime series offenders, and gangs as well as create leads necessary to address dated and unsolved cases. It should be pointed out that the main impression of the CSI television series is that everything is somewhere in a database and that general categorisations of criminal types are invariably true, but this is unrealistic. What is realistic, however, is for a properly structured forensic service to manage and handle the real forensic recoveries they retain effectively to make best use of them, within their finite resources.

Does Your Forensic Services Staff Have Access or Input to Your Intelligence Systems?

In police services, forensic staff may not have direct access to the crime intelligence systems because, in my experience, organisations are often slow to change working practices. Intelligence is associated with attitudes toward confidentiality for reasons associated with sensitive casework and is usually administered by individuals associated with that top-end casework. Those attitudes and resistance to change can lead to a situation where stakeholders involved in routine volume crime are either denied access to intelligence systems or very restricted in what they are allowed to do. Consequently, in some organisations little or no input is received from CSIs in this area owing to lack of training and access rights—even to have input-only rights.

Until 2001, for example, the Metropolitan Police as an organisation had not realised that CSIs and fingerprint specialists could make use of both intelligence gathering and input to intelligence systems with mainly the 'restricted' but not normally the 'confidential' areas of the system. The term 'restricted' means that the contents must not be discussed or disseminated outside the police organisation unless specific permission is given. Most crime reports for volume crime cases are restricted, as would be intelligence logs at the volume crime level with the exception of confidential informants or features of the case that cause the records to be graded 'confidential'.

Obviously, intelligence systems have security facilities designed for officers, who can allow input to and search of certain records around forensic recoveries and links with permission. Yet, supervision processes are built in as essential elements to ensure the smooth running of the system. Restrictive practices deny key staff and stakeholders the ability to participate in the detection, prosecution, case linking, and intelligence gathering sections of police business models.

Access to Forensic Support Resources

An adequate forensic strategy is required to collect forensic intelligence from crime scenes; part-time forensic 'cherry picking' business models or the lack of any forensic business model will prevent the proper use of forensics, inhibit performance, and, in some cases, obscure issues. In addition to visiting scenes of serious crimes, a properly funded forensic support team should be able to visit most suitable crime scenes, such as burglary, robbery, theft, and vehicle crime scenes within respective police jurisdictions to enable a useful level of forensic evidence recoveries. At the very least, the forensic support should be able to handle the priority crime types as currently decreed by the organisation and those scenes targeted as part of intelligence-led operations.

The approaches to improving the use of forensics explained in this text (Chapters 4 and 5) do not require a large amount of additional manpower or resources. Across the world, standards vary considerably in police services, and forensic services are often under-resourced. Best practice in forensic recoveries is essential in order to recover evidence in sufficient volume and give a clear picture relative to the nature of the crime, especially in forensic marks evidence such as finger marks, shoe marks, and tool marks, where third-level fine detail is required for expert matches to be made. For those unfamiliar with the '1 to 3' level grading of detail in forensic marks,

- Level 1 detail covers marks where only the basic outline of the marks can be seen.
- Level 2 detail covers marks where the main features are clearly visible, such as fingerprint ridge characteristics or pattern and wear areas on shoe marks.
- Level 3 detail covers marks where microscopic detail is evident, such as feathering on shoe marks, small damage features, and, in the case of finger marks, details of the structure of the friction ridges and individual sweat pores can be seen.

Recovering forensic evidence in sufficient volume and quality enables the processes of establishing crime clusters and links, which in turn greatly aids crime analysts in their work. If the forensic recoveries are patchy and insufficient, then the ability to improve performance in intelligence-led policing is compromised.

Forensic Intelligence in Intelligence-Led Policing

Where should a forensic intelligence capability sit within an organisation?

I had some excellent advice in 2008 from John Minderman, a retired agent from the FBI Behavioural Science Unit who was involved in the Watergate inquiry with his commander, who was known in the press as 'Deep Throat'. John was present at the White House when President Richard Nixon was impeached. John said, 'Forensics are like behaviours, in that they can appear at any crime level at any time and when your developing unit has success, management will try and put you in the serious crime part of the business, *where you will only be allowed to look at certain priorities*'. He believed that this prioritisation was the downfall of the original FBI Behavioural Science Unit, and John's advice was that 'this move will do your unit in'.

I agree with John and believe that such a move toward restriction will stifle development and research in new techniques because serious casework operates in a very sensitive environment where there is a nervousness about anything that may be questioned about processes. A forensic intelligence capability should sit across all police business from volume to serious crime; otherwise, its use will be inhibited.

Fortunately, the concept of forensic intelligence is becoming more robust, practised, and developed in many police services around the globe. In the UK, for instance, employment advertisements in some police services for crime scene investigators cite forensic intelligence as a key part of the candidates' skills, with respect to their having an appreciation of how to use their findings to support the investigative team in providing analysis and intelligence products.

The goal of this text is to provide a reference for investigating officers, forensic scene examiners and their colleagues in forensic science identification services (i.e., crime analysts, intelligence gatherers, and coordinators of tasking in police business groups). The following breakdown is a short guide to the content of the text, to be detailed in the chapters that follow.

I have visited the Guardia Civilia in Madrid and seen the forensic intelligence work there in the Madrid Police headquarters using Integrated Ballistics Intelligence System (IBIS) and work on tool marks on 'Euro locks', fingerprints, DNA, processing, and the general work of the scenes of crime department staffed by sworn officers. In 2008, whilst working as forensic intelligence manager, London, I met with the team from Taiwan in London who introduced footwear forensic intelligence into Taiwan; this team used Treadmark software. Taiwan is seeking to expand the forensic intelligence capability with respect to footwear marks across the country. Olivier Ribeaux, an academic from Switzerland who was working with the Swiss police service, visited me at the Metropolitan Police Forensic Intelligence Unit, Hendon, London, during the volume crime development phase of forensic intelligence and shared the methods used in the Swiss cantons in dealing with forensic intelligence with respect to footwear evidence. This approach using increases in pattern finding frequencies is covered and illustrated later in the text.

The text sets out how large a subject forensic intelligence is covering: methods, evidence types, and their characteristics together with advice on making best use of these features toward supporting intelligence products for action. The outlines of police intelligence models are covered with the language of intelligence-led policing. The three main intelligence assets that drive intelligence-led policing are covered, detailing knowledge assets, system assets, and intelligence assets. The generic intelligence products in the form of strategic, tactical assessments and problem profiles are covered together with the five by five model for grading intelligence. Forensics is considered as intelligence sources, and police business models with some case examples are given. The properties of forensic evidence types with respect to their potential intelligence value are reviewed as well as the uses of forensic legacy data accruing from laboratory casework. The nine main analytical techniques described in Chapter 3 are then related to the daily work of the crime analyst contrasted with daily work of a forensically aware crime analyst.

Structures for dealing with forensic intelligence are covered together with common inhibitors to forensic intelligence. For CSIs, forensic coding methods are covered with advice on setting up forensic intelligence databases. The uses of DNA results such as estimating the number of potential detections from unsolved crimes at DNA-linked scenes and the use of forensic intelligence to expand DNA results are explored. The setting of forensic strategies in response to crime problems and best use of the Automatic Fingerprint Identification System (AFIS) are covered and the use of modern forensic marks software such as Foster & Freeeman SICAR and Crime Scene Products, Inc. (Florida)'s Treadmark. A copy of Treadmark with a 30-day licence is included with the text for readers to use.

Chapter 5 highlights best practice for crime scene examiners with respect to the main forms of evidence recovered from crime scenes. This chapter is aimed at producing better recoveries from crime scenes as a forensic intelligence enabling issue. Chapter 6 is aimed at those who may wish to create or improve their current organisation in the area of introducing or developing forensic intelligence covering the setting up of a forensic intelligence capability. Pitfalls encountered in setting up forensic intelligence facilities are covered with examples from a sample of police services of how they deal with the issues. An account is given of the experience of the introduction of an intelligence-led policing model in the Metropolitan Police in 2004. The final chapter deals with potential ways ahead in improving technologies and concepts to take forensic intelligence forward.

The majority of readers will make up the full spectrum of interest in forensic science, crime analysis, academia, investigation, and crime scene examination. It is further expected that the text will give indications to those in other working environments with an interest in developing forensic intelligence. The following chapters provide experience-based ideas for adapting new and creative methods for expanding the use of forensic intelligence, regardless of available resources. The idea that passionate people from all walks of life could push forward credible business plans for adding resources and creating change in working forensic police practices may be off-putting to some, but the reality is that forensic services need to move forward; adding healthy inputs to the intelligence development field can only be advantageous.

The Origins of Forensic Intelligence

The concept of forensic intelligence for me had its roots in personal experience with changes in the forensic business model at the London Metropolitan (Met) Police in the late 1960s. The subsequent development of working practices combined with forensic technologies paved the way to the introduction of modern ideas of applying forensics to the new developments in intelligence-led policing in the twenty-first century. In addition, the introduction of information technology from the 1990s onward enabled the mass handling of data and images generated from police investigations. Prior to 1967, Met Police forensic services were delivered almost exclusively by sworn officers trained by the Met's Detective Training School, for such training was not generally available outside the police service at that time. The working practice with regard to serious crime investigations was to examine major crime scenes thoroughly, but in the volume crime area (e.g., vehicle crime, burglary, assaults, sex crime, robbery, etc.). Whether or not any forensic examinations were made was at the discretion of mainly Criminal Investigation Department (CID) officers.

To assist CID officers with fingerprint examinations the Fingerprint Bureau at New Scotland Yard employed 32 (mainly civilian) divisional fingerprint officers (DFOs) supporting the CID in vetting quality finger marks for bureau search. This meant that one fingerprint expert was responsible for one London borough because there are 32 London boroughs. Clearly, this support was not enough to examine the vast amount of crime scenes adequately in London, a city with a population of eight million people.

In 1967 a decision was made to introduce civilian scenes of crime officers (SOCOs). Under the working practices prevailing up to that time, it was not compulsory for detectives to examine volume crime scenes forensically. After the introduction of specialist SOCOs, it was expected that they would examine as many crime scenes as was practicable; the quantity and quality of their examinations were performance managed.

With the requirement to serve 5 years at the Met in order to qualify as a fingerprint expert before they could work on casework external to the Fingerprint Bureau, not enough manpower could be brought to bear on delivering the crime scene examinations required in a timely manner. Likewise, sworn officers were often not employed in fingerprinting because it was not beneficial for officers whose career goals were to secure posts in other departments; therefore, promoted sworn forensic officers often would move out of forensics, leading to a loss of expertise. The SOCOs were well trained in fingerprint and forensic recoveries, yet were not used as experts to prove identifications or forensic matches because of the requirement to serve 5 years in a fingerprint bureau to become a certified expert witness.

The UK fingerprint system in the 1960s was entirely manual and the only computer available in the Met was located in the pay branch in the form of a large mainframe machine; no small computer systems or networks were available at that time. There was no police national computerisation of criminal records at that time, so record keeping was maintained in paper Criminal Records Office files. The introduction of SOCOs solved the problems of bringing enough trained manpower to bear on increasing the number of forensic examinations of crimes scenes. The SOCO management had one main objective and that was to maximise forensic examinations.

To support this expansion in crime scene examination capability and because manual searching of local crime scene marks in the National Fingerprint Collection of over 4.5 million sets was too large a task to be practical,[5] the Met Fingerprint Bureau changed its methods in the recovery of crime scene marks. It switched from photography to adhesive tape lifting of marks because chemical film methods could not cope. With the use of the new, improved generation of photocopying machines, approximately 38,000 fingerprint forms were photocopied from the National Fingerprint collection of 4.5 million forms to create a 'breakers' collection for London of known burglary and robbery offenders.[6,7]

These were filed manually in Henry fingerprint classification order to enable manual scenes of crime marks against searches of prints of offenders. Likewise, further copies of crime scene finger marks (latent prints) were filed on the Fingerprint Bureau's scenes of crime teams and copies of offenders' 10-print sets in crime type bundles. Scenes of crime teams within the Met Fingerprint Bureau had a responsibility to cover defined geographical areas of London in order to focus local scenes of crime marks searches on local criminals. Specialist scenes of crime teams also covered serious crimes such as armed robbery, homicide, and terrorism with no geographical remit. Scenes of crime finger marks were then indexed on the teams, enabling comparisons of offenders' 10 prints to scenes of crime latent marks and scenes of crime marks to offenders' 10 prints. In this way, newly filed offenders' 10-print sets could be searched against filed unidentified crime scene marks and newly submitted marks from crime scenes could be searched against filed offenders' 10-print (exemplar) sets.

To facilitate the processing of additional cases by the thousands per year, the Met Scenes of Crime Branch ceased to use cameras routinely to photograph powdered latent marks. Instead, aluminium powder was used to develop most latent finger marks and low-adhesion transparent tape was used to lift the marks. The old process of photographing latent marks with chemical film could not handle the vast increase in scenes of crime marks submitted by the new SOCO field force. Lifting latent marks on to adhesive tape was quick and easy. The lifted marks were mounted on polycarbonate sheets, documented, and submitted to the bureau for photography and search. The other advantages of lifting marks were that the original mark was the exhibit and in later years, although not foreseen at the time, micro-DNA could be recovered from marks with insufficient detail—a useful method in cold case reviews.

The photographic process of the fingerprint lifts was automated using commercial printing machines using the transparent fingerprint lifts directly to print onto photographic paper, instead of creating photographic negatives. With 180 newly recruited SOCOs plus the 32 DFOs in the field force, literally thousands of fingerprint cases were submitted to the bureau, resulting in a massive expansion in identifications.[5]

The Met Police had created in the 'breakers' collection project an incredibly useful forensic intelligence coded reference database that had the capability to detect a large number of offenders. It should be noted, however, that the terms and concept of forensic intelligence in order to consider the project in that context were still in the future.

Crime scene marks were being identified against offenders and crime scenes linked against the previous situation. Whereas hundreds of identifications had been made per year, the Met bureau was now producing identifications in the low thousands. The Met's approach to civilianisation, or creating a business model, which then could service the majority of crime scenes, set the bar for further development. The SOCOs (CSIs) were trained in all forms of forensic search and recovery techniques, whereas before the DFOs were restricted to fingerprint examinations.

In the precomputer era before DNA techniques were developed, other forms of forensic evidence, such as footwear marks and tool marks, were dealt with on a case-by-case basis. A pre-DNA technology called the laboratory blood index dealt with scenes of crime blood and body fluid stains, providing frequency data for linked cases and matches along with percentage assessments of the population to which the grouped stains could be applied. The process used by blood index scientists was to wet dried bloodstains with saline solution and then group the stains in the 'A', 'B', 'O' system in a similar manner to that used in hospitals.[8] This development not only provided linked scenes with a probability figure associated with each link but also could provide elimination evidence in cases where suspects did not have the same blood groupings as the stains at the crime scenes. An important feature of the blood index was that it indicated whether or not the persons leaving the blood or body fluid had secretor status, which indicated whether or not that particular person's ABO blood grouping could be established from just his or her body fluids. This was a useful factor in eliminating persons from enquiries, for DNA profiling was a long way off in the future.

Before the discussed developments, most police services were not intelligence led. The concepts of intelligence-led policing and problem-solving policing are late twentieth century developments. COMPSTAT in the United States is an example of a statistics-based approach to problem-solving policing. The National Intelligence Model (NIM) in the UK, introduced between 2000 and 2004, is an attempt at intelligence-led crime analysis and statistical problem solving in policing. Before the NIM's introduction, police managed their business partly in a traditional command-and-control process developed over a considerable period of time and partly through crisis management, reacting to problems as they arose. Performance management was not on the agenda until the latter part of the twentieth century.

Prior to intelligence-led policing, detectives were grateful for fingerprint matches, but discharged these mainly on a single-case, single-identification basis. They were thus unable to maximise detections by analysing crime scenes in the identified offenders' neighbourhoods. Indeed, the intelligence office in each police division consisted of an officer called a collator who collated information on suspects and offenders on cards filed in metal drawers. All police records, including crime reports, were on paper and as such the ability to share information of searches across areas was extremely compromised.

Estimating the Number of Current Offenders

Previously, as an operational SOCO, I worked for a typical police division with a few hundred police officers and was attached to the divisional CID office, working for perhaps a dozen or so detectives. In this role, it was required to visit each reported crime scene and conduct forensic examinations. The experience meant that SOCOs were moving around in the activity spaces of what are now known as marauder and commuter (traveller) criminals, unlike police colleagues who would share a small percentage of the work among their group so that they did not have to visit all reported crime scenes. In 1969 when I started work on my first scenes of crime team in the Fingerprint Bureau of New Scotland Yard covering Northwest London divisions, each scenes of crime team had traveller bundles of fingerprints of known travelling criminals who were not in the main marauders around their own neighbourhoods. In 2000, Prof David Canter used the term 'traveller' in his book *Criminal Shadows* to define a method and behaviour of a criminal type, giving the first modern meaning and context to the term within the world of academia.[9]

As SOCOs, we had a large workload for which we were getting enough results from our techniques to hold the level of reported crime, in our opinion, in a relatively stable state. This statement relates to the fact that if a division has a low forensic identification rate, the crime rate climbs simply because, as the criminal population shifts, undetected offenders are added to by new ones, adding to the reported crime level. In my service, I have taken over areas where the crime rate was high and, after a considerable amount of forensic identifications and police teamwork, the crime level has been reduced significantly. This is the main reason for the adoption of problem-solving intelligence-led techniques such as the NIM and COMPSTAT to detect and reduce crime.

Has Modern Forensics Had an Impact on Crime Reduction?

In this section, the graphs are reproduced from the UK and San Francisco showing crime rates prior to and after the introduction of automatic fingerprint identifications systems (Figure 1.1) and, in the case of England and Wales, the introduction of the National DNA Database (NDNAD) (Figure 1.2). There is an apparent correlation between the years the systems came in and significant drops in the burglary rates; although some argue that the drop is due to increased affluence and social factors, this does not explain the similarities in different countries with different economies. DNA databases add significantly to identification rates also. After all, it is generally agreed that criminal populations are small compared to the size of the general population and identifying thousands of offenders who are then prosecuted may have a significant effect on the activities of the criminal population.

Being involved in the daily examinations of the majority of reported crime in our division, we were aware of the various locations preyed upon by offenders across the area. The question as to how many offenders were causing the police workload was one of interest because the general perception was that things were always in a steady state—but could this perception be based in truth?

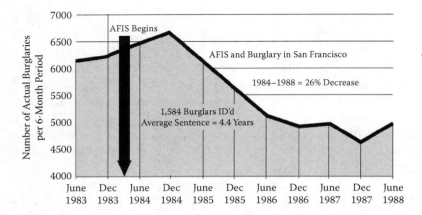

Figure 1.1 Statistical study of AFIS hits versus burglaries in San Francisco, 1984–1988 (Bruton 1989). Is the use of AFIS a significant factor in reducing burglary?[14]

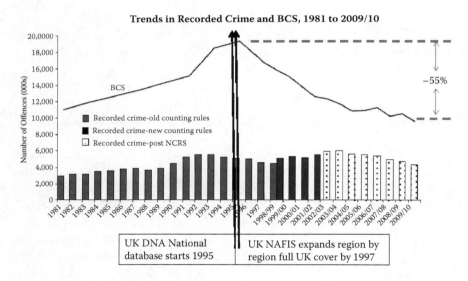

Figure 1.2 Reported crime in England and Wales, UK, prior to and after the introduction of the DNA database and the start of NAFIS. Could forensics have anything to do with the crime reduction or is it a coincidence?[15]

Those involved in dealing with daily reported crime, even in busy inner city areas, will note that, at most, two dozen crimes are reported each shift, with no more than approximately 10 being burglaries; however, in a city jurisdiction, 2,000+ burglaries may be reported, for example, over the course of a year. To illustrate the process of estimating the range of the potential number of the divisional active offender population, an examination of the published figures for burglary, 2010 to 2011, on the Metropolitan Police London website[10] is useful for illustrative purposes. The total number of reported Met burglaries 2010–2011 is shown as 95,082 offences. These are split between 32 London boroughs (i.e., police districts), so the simple average number of burglaries per division is 98,082/32 = 2,971 offences per annum. Dividing this number by 365 gives an average number of approximately eight offences per day per borough. Does this mean that nearly 2,000 burglary offenders are active in the borough or even a number in the hundreds?

To generalise, as a hypothetical scenario, it is known that most burglary offenders operate in their own neighbourhoods, so with an average Met rate of eight reported offences per day, it is obvious that on any particular day the number of persons active must be a relatively low number, taking into account gangs', criminal networks', and single offenders' activities. Again to generalise, when dealing with prolific offenders postarrest who have been active for over a year, admitted offending rates by offenders are typically in the 100 to 150 offences a year range. (*See postarrest detection maps in Chapter 6, p. 178.*) This figure relates to typically about three offences per week per offender on average; considering the offenders' logistics, this seems to be a reasonable ballpark figure. The offender has to commit the burglary, dispose of stolen property, buy drugs, etc. and enjoy the profit from the activity and then commit another offence. This is a generalisation because some will commit offences every day and some once in a while, but on average the indications are always that the active criminal population is a small subset of the general population. Consequently, the marks and evidence left are representative of that small subset.

From my experience over 40 years' service in Met Police divisions, many of the criminal offences happening are not reported during the same working day. Instead, crimes may be reported in the subsequent days or, worse, not at all. As some offences may be committed by the same offender on the same day, it is obvious that the ability actively to track the criminal population involved in prolific offending on any one day to a week is diminutive from the point of view of on-the-street policing. Further, if the distributions of the crime scenes are discussed with operational police officers, usually a fair number of useful prospects will be accurately suggested as suspects. By using an intelligence-led approach coupled with advanced forensic techniques, it is possible to reduce the crime rate for certain crime types in an area dramatically.

The crime scene investigator's view of crime is quite a different one from those of most of his or her police colleagues in that the CSI sees closely in detail all of the evidence left at the scene and methods used by offenders in reported crime scenes; therefore, he or she has an intrinsic knowledge of crime in the area operated. It is important for police and forensic services managers to understand that CSIs at times may not communicate with crime analysts or view it as necessary to link crime scenes unless instructed to do so. CSIs, like analysts, may not be aware of the activities, methods, principles, business, or working language of each other's departments.[11] Chapter 2 talks about the propensity for police and CSIs to do the work necessary to attain conviction rather than to fuel systematic research.

One simple approach to this problem is to give copies of CSI notes to the crime analysts responsible for searching for crime links and intelligence police tasking products a practice, which, from my experience, usually creates a pile of unread notes in the analyst's office. The dumping of CSI notes into an intelligence unit for analysis is far from a solution because analysts are often not forensic practitioners, and a simple scan through textbooks and course work will show that they usually have little training or real knowledge in this forensic science/criminalistics area.[12] Checking the International Association of Crime Analysts website on 3 November 2011 reveals the word 'forensic' is not mentioned on the site. UK training of analysts has taken its lead, I believe, from this association. Lack of performance because of these omissions will certainly be a result of the current system regarding not using forensics efficiently. The process of using forensics in intelligence, like other issues in policing such as crime analysis, has to be managed or else it may not happen.

A strong police business model (as discussed further in the text) has a high forensically sanctioned detection rate and standard operating procedures in place for dealing with forensic evidence, which ensure that hard-evidence DNA and fingerprint hits do not pile up on police teams desks, not acted upon and resulting in offenders further adding to the workload. This causes a scenario where offenders are left for days on end to continue offending, whilst the officers dealing with the forensic hits leave themselves no proper working time to follow up and obtain more detections from the grade A1 forensic intelligence identifications they have been given.

Using the 'Breakers' Collection in the precomputer era, the Met Bureau had spectacular success in linking scenes and detecting serial offenders in that literally thousands of identifications were made. It was in that working environment in 1975 that we had the first experience of how an organised attempt at analysing forensic recoveries could be successful against volume crime.

The Beginnings of a Concept of Forensic Intelligence

In Barkingside Division in Northeast London in 1975, I was posted as the divisional SOCO and was confronted with 6 to 10 burglaries a day in addition to vehicle crime, thefts, and a sprinkling of robberies and sex crimes. Based on assessments of the possible number of offenders responsible for these crimes, the overall crime rate implied that the population causing the

crime problems approximated at between 25 and 30 persons. A simple calculation indicates that if 30 offenders commit one or two offences a week,
then over a year the total will be in the ballpark of 3,000 offences per year,
which approximated the real casework total for burglary that year (30 × 2 =
60 offences per week × 52 = 3,120). There were no computers or other technological facilities available, so notice boards and flip chart paper were used to
record the series of burglaries on the office wall. Entries were posted in red for
fingerprint cases, green for other forensics such as shoe and tool marks, and
blue for cases with police information, intelligence, or feedback from arrests.

Our efforts, starting mid-1975 into mid-1976, solved one series after
another by the use of fingerprints, footwear matches, pre-DNA technology
blood index hits from blood typing, and police activity. The total number of
active burglary offenders prosecuted in that period from this work totalled
27, concentrated mostly around the burglary series. The number of reported
burglary offences dropped from up to 12 per day at its peak to just three per
week due to our concerted efforts at forensic detection and problem-solving
police work. The estimate of 25 to 30 criminal burglary nuisances tying down
the division proved to be accurate, but without Home Office, government, or
academic research to support our experience, the forensic detection technique
developed at Barkingside Division was not adopted by other teams within the
Met force. Even still, with continued efforts using these techniques, the divisions I was subsequently posted to achieved top results in forensic detection
and crime reduction for the Met—particularly Newham borough in the early
1980s, which for a number of years was amongst the top boroughs for results
for forensic identifications amongst the London boroughs.

The Introduction of Information Technology: From the 1980s Onward

In the mid-1980s, changes to the structure of Forensic Services in the Met
Police enabled innovations to take place. The installation of a Printrack AFIS
computer system had advanced the process of forensic intelligence, making
the manual 'breakers' collection obsolete because the scenes of crime teams
could now electronically scan in scenes of crime marks for search against
10 print fingerprint sets, thus speeding the process and enabling pan-London
searching. By the 1980s, the police national computer (PNC) had been networked to every division in the whole of the United Kingdom and a number
of police forces had installed their own AFIS systems.

The lessons learned from the manual fingerprint Breakers System, plus
the use of modern information technology and the other evidence types such
as footwear and tool marks, could become more dynamic in crime analysis

applications using the following methods. By basic methods of coding and sorting out the coded forensic evidence against other crime, information links and clusters of offences could be established. The experience with the manual fingerprint Breakers Collection's success had indicated a way ahead in dealing with other nonautomated forensic evidence forms.

At this stage, it should be pointed out that the way police services in different countries deal with forensic examinations varies considerably. In UK practice, crime scenes forensics recoveries and the processing of evidence from those scenes are largely in the domain of civilian specialists. The objective is to examine as many crime scenes as possible to maximise results from the DNA and fingerprint recoveries. At the same time, other forms of forensic evidence are searched for, noted, and recovered, so there is a tremendous amount of potential forensic material available for intelligence and detection uses.

In other police services across the world, some forensic services are not so well resourced even to the point that, for example, burglary scenes are not forensically examined unless there is a suspect or sometimes not at all. Within such a business model, the intelligence with detection opportunities is compromised and many victims of crime are not given the level of service that, as taxpayers, they should expect. Worse still, there are police services where forensic examinations are left to individual officers' discretion or largely not done at all unless the crime is a very serious one. From personal experience, I have lived through working scenarios covering both extremes, and progress is only made in general crime reduction if a modern business model is followed covering forensic examinations of most reported crime. Thus, it is quite feasible for a police service of any size to adopt a forensic intelligence approach within the concept of problem-oriented policing (POP). In fact, the smaller police services in the UK, such as West Yorkshire and Lancashire, have been very successful in achieving high detection rates with forensic intelligence because small departments covering forensics and intelligence can share offices, with improved communication.

It may be assumed from the television programme *CSI* that all that has to be done is to pop an exhibit in a slot and the computer reveals all that needs to be revealed to solve a case. That is, in the main, a ridiculous set of scenarios presented in the *CSI* television series. New technologies such as AFIS and DNA are useful but are not magic fixes to resolving crime problems.

It is important to realise that in a police service with good forensic performance, finger marks are recovered from 25% of burglary scenes and DNA from 5% to 9% of crime scenes. There is a cap on DNA recoveries because the offender has to bleed or shed body fluids, hairs, or tissue. This means that in the preceding good performance scenarios, DNA is *not* found at approximately 90% and no fingerprints at approximately 75% of burglary scenes.

In many police services across the world that negative 'not found' percentage is considerably higher. It is important in a good working forensic business model, therefore, to consider the other forms of evidence commonly found at crime scenes and not to trust to luck that a serial offender will suffer a cut or forget to take gloves to the scene. Remember that it is a fact that offenders cannot fly or pick locks like Tom Cruise in *Mission Impossible* movies, so footwear evidence recovery at crime scenes is very useful, as is the recovery of tool marks; both evidence types can show geographical distribution and provide conclusive matches.

COMPSTAT

With respect to the United States, the New York Police Department (NYPD) has had success largely achieved through a thorough revision of the business model and working practices realised through COMPSTAT ('computer statistics' or 'comparative statistics'). A visit to the NYPD website clearly indicates the success achieved through the significant investment made by the city.[13]

Unfortunately, not all police services can benefit from such massive investment and levels of manpower; however, significant improvements can be made within available resources, without overstressing the existing staff. The New York model does indicate, however, how it is possible to bring the reported crime situation under control, thus enabling economies in ultimately not having to resource an enormous amount of crime scene visits and examinations. This is the true value of intelligence-led policing. The success that New York experienced with COMPSTAT has not always been repeated elsewhere—perhaps through lack of manpower and forensic resources to back up the implementation of the COMPSTAT model together with a great number of officers patrolling every 50 yards or so, as is the case in Manhattan.

The true economies for the taxpayer dealing with policing are to create working practices complementing business models using intelligence and forensics, to reduce crime in order to enjoy the later benefits in public safety with reduced costs.

Police Intelligence Models and the Language of Intelligence-Led Policing

In order to give an idea of the structures and language used in police intelligence models generally, the intelligence assets products described in the UK NIM and their functions are covered next as an example for readers to compare against their models.

All intelligence-led policing models are about setting strategies and tactics and providing live intelligence assessments as products to take the business forward, operation by operation; thus, the UK NIM is a good benchmark against which to compare others. In intelligence-led policing, the identified strategic issues, although important, should be seen just as necessary parts of the business and should not be the only issues pursued to the detriment of other issues. By default, this creates other strategic problems if they are allowed to develop.

'Intelligence Is What It Does': A Definition

Amazingly, most of the texts written about intelligence-led policing and crime analysis in their contents do not mention the words 'forensic' and hardly ever 'intelligence'; nor is any guidance given as to the creation of original intelligence products found by analysis of forensics. These textbooks are more about performance-statistics-led policing that say, 'This or that is going on and let us send out the troops', but what about actual detections and evidence for prosecutions? When presenting their findings, the authors of these approaches always say something along the lines of, 'When we mapped the crime in the area, the amazed police chief said, "Hey, I was sceptical at first but I need to know this stuff"'. From my experience, someone in that position of authority with such a lack of a grip should get some help or quit—or could it be that the proponent of problem-solving techniques has no forensic background and has never been to a crime scene in the role of someone who has to provide the evidence to solve the case?

The main purpose of this book is to improve the situation in crime problem solving and analysis by introducing the value of forensics in intelligence. Through this awareness, new drivers can be created in developing true intelligence models, which can find new crime problems and solve them in constantly changing new and novel situations. After that, the entire problem-solving function is at the heart of this definition of intelligence: **'The ability to use knowledge and skills in solving problems to produce solutions in new and changing situations'.** This is the definition I preferred to work to in my service.

Police Intelligence Models

Police intelligence models, including the UK NIM and US COMPSTAT model, all have their roots in the work in problem solving, typical of the work produced by the problem-solving laboratory in Washington, DC. The thinking is to create a pyramidal business structure to enable organisations to realise priorities, set tactics to deal with the priorities, and analyse known data

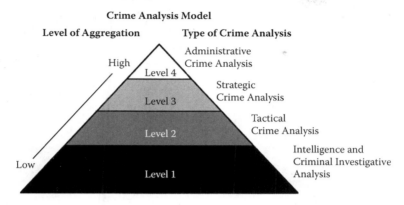

Figure 1.3 Pyramidal problem-solving model. (NIJ 8th Crime Mapping Conference, United States, 2005.)

around those priorities utilising intelligence sources, whilst at the same time dealing with the bulk of cases to some extent being reported to the organisation. The problem-solving pyramid described by the problem-solving laboratory has four levels of crime assigned to it (Figure 1.3). However, most police models quote only three levels of crime, ignoring the top 'administrative level four', where directions are given by government to law enforcement agencies in pursuit of its objectives, which usually have to be included in their strategic objectives products, sometimes irrespective of the actual real situation across the spectrum of their particular jurisdictions. For simplicity, the universal structure discussed in this text is related to a three-level model.

The Four Levels of Crime Divisions in Crime Intelligence Models

Crime within intelligence models is split according to the perceived seriousness of the offences. For example, under the UK NIM and in the US COMPSTAT model, the levels are defined as follows:

- Level 1 crime: general volume crime within a police division
- Level 2 crime: cross-divisional and cross-force volume crime; also, more serious crime within divisions
- Level 3 crime: serious crime, which may be within a division, across divisions, across forces, or even across national boundaries
- Level 4 crime: administrative level included for completeness, where government wishes police to follow a strategy for political, social, or other reasons as perceived by government

Clearly, these crime levels define to a certain extent at what point decision-making processes kick in as to who will deal with a crime problem as it develops. Further, as intelligence products are really business cases for the coordination and tasking processes within policing organisations, there has to be a business model to enable those resources to be applied to the crime problems as they arise. The UK NIM mixes crime levels with geographical links and levels of crime, requiring a somewhat bureaucratic approach to advancing casework through a tasking and coordination cycle. COMPSTAT also has a cycle, which is very publicly aired in the media as a driver. Both models generally work in a 2-week review cycle.

The UK NIM operates at each of the crime levels, so the local division has its own tasking and coordinating process, as do the business groups dealing with level 2 and level 3 crime. Through each crime level, tasking and coordination of casework progress up to and down from and to the next level. Level 4 is somewhat different in that government influences the strategies of police services at their highest strategic level.

The pyramidal intelligence model in Figure 1.3 also gives a false impression of less manpower dealing with serious crime at the top, but in reality serious crime and murder investigation teams have high levels of manpower and can afford to explore every avenue in a non-Bayesian (nonprobabilistic) approach to crime investigation. Thus, perhaps a better suggested model would be to create intelligence route maps for advancing casework. These would kick in when a case develops from whatever crime level upward or downward, defining direct action to whoever deals, in order to refer intelligence products for action at the right level. Such a model would have more of a 'snakes-and-ladders' appearance than a pyramid, and this approach may be considered for development in the future.

New York Police Department: COMPSTAT

In the NYPD COMPSTAT model, everything from, for example, bicycle thefts upward is considered and comparisons are made between where the department is at the present and the crime levels historically (see Figure 1.4). This process is reviewed in a very public forum and acts as a process where public views and pressure are considered in the NYPD's dealings with crime at all levels. In contacts with the NYPD and other American police professionals, it was not clear how they viewed the concept of forensic intelligence or how it fitted in with COMPSTAT. One thing is clear: As a discrete issue, forensics is not mentioned in the model; yet, in the NYPD, there has been a considerable investment in forensic support. Reference is made to inputs from prisoner debriefs in the COMPSTAT diagram but not expansion of forensic hits, and in the relentless follow-up section, a performance indicator identifying offenders is listed as a feature considered in measuring performance.

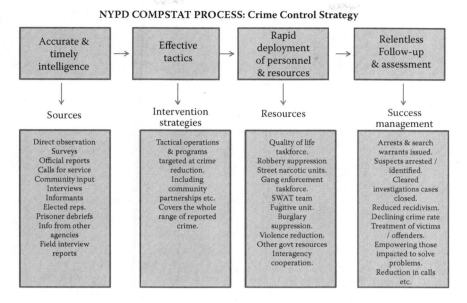

Figure 1.4 COMPSTAT diagram. (From NYPD Internet site. With permission.)

In this section, it is stressed that, when referring to intelligence models, these should encompass crime analysis, geography, and forensics. In reality, if all these components are not considered in the round, then the ability to see the whole picture is compromised. With this loss, the risk to the organisation is increased through the possible inhibition of casework progression, leading to poor performance or to a major scandal leading to the removal of top management in a worst-case scenario.

Intelligence Assets

A generic minimum number of assets is required for an intelligence-led police business to function; these encompass all of the personal training, data storage, knowledge references, and technology to enable those involved in an intelligence-driven model to function. All properly constructed criminal intelligence models use the following three assets as defined in the UK NIM, although these three assets can be applied to any police business:

- Knowledge
- System
- Intelligence (people and sources)

These three assets apply universally, for even small police services with few officers pass on intelligence and analytical information to the chief for action, even if it is 'from the hip' in the process of day-to-day work. This intelligence and analysis is derived from intrinsic knowledge of law, processes, policing business structure, what is happening in their jurisdiction, and the use of information technology systems and intelligence sources, plus what forensics can reveal or support. What they are in fact doing is using the main intelligence assets and products without formalising the process; however, in so doing, the records of what caused actions to be taken will be incomplete and, consequently, the learning may well be lost. This was evident in policing organisations prior to processes like the UK NIM or COMPSAT; otherwise, there would have been a need to advance these ideas in improving the results of modern policing.

Through use of the three main assets, the UK NIM is used to create four key intelligence products. Indeed, versions of those products are also present in the COMPSTAT process, for it is within the framework of both models that the national or local rules and laws define how the processes, business, and best practice are delivered. Both processes are about tasking, coordination, accountability of police services, and improving results.

Knowledge Assets

These assets are concerned with staff training, the legal framework in which staff members work, the understanding of standards, and best practice to deliver intelligence products for action in tasking and coordination. It is important that staff members have access to the right information and facilities to enable their work. Within knowledge assets, the legal framework required is defined to enable legal intelligence gathering as required for progress in casework. In the UK the Regulation of Investigatory Powers Act 2000 (RIPA), for example, defines intrusive and directed surveillance and what permissions are required for surveillance to be carried out legally. In the United States, there is also a legal framework defining correct practices for investigators and defining what is admissible and what is not, depending upon whether or not the right permissions and due processes were used.

System Assets

These are the manual and information technology systems that enable the security of data as well the grading, evaluation, and analysis of data to enable the intelligence model to work. System assets provide the background against which to check intelligence information for validity. For example, an informant (covert human information supplier, CHIS) reveals that a specific individual is committing crimes. The first stage on checking this intelligence is to interrogate systems to ascertain if indeed those crimes were reported and, if so, the details of the case. Could the details of the case(s) be checked plausibly against the supplied intelligence to enable analysis and decision making to be made to advance the case?

The following typical core system assets in modern policing are from a Met Police UK perspective, but those in other countries will recognise generically their versions of these systems, some of which are marketed internationally to many police services:

- Crime report system
- Intelligence system
- Custody records system
- Stopped-persons database
- Intranet within the organisation enabling knowledge repository, communications analysis, and statistics production
- Internet for open source information and communications externally
- National criminal records system (e.g., UK police national computer, PNC)
- Computer-aided dispatch system (CAD)
- Automatic fingerprint identification system (AFIS) or national system (NAFIS)
- National DNA Database (NDNAD)
- National Ballistics Intelligence Database (NaBID)
- Forensic intelligence data and forensic legacy data
- Crime mapping system
- Major investigation system (e.g., HOLMES [Home Office Large Major Investigations System] in the UK)

Some countries have yet to create NDNADs, NaBIDs, forensic intelligence and legacy data, and major investigation systems or are using old systems; however, in consideration of the perceived desire of police services to develop them, they are included.

When engaged in planning changes and the development of crime intelligence system facilities in the information technology area, the best advice is to try to see the whole picture. In implementation of new intelligence systems, it is best to avoid the use of people who are 'intelligence hawks'—who will try to declare in advance, by category, what is intelligence and what is not. The truth is that any information can become useful intelligence and restrictions that are too tight should not be placed on system inputs because such an approach will inhibit performance through intelligence loss. The best approach is to supervise daily intelligence logs input to the intelligence system and work with stakeholders in getting the business right. After all, the computers involved can handle far more data than most organisations could generate in a decade or more. Bad handling of intelligence and information policy can actually generate a threat to an organisation's performance.

In the Met, since 2006 and 2007, there has been a move to integrate searching across multiple system assets with the creation of the Integrated Intelligence Platform (IIP), enabling investigators and analysts to use one search to look for a name, place, or topic across most of the systems listed before. The current development is toward 'entity'-based records to move away from the older records-based police systems. The concept is that persons, places, vehicles, locations, forensic exhibits, etc. are real entities, so a search carried out against any entity should produce responses about that entity. The current records-based police systems cause searches against entities to be made by proxy; records are sought where the entity may be in a field in the entry. The FBI has an entity-based records project at this time and some companies are producing software to assist the COMPSTAT process by data mining relevant records to the entities being researched.

Intelligence Assets

Intelligence assets range from the officer on the beat to the top level 3 staff in crime intelligence working in confidential units managing undercover police officers and the supervision of the handling of confidential informants, who are intelligence assets also. Intelligence assets are in all parts of the policing business, from level 3 down through levels 2 and 1—units that mirror those functions in their own business groups. Through intelligence assets, confidential information is processed, surveillance carried out, and the intelligence services within the policing organisation managed.

The Four Generic Intelligence Products and the Aims of COMPSTAT

The **knowledge, system, and intelligence (people and sources) assets** enable the production of the four main intelligence products and, even in COMPSTAT, the process has those products. They may not be named as in the NIM, but the four published aims of COMPSTAT are to provide

- Accurate and timely intelligence
- Effective tactics
- Rapid deployment of personnel and resources
- Relentless follow-up and assessment

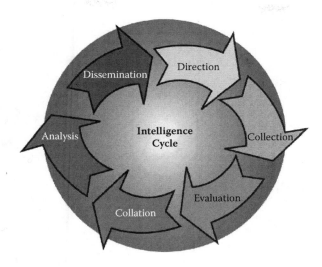

Figure 1.5 The intelligence cycle. (From R Milne presentation to Forensic Science Society, 2009.)

These are broadly what the UK NIM and COMPSTAT are about, and each business model fits into the intelligence cycle in Figure 1.5.

In the NIM (Figure 1.6), as in COMPSTAT, accurate and timely intelligence is used in the two overarching products:

- **The strategic assessment** identifies the key issues to be dealt with by the police organisation, enabling judgements to be made around prioritisation of those objectives. Strategic assessments are made in a quarterly to half yearly cycle (some cover longer periods for delivery), but emerging threats can accelerate their production. Strategic assessments can be generated by an emerging threat, increase in a crime type, government objectives, or matters of concern to the population in the policed area.
- **The tactical assessment** (US COMPSTAT 'effective tactics') covers the practical issues around the implementation of the strategic assessment(s). Several tactical assessments around different crime types and within different police business groups can be generated in achieving the goals set in the strategic assessment. The tactical assessment in the National Intelligence Model covers the second objective of COMPSTAT in using effective tactics in dealing with crime problems. A tactical assessment defines the scope of the problem and proposes operational solutions in prevention, detection, or diversion of the problem.

In the NIM, two further products are produced that give the business case for the deployment of personnel and resources, which is the third main

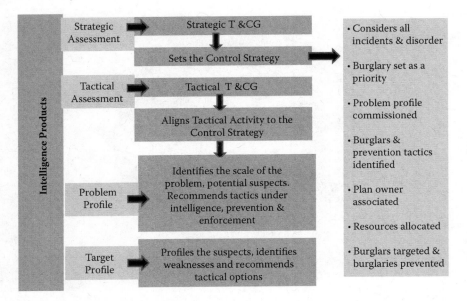

Figure 1.6 UK National Intelligence Model products. (UK National Police Improvement Authority, NPIA, NIM CD.)

objective of COMPSTAT—the 'rapid deployment of personnel and resources', which also operates along similar lines in both models. Those two products are the following:

- **Problem profiles** are usually written around crime problems where definite suspect(s) are not precisely defined but named suspects may be included in the profile. Problem profiles are generated for two main reasons:
  - The first is in response to maintaining problem profiles routinely for each priority crime type identified in the strategic assessment to keep track of the crime type. The up-to-date problem profiles of this type are used in the intelligence cycle to compare and evaluate progress in dealing with the problems. In the COMPSTAT process, a similar product would be an enabler in the areas of deployment of resources and in the follow-up.
  - The second reason for creating problem profiles is that research, analysis, and forensics identify crime problems or crime series. This form of the product can be specific around a crime series or, for example, an organised crime group.

  Problem profiles are created around crime series and problems; however, in the case of targeting individuals or defined groups, another profiling product is used:

- **Subject profiles,** sometimes called target profiles, are created around and about individuals or groups of individuals. Subject profiles under the National Intelligence Model fulfil a similar function to achieve the COMPSAT aims of effective tactics, follow-up, and assessment. Subject profiles may suggest surveillance and the issues of obtaining permissions or lifestyle research into the subject(s) to ascertain if they are living from the proceeds of crime.

In the areas of problem and subject profiles, with respect to criminal networks, the definition of a criminal network used in the Metropolitan Police is as follows (there may be variations on this definition in other police services): *three or more persons engaged in criminal activity over a prolonged period for the motives of profit, power, or self-gratification.*

In the NIM, problem or subject profiles are in the form of proactive assessments, which are in fact business cases put forward for the tasking and coordinating group to deploy policing assets to deal with the problem or subject profile. In smaller level 1 volume crime cases, the proactive assessment can serve as the problem or subject profile and will suggest tactical solutions. The intelligence products in this form in the UK Metropolitan Police service include calculations of projected manpower costs and overtime to advance the business.

Intelligence Sources

In criminal intelligence work, strategies, tactics, and analytical products are produced through the processes of research and analysis of intelligence from many sources. These can be broadly categorised into three main categories:

- Confidential sources. These are usually in the form of either information from covert human information suppliers (CHIS) (in other words, informants). Intelligence from confidential sources is often marked secret and access to confidential source data is restricted on a need-to-know basis. Undercover officers work through a confidential unit in police organisations, which usually sits within the main force intelligence bureau (in other words, mainly within police intelligence and systems assets).
- Restricted sources. Examples of restricted sources are official records such as crime reports and most crime level one and two intelligence logs in the volume crime area (in other words, mainly within police systems assets).
- Open sources. These are literally open and available to everyone; examples are press reports, information published on the Internet, published social demographic data, etc. In the 'open source' domain, the knowledge assets are usually available to all.

Intelligence Handling Codes

In the NIM and most other international intelligence systems, handling codes in a five by five by five (5 × 5 × 5) system are assigned to each intelligence log and define the reliability of the intelligence and who is entitled to view it subject to permissions and the status of individual system users. The first two codes are usually assigned by the person creating the intelligence log, subject to supervision, and the third handling code is usually assigned by the intelligence supervisor.

The 5 × 5 × 5 System as Used in Grading Intelligence

This model grades the source of the intelligence by five letters: A to E. It evaluates the information as a score of 1 to 5 and on the same basis indicates who has access to the information:

- 5 × 5 × 5 intelligence report
  - Source evaluation
    A: always reliable
    B: mostly reliable
    C: sometimes reliable
    D: unreliable
    E: untested source
  - Intelligence evaluation
    1: known to be true without reservation
    2: known personally to source but not to officer
    3: not personally known to source but corroborated
    4: cannot be judged
    5: suspected to be false or malicious
  - Handling codes are to be completed at time of entry into an intelligence system and reviewed by a supervisor regarding dissemination levels:
    1: may be disseminated to other law enforcement and prosecuting agencies, including law enforcement agencies within the EEA and EU compatible (no special conditions)
    2: may be disseminated to UK nonprosecuting parties (authorisation and records needed)
    3: may be disseminated to non-EEA law enforcement agencies (special conditions apply)

4: may be disseminated within the originating agency only

5: no further dissemination: refer to the originator; special handling requirements imposed by the officer who authorised collection

It is standard practice when dealing with an informant or CHIS known to be totally reliable and known personally to an officer to code the highest intelligence code as 'B1'; then, a handling code is added as appropriate. Only forensics can be graded in the case of conclusive positive matches or links as A1. The third number is added to define at what level the intelligence can be disseminated. Thus, a log of intelligence from a reliable CHIS, which may be disseminated to others, would be graded 'B-1-1'. If the source was unreliable and not well known to the originating officer, then the log could be graded 'E-4-1'.

Forensics as Intelligence Sources

In the case of forensics, the results of forensic examinations from crime scene examinations, fingerprint bureaus, or forensic science laboratories can be viewed as intelligence sources for development into intelligence products because forensics can

- Imply links between events
- Prove links between events
- Identify or match individuals to events
- Identify or match individuals to other individuals as victims, associates, or others involved in inquiries

Forensics can be used to produce stand-alone intelligence products for action or used to corroborate or prove other source material to enable higher confidence levels around intelligence products. Just like any other source, forensics can start, progress, or finish investigations or provide a range of inputs and outputs to assist investigations.

Forensics can provide the material for the production of problem profiles around crime clusters and links. Forensics can also provide the material for subject profiles and as such is as valuable a source of intelligence products for action as any quality information from a covert human information supplier (CHIS). Forensics can also prove the value or otherwise of CHIS information.

The Collection of Forensic Intelligence

When crime scenes and individuals are examined, methods, timings, locations, behaviours, and forensic exhibits are recovered and recorded. The
forensic exhibits and information gleaned are case specific but add collectively to global (across the police business group) collections of information
and evidence. If properly organised, this can be viewed by evidence type or
crime type in collection or database.

Collections can be a data set—for example, in the UK, the National DNA
Database—or a physical set of exhibits such as the old national fingerprint
collection now represented by NAFIS. In the case of shoe and tool marks,
these are stored locally on divisions but for reference can be databased on
systems for sharing across police business groups for data search and scene
linking, providing forensic intelligence input. These softer forms of forensic
evidence can be submitted to laboratories to establish matches and confirmation of links for intelligence purposes.

Arson data, for example, is case specific, but also provides a set of global
in-force and cross-force data, covering methods, behaviours, locations,
times, materials used, and other forensic evidence giving specific information about accelerants, physical marks, and biometric results from fingerprints and DNA. The application of forensic intelligence methods enables the
merging of stakeholder data sets such as fire service data to set the reported
crime data in context.

Police Forensic Business Models

In the modern intelligence-led policing environment, scene examiners
(CSIs) should use their knowledge assets from experience, available force
knowledge products, and training to input forensic data into police systems
assets to record the examinations and provide input into the intelligence
systems. Through access to the police briefing and intelligence systems, the
scene examiner can make use of intelligence products for awareness and provide the opportunities for police intelligence assets to create new intelligence
products, as well as adding value to existing intelligence products being used.
Forensics can also be invaluable in distinguishing superficially similar crime
scenes, which normal analysis techniques would find difficult or impossible
to do.

A major function of this text is to provide awareness to crime and intelligence analysts about the true value of forensic recoveries and not just those
valuable results from single fingerprint and DNA matches. Most publications covering the topics of crime analysis and intelligence processes do not

adequately cover forensics as a valuable contributing source to the creation of intelligence products. Further, there is a mistaken view that all forensic results are reactive after the fact, but nothing could be further from the truth. Techniques such as 'upstreaming' and the mathematics of scene linking enabling levels of significance to be put around forensic problem and subject profiles are covered later in the book.

In upstreaming, forensic links between, say, drug seizures enable assessments of the common sources (across national boundaries) to be made, leading to a capability to take the investigation back to those common sources and shut them down. From a 2005 drugs forensic intelligence workshop held at New Scotland Yard by my forensic intelligence desk and the SCD forensic intelligence desk, the concept of using drug test purchases and user seizures laboratory analysis of larger amounts for drug seizures in Southwest London was taken back to the Serious and Organised Crime Agency (SOCA) by its forensic liaison officer. This led to SOCA creating its own Operation Endorse, which has had a serious effect in cutting the illicit drug trade to the UK.

In some police services in the twenty-first century, there has been vast expenditure to the point of overkill in buying intelligence and analysis capabilities, whereas the forensic services department has often been treated as a Cinderella service. It is always worth remembering that a good CSI in a detective department or division can detect more unwitnessed and cold cases than all the rest of the department put together. Through working through the actual crime scenes, the scene examiner has a valuable intrinsic knowledge of what is happening on the ground. Teamwork is the key and arranging a model to capture vital evidence information producing intelligence for researchers, analysts, and investigators is what is required.

A Short History of Forensic Intelligence in the Metropolitan Police

Prior to 1986, all scenes of crime forensic databases other than the Fingerprint Bureau's collection were maintained inside the Metropolitan Police Forensic Science Laboratory (Met Lab), which at that time was owned in house by the Metropolitan Police but operated along the same business lines as the other Home Office Forensic Science Laboratories in the UK. These databases comprised

- Blood index derived from grouping bloodstains and body fluids from crime scenes and samples from suspects in custody
- Shoe mark index and reference data collection maintained for serious crime only from armed robbery upward in severity

- Instrument mark (tool mark) index covering London and the surrounding Home Counties
- Gun collection and ballistics comparisons in mainly Met cases
- Drugs reference collection
- Various reference databases—for example, vehicle paint, fabrics, etc.

In 1986 I created Operation Bigfoot—a coded database of scenes of crime shoe marks utilising the Metropolitan Police forensic science laboratory (Met lab) shoe codes from their reference collection (Figure 1.7).[4] This collection became the Forensic Science Service 'Chorley' coded collection when the Met lab was sold to the then new UK Forensic Science Service Agency, whence the Met had to pay for the information!

Prior to Operation Bigfoot, shoe codes were not entered on crime reports and the only way an investigator could search for a shoe pattern was to visit a scenes of crime office and go physically through the exhibits. As the facility was precomputerisation of crime report records, the Bigfoot reference database was distributed on microfiche film to all 32 operational command units in the Met Police. Each CID office had a microfiche reader for reading criminal record files and most had a microfiche copier enabling the printing and copying of footwear images for dissemination to police.

Together with Operation Bigfoot, an instrument mark coding system was developed using the coding protocols in use at the Met lab. Footwear mark and tool mark data were entered on crime reports in the SOCO field,

Figure 1.7 Bigfoot shoe mark coding microfiche update issued to all Met scenes of crime staff in 1987 before computerisation. (Source: R Milne.)

making the data available for investigators and arresting officers. The data were then manually input into a spreadsheet, enabling analysis and statistical performance data to be created.

The change in working practices by the CSIs was to make them aware of the use of Bigfoot data in crime scene linking and to share this information with investigators. This was 16 years before the UK adopted intelligence-led policing under the NIM. The almost total lack of access to information technology by the Met's forensic field force limited the development and use of forensic intelligence at that time.

In 1996, the Met Police installed their first computerised Crime Report Information System (CRIS), and in 1997 a few desktop computers began to appear in the offices in Forensic Services. However, most staff, especially the scene examiners, had virtually no access to e-mail or the emerging internal force intranet. As an innovation, I obtained funding arranged by Roger Shearn, scientific support manager, Northeast London, for two CRIS 'screen scrape' computers to be built. According to search parameters in the form of Boolean operators, these machines could extract up to 1,000 cases at a time with coded forensic recoveries, in Microsoft Excel format, giving the Bigfoot footwear and tool mark codes, with locations, methods, fingerprint and DNA status, etc.

This enabled immediate research and analysis of hitherto unseen crime series and, for the first time, on demand, we could visualise whole crime types against evidence and whole evidence types against crime types across Metropolitan London. Because the structure of the Met Police was split into four geographical areas at the time, only Northeast London's area had the facility, although we could look across into the other areas of volume crime forensic recoveries, seeing level 2 cross-divisional crime series.

An Early Forensic Intelligence Tool Mark Case Example from the Late 1990s

In the first week using these data, formerly unseen crime series were sent in report format to various police divisions. One of these was a burglary series revealed from tool mark data. Harrow and Edgware police were contacted in the Northwest London area and informed that they had many more 10 millimetre single blade lever edge tool mark residential burglaries (code SBE10) than the whole of the rest of that quarter of London. Their response was that they thought SBE10 levers like screwdrivers must be common—a fact that they could not possibly know because they had never before seen the real data in this format and obviously knew nothing about probability techniques in estimating the significance or otherwise of the links. The SBE10 marks were found only in the northwest area at less than 1 in 30 burglaries, so to find a cluster straddling two divisions was highly significant; otherwise, why were they not spread about elsewhere uniformly? In addition, the cases were all midweek (Tuesday to Thursday) and mainly midafternoon; only cash and jewellery were taken. The mapping of the scenes revealed an activity space and possible journey to crime routes restricted to an area bordering the two divisions.

Whilst the police were pondering a course of action, things rapidly came to a head when a man returned home early from work and disturbed a burglar, who stabbed the man to death with an SBE10 screwdriver as the murder weapon. The suspect was arrested within a week and it was found that he lived in the town of Peterborough north of London and commuted by coach to the area, sleeping rough midweek and burgling houses. He took only property he could carry and convert easily to cash. It transpired that he had been committing six to eight offences per week and had not been arrested for 3 years. In that time, he had committed literally hundreds of offences as a travelling burglar, for if he had been active in his hometown, where he was known to police, he would have been subject to being routinely stopped during his activities. It was found that when the suspect had been arrested previously for burglary, he had admitted about 800 offences—or about the sum of 2–3 years' activity for this person.

The series had not been picked up by local police for three reasons:

- The local analyst was not using the analysis of forensic recoveries as a standard main technique and consequently did not have the extra data to enable the sifting of lever-entry burglaries of one series from another.
- It was assumed that the SBE10 levers were common and the method was too common to sort out the cases from hundreds of others. This was not the case, for in seeing the whole picture, the SBE10 lever marks were only common to a restricted area and nowhere else in a similar context.
- Without the forensic intelligence data, the frequency of the finding of the evidence type combined with other data could not be ascertained, so it was difficult to decide what clusters were significant without this knowledge.

Another problem was that, in the late 1990s, the Metropolitan Police did not have an intelligence-led policing culture; consequently, their business model was not fit to deal routinely with this type of intelligence and task responses to it.

The Metropolitan Police Modernise
for the Twenty-First Century

In 1997, forensic intelligence was as a facility developed in only one business group in the Met's Northeast London area at the Northeast Forensic Science Support Unit (NE FSSU) under the direction of Roger Shearn, the scientific support manager. He had the foresight to obtain funding enabling progress to be made. Through studying the relationship between forensics and other crime data in crime problem solving, it was realised that there was scope for improving the techniques of the CSIs and their working practices. For example, the way footwear marks were dealt with compromised third-level detail and affected results. Reports were made about the inadequacies of the Police and Criminal Evidence Act 1984, in clarifying the right to take footwear from those in custody for search. (This matter was not resolved by the UK government until 2006.) This work in relating forensics performance to make it fit for a forensic intelligence capability led to the following:

- A best-practice guide with refresher training for all Northeast London staff in quality marks recovery with a guest forensic scientist specialist invited to each training day. Refresher training was later spread to the whole Met organisation.
- The design and installation of modern sequential treatment fingerprint laboratories to deal with volume crime efficiently, using internal filtration cabinets, designed in partnership with a fume cabinet manufacturer to our top-down design but now copied by manufacturers everywhere. The introduction of digital fingerprint imaging for volume crime gave a capability to deal with street robbery property resulting in approximately 500 Met fingerprint hits plus a similar amount of DNA hits per year against street robbers. Before the changes in working practices, hardly any street robbers were identified. All volume crime in the northeast area was handled by the laboratory in a 90-hour turnaround time.
- My design of a compact electrostatic wireless dust mark lifting device—the Pathfinder—to boost the recovery and awareness of recovering quality third-level detail footwear marks.

In 2001 the Met appointed Gary Pugh, OBE, as the director of forensic services—the first scientist to be appointed to this role. Gary set about the modernisation of forensic services in the Met and secured over £100,000 funding to equip 76 Met scenes of crime offices with networked desktop computers. Gary reviewed the northeast volume crime sequential treatment laboratory and immediately saw the value in creating a similar laboratory in each of the other areas, thus efficiently dealing with volume crime and relieving the central fingerprint laboratory to focus on serious crime. The volume crime fingerprint laboratories had a 90-hour turnaround time target for casework and could deal with urgent cases on the same day.

Gary not only procured resources to provide the laboratories, but he also brought about the business change to introduce forensic intelligence as a development issue. It was not known at that time how far we could develop the concept, but the feeling was that, through tackling the problem of effective uses of forensics in crime intelligence, we would improve our working practices, develop new technologies, and maximise the return on the investment in forensics.

Forensic Intelligence Development in the Metropolitan Police, 2002–2008

Two forensic intelligence offices were created in 2002 to work on development in the two main Met Police business groups: Territorial Policing (TP) and the Specialised Crime Directorate (SCD).

My office then was with the TP Directorate and had the largest share of the forensic field force of crime scene examiners, servicing all of the volume crime in London and covering level 1 and level 2 crime. When the Met Police adopted the NIM in 2004, my office was aligned to the TP Intelligence Unit, producing pan-London intelligence products for tasking and coordination under the Metropolitan Police model and delivering the objectives of the NIM. During this development phase, 10,000 crime scenes were linked on hundreds of series and up to 300 problem profiles written per year. The crime report system (system asset) research revealed that 3,000 detections had logged on crime reports relating to those crime reports covered in the problem profiles. Figures 1.8 and 1.9 show the auto route mapping from the TP Forensic Intelligence Unit supplied to detectives for transporting a suspect around the crime scenes listed in the intelligence problem profile, following his arrest, to enable the offender to pick out the properties and describe what he stole and other facts to clear the cases. This would be an activity listed under 'relentless follow-up and assessment' in the COMPSTAT process.

In territorial policing, the Forensic Intelligence Unit explored techniques that could be developed to research and test concepts, but in the SCD Forensic Intelligence Unit, they were only tasked to deal with certain issues in order to try to add value to investigations. This feature of the strategic end of the business related directly to John Minderman's (FBI Behavioural Science Unit Retired) advice cited earlier in this chapter.

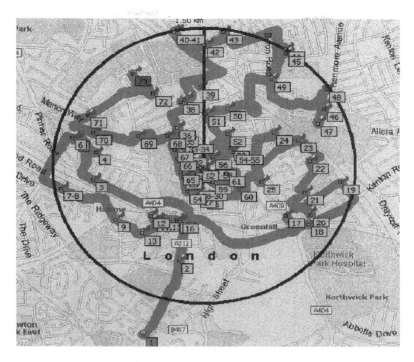

Figure 1.8 Brantingham crime pattern involving 91 detections in Northwest London in 2004.

In the TP side of the business, concepts such as the journey to crime, the living space of offenders, and the mathematics of scene linking related to evidence recovery frequencies were explored. Partnerships with other bodies such as the London Fire Brigade, the Government Office for London, academia, etc. were also explored to ascertain the extra potential value that could accrue from such partnerships.

The SCD unit under the management of my colleague, Julian King, looked at issues such as why legacy data from forensic science provider laboratories were not always easily available. With both forensic intelligence units working together, the following avenues were explored:

- Workshops with forensic science provider laboratories involving the Met contracts manager, scientific advisors, scientists, and account managers focussed around discussions about products procured and changes to working practices to enable better use of case and legacy data.
- The cross-force Home Counties forensic intelligence group was set up to explore cross-force forensic intelligence links and met quarterly in the city of London police office.

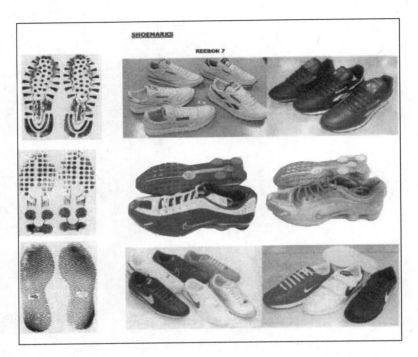

Figure 1.9 Images from the Bigfoot shoe collection from the 91-case series shown in Figure 1.8.

- Links with other development strands in the Met Police Forensic Services Directorate and externally (e.g., NaBIS and other forensic services sections were developed and service level agreements were arranged around delivery of tactical assessments in moving on casework results.

During the development of the forensic intelligence concept, forensic intelligence units, in partnership with stakeholders, produced the following facilities:

- Operation Bigfoot footwear and instrument marks database
- Best-practice guide for CSI forensics in intelligence, a Met Police report
- Operation Bigfoot, *Journal of the Forensic Science Society,* 2001, and the presentation at the Forensic Science Society meeting in Amsterdam in 2001
- Forensic applications using the Interactive Offender Profiling System (IOPs), which was developed in partnership with Prof David Canter's team at the International Academy for Investigative Psychology now based at Huddersfield University; a system combining behavioural profiling with geography and forensics in the forensic intelligence

applications; used in workshops and real casework; workshop lead-
ing to briefing SOCA's head of emerging developments
- The creation of a cross-force forensic intelligence group
- Presentations on the mathematics of scene linking and the mapping
  of forensic evidence (R Milne and C Leist for the Jill Dando Institute
  of Crime Science, National Crime Mapping Conference, London
  University; and the 8th National Crime Mapping Conference,
  National Institute of Justice, United States, 2005)
- Various forensic science provider workshops
- The shared data partnership between the Met Police and London
  Fire Brigade and the creation of a forensic intelligence shared data
  structure; data structure being incorporated in the format of the
  eFIT1 electronic means of notification to police of deliberate fire setting in Metropolitan London
- Proactive assessments in the forms of forensic strategies, problem
  and subject profiles covering thousands of cases and hundreds of
  identified offenders
- Work on the Met's forensic intelligence process map of the handling
  system for ballistics intelligence
- Forensic intelligence products around gun conversion criminal networks, organised cannabis production, and sex offenders, and support casework around serious crime investigations

Where Forensic Intelligence Should Fit within Police Organisations

In the development phases from 2002 to 2008, a number of business changes
were made in developing a forensic intelligence capability. The following
approach is the one that I believe is the most useful and, from experience and
advice, is the right place to site the main part of a forensic intelligence capability.

Forensics-like behaviours can arise anywhere in any casework across any
organisation at any level, so the very piece of evidence sought to lead to an
offender could arise in the volume or serious crime areas. Forensic intelligence should be visible and researched across the various crime levels; otherwise, it is likely to be missed. Forensic intelligence starts where evidence is
collected from all crime scenes and should provide input at all crime levels
from serious to volume levels. It should not be centred only in a specialist
unit dealing with serious crime, but the specialist serious crime investigators
should be able to look across the whole business. Likewise, the units dealing
with volume crime should not be denied a capability to make best use of all
forensic recoveries in an intelligence-led environment.

Summary

This chapter has offered a broad view of what forensic intelligence is about. It has provided basic terms in the subject of police intelligence models and products with respect to the UK NIM and COMPSTAT. A brief history of forensic intelligence in the Metropolitan Police has been detailed.

Country-Specific Considerations

United States	United Kingdom
Many small police services and fewer large policing organisations; over 10,000 services	Forty-three police services
National Institute for Justice gives guidance only	Strong direction from the Home Office NPIA and ACPO
COMPSTAT was recommended to be adopted, but not universally	The NIM country wide
Forensic services patchy and undermanned; no national DNA database, with some states not yet passing legislation	Civilianised forensic services working broadly to similar standards
9/11 and Homeland Security	NPIA project to move forward and avoid mistakes of the past
Desire by smaller police services to improve intelligence-led policing	NPIA forensic intelligence projects (e.g., National Ballistics Intelligence Service, NaBIS; National DNA Database, NDNAD; National Fingerprint System, NAFIS; ANPR; National Footwear Project, NFRC)

The Value of Forensics in Crime Analysis and Intelligence

2

Intelligence Features of Forensic Evidence Types

By their nature, forensic evidence types are best viewed in two main categories as the biometric forms of evidence; fingerprints and DNA are for practical, near infallibility purposes specific to individuals or conclusively link crime scenes and individuals to those scenes as well as establishing identity. The other forms of evidence derived from matching physical marks, such as shoe and tool marks or trace evidence transferred between suspects and scenes, are viewed as softer forms of evidence. By looking at these main evidence types in turn it can be seen that they have properties that lend themselves to different practices in processes and interpretation; nevertheless, they can produce a range of links graded in descending order as

- Conclusive
- Highly significant
- Moderately significant
- Little significance
- Not linked

These terms are used routinely in forensic science to assign values to findings in court statements and reports. It is recommended that the same terms should be used by analysts and investigators when using forensics in crime intelligence as a guide to the value of the research and analysis.

Process and interpretation are in the areas of assessing how much detection may be possible from biometric identifications or the significance or otherwise of linked crimes in perceived clusters. After all, police intelligence-led models are about improving detection and driving crime reduction, and a major part of the work of the intelligence crime analysts is to prepare the business cases for tasking and coordination. This is as true for the National Intelligence Model (NIM) as it is for COMPSTAT. Later in the chapter, explanations are given as to what is meant by linking cases and then taking each evidence type in turn and revealing whether or not it provides the forensic intelligence potential in the following areas:

- Individual case match capability
- Global in system collection of matchable suspects data
- Global in system collection of matchable crime scene data
- Cold search identification capability
- Case-linking capability
- Evidence recovery frequency data
- Sharing of data in force, across forces, or nationally
- Sharing data internationally

Linking Cases and Comparative Case Analysis

In consideration of what problems are resolved in scene linking, a review of the subject reveals the following factors[11]:

- In the development of information for offender identification, the more factors that can be associated with the same case, the higher the confidence level around the significance of the results of the research will be.
- If significant links can be established between scenes, then this enables the prioritisation of forensic examinations, strengthening the follow-up processes in the NIM and COMPSTAT.
- The better the intelligence and analysis tied to forensic evidence recoveries are, the more likely it is that an offender will admit other offences committed, thus increasing the detection rate. Often, offenders will only admit cases that they are responsible for committing and that they think the police can prove.
- Cases in court are strengthened by similar fact evidence gleaned by analysis supported by forensic results. Convictions can be realised through cases established by a system used by offenders to commit crime, combined with forensic links.

Forensic intelligence gives opportunities to set the forensic links within the other circumstantial and behavioural evidence. It gives factual links to other analytical links based on probability around timings, locations, and methods. The use of forensic intelligence offers opportunities to develop case-work derived from behavioural science analysis from the realms of investigative psychology assessments, particularly in serious crime casework.

The Different Forms of Case Linking in Criminal Analysis

The linking of crimes and individuals to crimes has a number of varieties of linking problems and each requires a different form or criterion for answering the linking problem. The strength of applying forensic intelligence to crime analysis from a great number of crimes, even across vast areas, is that it often enables resolutions of the linking problem. Further, once the correct person or persons are targeted, forensics can solve the cases because forensics

- Is specific
- Is persistent
- Is graded in support or otherwise of suggested hypotheses
- Implies links
- Proves links
- Identifies individuals
- Profiles individuals

Forensics can start a case, advance a case, end a case, or solve a case.

Varieties of Forms of Case Linking

- One to one
- One to some
- Some to some
- Few within many[11]

Any analytical process based on probability and facts such as geographical profiling, psychological profiling, or general analysis on general reported crime statistics, method, or temporal data can generate the following questions:

- Are the cases actually linked?
- Can any cases be unlinked?
- Have any cases been missed in the linking process?
- Are there any false alarms in the linking process?
- Can we establish that the rejected cases have been correctly rejected?

A mix of probabilities can be illustrated mathematically and may offer some guidance in evaluation of scene-linking intelligence products. Obviously, if a method is so unusual, for example, as to be very rare, then it is more likely that a repeat occurrence has a higher probability of being linked, whereas a common method on its own needs other supporting factors such as forensic evidence. A good example would be a generic method of breaking into houses by kicking in the front door. Here, the likelihood of recovering shoe marks from the attacked doors is very high, so clusters of cases with the same shoe pattern or in combination with other analytical evidence give a higher probability of links from a few cases within many. In this situation, crime analysts with little forensic awareness assume that everyone is walking about with common designs of shoes. Those assumptions are about the general population and not the small subset of the population who are burglars. Further, without knowledge of the vast number of thousands of shoe sole patterns on the market or any idea of what the offenders are wearing, no sensible assessment can be made of the significance of a cluster of the same patterns.

To solve this problem, a forensic intelligence database will provide the pattern frequencies for the bulk of recovered marks from real crime scenes, thus assigning a value to the recoveries and indicating how rare or otherwise those recoveries are within the context of reported crime. These data have nothing to do with general shoe sales to the general public. The recovered shoe patterns could be statistically rarer than the unusual method, to which value was given in the hypothetical case and the forensics are more significant as a linking factor. It is really essential that crime analysts be given a proper awareness of the value of forensics, for in real work experience, I have found this is not usually the case. It is equally as important that police departments invest in their forensic support and make the effort to supply quality information technology.

The mixtures of possibilities in case linking mentioned before shows that the judgement as to whether or not cases are linked can miss cases that are linked and unlink cases that are part of a series, as well as validly link cases. The more effective the linking factors are, the less likely it is that errors will be made, resulting in a lower proportion of misses and false links.

A method of exploring this problem is the technique of **receiver operator characteristics (ROCs),** which determine the criteria for linked cases. This approach enables the plot of an ROC curve.[34] The larger the area under the curve is, the more effective the case-linking criteria are.

The following probability approach can be used to illustrate the strengths or weaknesses of links between cases:

$$pH = \frac{a}{a+c} \qquad\qquad pFA = b(b+a)$$

$$pM = \frac{c/(a+c)}{a+c} \qquad\qquad pCR = \frac{d/(b+d)}{b+d}$$

where
  p = prediction
  a = linked
  b = false positive link
  c = miss
  d = unlinked
  H = hits

FA = false alarms
M = misses
CR = correct rejections

Receiver Operator Characteristics

The ROC was described in a paper by T. Fawcett in 2006.[11] The ROC approach can be useful in evaluating the values for ROC assessment. Obviously, a biometric fingerprint or DNA link is evaluated as 1 and a shoe pattern link from the commonest pattern type with no expert confirmation of the link may be 0.3. Other values have to be assigned according to some assessment of probability. Assessed '1' links in a series obviously will create a very fat area under the curve (AUC; see Figure 2.1), whereas common methods or behaviours on their own will give a pretty slim curve, with much less of a confidence level that the series is firmly linked. This gives mathematical proof of the value of forensic intelligence. This makes the lack of appreciation of this area in crime analyst training staggering—especially when considering that the current state of crime analyst training in many police services generally contains virtually no serious awareness of forensics.

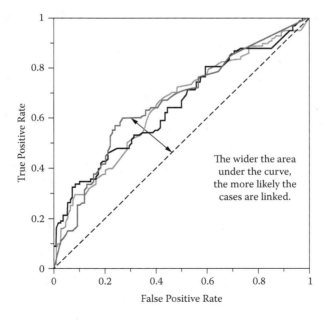

Figure 2.1 The AUC curve. The larger the area under the curve is, the more effective the criteria are.

Truth and Probability

When police investigate crimes, facts are recorded, as well as resources and training; from those facts, hypotheses are produced. From those hypotheses, strategies and tactics are produced for action. Is the truth, however, being dealt with or just calculations and opinions that real truths are being dealt with? After all, at most crime scenes the people dealing with the investigation do not witness the commission of the crimes personally and have to rely on secondhand information collected by others. Can the opinions derived from the collected information be tested or can alternative explanations be given to describe the problem or situation?

This consideration of truth and probability may seem to be probing into the philosophy of criminal investigation, but the word philosophy itself means 'love of truth' and, in consideration of the concept of forensic intelligence, truth needs to be explored for the simple reason that most texts on criminal intelligence analysis concern themselves solely with problem solving and handling of information arbitrarily deemed to be intelligence. They do not, in general, explore the actual processes of proof, provision of evidence, and detection leading to prosecution in the courts.

The removal of offenders by the processes of detection and prosecution is just as valuable as the process of using crime data and statistics in a business model in an effort to solve crime problems. Indeed, it could be argued that training under 1% of a police service to deal effectively with the forensic examinations of the bulk of crime scenes is actually a more economical process than hiring a large number of personnel as analysts and researchers to deliver a bureaucratic police intelligence model that, by its nature, will tend to be seized on by performance managers to provide impressive crime statistics in pursuit of management objectives, instead of providing real intelligence for action. Performance analysis has its place and the management of the deployment of manpower, based on analysis and intelligence, is a necessary ingredient of modern policing. Without evidence provision and prosecutions, however, the effect of the analytical effort will likely be merely to displace a crime problem onto another jurisdiction or temporarily suppress the activity.

The model used in illustrating the concept of the minimum factors needed for a crime to occur is the 'crime triangle', where each of the three factors for a crime to have been committed is assigned to each side of the triangle—the offender, the victim, and the location. If one of these three factors is missing, the crime cannot occur. The theory is that by removing or obstructing one of these factors, the problem is solved. This is true, but is this for an hour or two, a day, a week, or more? Who knows? A patrol car parked strategically from a tasking following analysis of robbery locations and times may cause a short break in criminal activity, or a CCTV camera placement may produce a more prolonged effect. What the crime triangle model does not include is a fourth factor—'evidence', but without it, detections and prosecutions will not take place. The four-sided model is introduced in this text.

The Crime Detection and Prosecution Rectangle

The Values of Forensics in Case Linking

Evidence takes many forms and may come from the victim, the offender, the location, or permutations of all three generic sources (see Figure 2.2); each in turn has the capability to link to other events outside the original crime. Forensics of all the evidence types is generally more reliable than witness evidence and offers the following features:

- Forensics is an independent aspect of the crime scene.
- Forensics offers another layer of intelligence.
- Forensics is a separate means of identifying clusters.
- Forensics can link cases across great spans of time and distance that would not have been linked by other means.

All police services deal reasonably well with single-case forensics but much of the crime scene examination effort is wasted if there is no training or business model in place to deal with the resource created by the collection of forensic marks and evidence from crime scenes. The purpose of forensic scene linking as part of a policing model has four main functions:

- To identify clusters using forensics to assist in sorting common crime types from one another
- To enable the analysis of crimes in clusters to enable evaluation that the scenes are linked

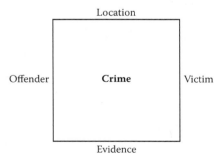

Figure 2.2 The detection and prosecution rectangle. (Source: R Milne.)

- To develop profiles of offenders from forensic analysis, crime analysis, and other intelligence available
- To use the resulting intelligence products for further use in investigations

Thus, linking crimes with forensic intelligence techniques gives the following advantages to the crime analyst:

- Identifying clusters using forensics assists in sorting common crime types from one another, thus improving UK NIM tactical assessments and problem/subject profiles, as well as improving the tactics and relentless follow-up in the US COMPSTAT model.
- Aiding the evaluation of crimes linked by analysis reinforces the evaluation that the scenes are actually linked, thus improving the NIM tactical and problem/subject profiles. The tactical and relentless follow-up processes in the COMPSTAT model are improved.
- The development of profiles of offenders from analysis and other available intelligence improves the subject profiles, tactics, and proactive business cases for tasking and coordination of police assets.
- Additional development of intelligence products for further use in investigations is enabled.

It is not enough to refer in crime analysis to forensics as 'check if there any forensics to support my analysis'. Rather, the question should be, 'Who is carrying out performance analysis on my force's forensics for quantity, quality, structure, data integration, development, training, etc.?' These issues are just as important as working out crime levels relative to fixed time slots or elucidating other statistics, which are not actually crime intelligence or detection processes. The processes in a true intelligence-led model should include probability and truth to function properly. This means getting a grip on forensic 'nonhuman' sources as well as human sources in improving a police service's perception of what is going on.

A Footwear Evidence Persistence Case Example

DNA technology has illustrated how dynamic forensic evidence can be in solving cold cases, but even the softer forms of evidence have been known to solve cases after many years have elapsed—for example, a robbery case solved in the south of England where, through information from an intelligence source, an armed robbery offender was convicted and sentenced to 15 years in prison.

When the offender was released over 10 years later, he tracked down the informant and murdered him. The scenes of crime officer still had old photocopies in the archive of the offender's shoes taken for speculative search years before (before the Police and Criminal Evidence Act 1984) and compared them with the shoe marks from the murder scene. To his surprise, they were the same design and size. Upon expert examination, the offender's shoes were conclusively matched to the murder scene marks. It appears that the offender had handed over his shoes, which were not required in the original robbery investigation, to the prison property store at the start of his sentence. On release, he collected them and wore the same shoes when he committed the murder, so excessive wear on the shoes between events was not an issue. This is an extreme case, but it illustrates how persistent and specific forensic evidence can be.

A Linked Homicide Case Example

In 2006 in South London, a man was found stabbed to death in his bathroom with extensive blood splashing in the room. No finger marks or stranger DNA was found at the scene, but the shoeprint pattern on the bathroom door that had been forced by bodily pressure was researched in the Met Police 'Bigfoot' forensic intelligence database and the pattern found to be recovered at only 1 in 3,000 crime scenes—a fact communicated to the murder investigation team (MIT).

A few days after the murder, some 20 miles away in another jurisdiction, a woman was attacked in her home by an intruder armed with a knife. The only room with a door that locked was the bathroom, so the victim sought refuge there. In this case, the attacker did not manage to break through the door to attack the victim and fled the scene. He left a fingerprint at this scene, leading to his identification within 24 hours; upon his arrest, his shoes not only matched marks at both scenes but traces of blood DNA from the murder victim also were found on his shoes, leading to his conviction for both offences.

The quick resolution of this case was possible because coded and pattern descriptor file details of all shoe mark recoveries in Metropolitan London were available at the touch of a button. Prior to this facility, the detectives would have had to circulate gazetteer or briefing pictures, asking if anyone had seen this type of shoe mark and then would physically have had to go through stored exhibits in many locations. The resolution of this case was so swift that it almost certainly saved another victim suffering at the hands of the offender, who had serious mental problems. Interestingly, the facets of both crime scenes generated by the suspect caused the same actions by both victims to result in seeking refuge in the bathroom. The text will later cover the effects of different facets (facet theory) in a criminal act or behaviours causing an effect called intermodulation or other facets to emerge as features of the scene.

Dealing with Forensic Crime Links and Clusters

Clusters can be spatial or temporal and can be identified forensically, by method, by behaviours, or by combinations of all these features. Most forensic identifications, matches, and links are capable of being made into intelligence products. Forensic clusters of similar evidence can also be used with other crime intelligence, or analytic data can likewise be used to create intelligence products for action by police under the NIM or COMPSTAT business models.

The system, knowledge, and intelligence assets of a policing organisation should enable the recovery of the following information:

- A means to determine the scale of offending
- The CSI/police recovery rates for each forensic evidence type
- The frequencies of recoveries of each forensic evidence type of forensic mark and evidence type

This information enables the estimation of the following components toward the construction of a problem profile intelligence product:

- The number of crimes in clusters where specific coded or described forensic marks or impressions have been found
- From the evidence type recovery rate, an estimate of the range of the total number of offences in which offenders could have been engaged
- From the finding rate for a specific type of mark, the estimated probability of finding another mark of the same type

A Footwear Mark Cluster Example

In researching a coded forensic intelligence database of crime scene shoe mark recoveries, a cluster of five burglary scenes is noticed in an area 1 kilometre in diameter. Two other scenes, one closer and the other further away, along a road heading west from the possible clusters are noticed; the farther away case is the first with that shoe pattern to appear at a similar method burglary—possibly an outlier. What is the probability that the seven-case cluster is possibly linked? Can the total number of offences be estimated?

The forensic intelligence shoe mark database should log the number of times the particular shoeprint pattern has been found in the time frame against the total number of shoe mark recoveries in the whole area, within the 1 kilometre circle. These data give the mark finding rate for shoe mark evidence in that area also. The Treadmark software supplied with this book gives the finding frequency as a percentage of the database of each pattern type file on the system. If shoe pattern codes are input into a modern crime report system, then the data can be recovered as a spreadsheet enabling the frequency data to be easily recovered.

In this case, the shoe mark finding rate for CSIs is 20% of burglary scenes,[16] so for a seven-scene cluster, the total range for scenes is between 7 and 35 scenes for the total number of scenes in the time frame (7 × 5 = 35). From other crime report data on method, timing, types of property taken, etc., it is found that the estimate is 12 scenes in the cluster, adding those scenes where shoe marks were not found.

If the total shoe mark recoveries in the 1 kilometre defined circle are 456 in the same time frame and the particular pattern in the cluster has a simple probability or finding rate of 7/456, this equals 0.015 or 1 in 65. This figure is highly significant, for the total probability would be for seven scenes (7/456) multiplied seven times, resulting in a very small number and giving very high odds that this is a series and not just an accidental gathering of marks of the same code. Otherwise, why are those marks not spread uniformly elsewhere? The binomial model can give a better indication that the cluster is very unlikely to be accidental, but for practical purposes the simple arithmetical probability assessment is adequate.

Footwear Evidence Frequency Evaluation

The same type of calculation can be applied to tool marks and other forensics where repeat occurrences of the same type are found. From a mathematical investigation of shoe mark clusters by Terry Napier and Fiona Pearson,[16] it was found that, for shoe marks, if the finding frequencies are assigned in the following ranges, then the following descriptors are appropriate:

- High significance: less than 1 in 100
- Moderate significance: between 1 in 50 and 1 in 100
- Weak significance: between 1 in 10 and 1 in 50
- Little significance: greater than 1 in 10

For the more statistically common patterns, of which there are relatively few compared to the vast range of patterns available, more scenes are usually required to improve the confidence level that there is a cluster.

In the case of footwear sole patterns, there are over 19,000+ designs in the UK market[17] and from real collected data there are only a few really common patterns found frequently at crime scenes. Consequently, this would attract the 'little significance' descriptor from the table produced by Fiona Pearson.[16] Most footwear pattern types require only between three and five scenes in a cluster to be significant.

The following tables highlight the strengths and weaknesses of the current state of the uses of the main forensic evidence types within a highly developed police service. The situation in less developed services around the world is much less complete. The tables highlight the areas to be targeted to improve the capability of an organisation to make best use of forensics with respect to crime analysis support and intelligence. Those evidence types that all answer 'yes' are from the UK (and, in the case of fingerprints, the United States), whereas the position is not so clear with other forensics in that things are not so well collated forensically. The United States still has to resolve the national DNA database situation and, in smaller police services, there is scope for improvement—for which purpose I hope this book will be found to be of use.

All police services, however, at little cost can improve and work on the applications of the softer forms of evidence usually stored locally. The material, equipment, and information technology required are either already in a normal office environment, and the costs of the crime scene investigation equipment are not large compared with a 'normal' police department's budget. The issues are largely awareness, organisational, and training issues. The tables cover the position in 2011 in the UK.

Properties of Forensic Evidence Types Reviewed with Respect to Intelligence Potential

Forensic Intelligence Properties	Status of Properties
	Fingerprints
Individual case data	Yes
Global data suspects	Yes
Global data crime scene marks	Yes
Cold search capability	Yes, subject to research to cause searches or new techniques to develop marks
Case-linking capability	Yes
Sharing data nationally	Yes, subject to finding force notifying originator of NAFIS reference number cross-force
Sharing data internationally	Via protocols on request
	DNA (if a national database is available)
Individual case data	Yes
Global data suspects	Yes
Global data crime scene DNA	Yes
Cold search identification capability	Yes
Case-linking capability	Yes
Sharing data nationally	Yes
Sharing data internationally	Via protocols on request
	Footwear and Footwear Marks
Individual case data	Yes
Global coded reference data of patterns and manufacturers	Yes; in UK the NPIA National Footwear Reference Collection (NFRC), available in Treadmark software and in SICAR (Shoeprint Image Capture and Retrieval) data

Forensic Intelligence Properties	Status of Properties
Global set of suspects' data in scanned images or on paper	No; practices vary between police services and countries; should be easy with scanners and proper software
Global set of scenes of crime marks	Yes, in coded forensic intelligence form in some police services; needs software such as Treadmark or SICAR to link suspects' shoes to scene marks for real quality screening
Case-linking capability	Yes, via forensic intelligence techniques and by physical comparison
Cold-case-linking capability	Yes, if the proper software is in use with digital imaging so that police can share data for search
Sharing data nationally	Yes, in the provision of the NFRC in the UK and Operation Liberal offering a national approach to footwear in travelling distraction burglary scenes
Sharing data internationally	On request; NFRC in the UK has the capability of linking in internationally
Tool Marks	
Individual case data	Yes, exhibits stored locally but coded descriptors enable search and filing to find the exhibits
Global suspects data	Not usually; depends on legality of seizing tools for speculative search. However, coding protocols are included in this book, enabling forensic intelligence searches; has potential for technological development
Global scenes of crime data	Yes, at a forensic intelligence level using coding and descriptors enabling exhibit location for laboratory submission and expansion of crime analysis in casework
Cold-case identification capability	Yes, in certain circumstances limited by poor business models around this evidence type, which often provides conclusive evidence of matches if it is submitted to a laboratory
Case-linking capability	Yes, definitely; if the same tool has made the marks, then the match is generally conclusive; similar to footwear in being very useful for scene-linking purposes
Sharing data across forces/ nationally	Sharing by request
Sharing data internationally	Sharing by request
Ballistics	
Individual case data	Yes
Global data suspects	Yes
Global data scene marks	Yes

continued

Forensic Intelligence Properties	Status of Properties
Case-linking capability	Yes, using IBIS (Integrated Intelligence Ballistics System) technology (e.g., UK NaBID—National Ballistics Intelligence Database)
Sharing data nationally	Yes, usually in a national or state ballistics intelligence service (e.g., UK NaBIS—National Ballistics Intelligence Service)
Sharing data internationally	By request although international links are being explored.
	Illicit Drugs
Individual case data	Yes, but within individual laboratories or police services
Global data suspects	Can be obtained as legacy data from individual laboratories and police services
Global data from seizures across departments	Can be obtained as legacy data from individual laboratories
Case-linking capability	Yes, was offered by FSS Gov Co in UK and FBI has a linking capability; can be requested from laboratories that may be able to offer a service
Sharing data nationally	By arrangement and via protocols set up by national serious crime units—SOCA, FBI, etc.
Sharing data internationally	On request via protocols
	Arson Forensics
Individual case data	Yes, split between police and fire service data sets
Global data suspects	Available via police records
Global data scene forensics	Yes, available from police crime reports and CSI notes as well as laboratory and fire investigator reports
Case-linking capability	Yes, through forensic intelligence data sharing and other forensics from scenes
Sharing data nationally	On request; most arson is committed by local marauders
Sharing data internationally	On request if required in specific cases

The concepts of how, through teamwork, the uses of forensics can be enhanced in modern intelligence-led policing are easily appreciated. The text thus far has been focused on the topics of intelligence assets, products, and the applications of forensic intelligence in the areas of crime scene forensics. Computer and mobile phone research and data are covered in later chapters, but through use of forensic links, individual phone records can be checked in a network analysis to find nodes to other contacts of interest. Analysts can produce a cost-effective facility for network analysis using Node Excel, which is available as a free download from Microsoft.[18]

Forensic Legacy Data

The data sets from crime investigations, crime scene examinations, fingerprint bureau, and laboratory examinations combined with intelligence gleaned plus recorded crime data are called legacy data. A good working model combined with good working practices gives those involved in investigations and crime analysis access to legacy data so that they can see the whole picture. A bad model or lack of any model can deny access to some or all of the legacy data. So depending on the working practices, issues can be clarified, obscured, or even totally hidden to the extent that an underlying problem is not perceived.

The access to legacy data is important as the wrong model or lack of a model in dealing with the issue of forensic intelligence applications can prevent or inhibit access to the knowledge, systems, and intelligence assets of external forensic science providers and police analysts. The inhibiting factors can be in the areas of the business model, working practices, or inbuilt for contractual or financial reasons.

Although it is appreciated that some intelligence has to be kept confidential, a good business model should allow all stakeholders access to legacy data categorised as below the level of 'confidential'. The levels of confidentiality are

- Top secret
- Secret
- Confidential
- Restricted
- Not protectively marked

Although not totally exhaustive, the following list covers most of the items that comprise legacy data or provide legacy data:

- Crime report information
- Crime intelligence system with $5 \times 5 \times 5$ evaluation of intelligence logs
- Scene examination data
- Method data
- Behaviours data
- Coded forensic marks with frequency data
- Forensic marks measurements and descriptors with frequency data
- Crime statistics
- Crime analysis
- Laboratory case files (includes X-force)—for example, FSS sexual offences intelligence service

- Laboratory reference collections
- National reference collections (e.g., UK NFRC)
- Laboratory global and case-specific evidence types of data
- Ballistics intelligence (NaBIS and laboratory data)
- Physical and chemical characteristics data
- Scientists' statements
- Victim and witness data
- Hard evidence (fingerprints and DNA) identifications and case links
- Geographical data and profiling
- Temporal data
- Knowledge databases

The legacy data items all fall into the categories of knowledge, system, and intelligence assets because any of those items provides information, which can become intelligence for action. The inability of investigating officers to have access to legacy data in forensic science laboratories has led to costly and serious failures in investigations. An example of one of those failures was the handling in the UK of the Damilola Taylor murder case, when a 10-year-old boy was murdered in Peckham in South London.

During forensic science laboratory examinations, extremely detailed notes and photographs are taken and extensive files covering the work are created. The output from the laboratory is in the final form of a statement for court use, but it is usual for updates of the progression of the case to be given to investigating officers. The laboratory files contain far more legacy data than is normally supplied to the client investigator.

In the Taylor case, the investigators were not in a position to ask questions about the status of the examinations of each blood spot, some of which were not sampled or sampled with an adequate method. Upon another forensic science provider's reexamination a few years after the initial laboratory examination, the DNA profiles of two suspects were actually found on the shoes and clothing of the victim. One of the blood spots on a shoe belonging to the victim was quite prominent, but were the investigating officer and the investigation team in a position to see the legacy data? Were they in a position to ask crucial questions about the status of the laboratory casework and ask the question as to whether the stain had been DNA sampled?

In work-shopping UK private laboratories around general forensic intelligence issues, I found a tendency to charge the customer for the legacy data generated during casework examinations. However, when the issue was pressed, some accommodation could be made in the provision of legacy data across a crime or evidence type. After all, the client has paid for these data or, in the case of state-owned or in-house laboratories, the issue involves the service-level agreements between the organisations and the users.

Legacy Data and the FSS Sexual Assault Forensic Intelligence Service

A good example of forensic intelligence legacy data use is in the sexual assault service offered by the former UK Forensic Science Service Gov Co (FSS), where the FSS provided a quality forensic intelligence service to most of the police services of England and Wales. They could do this because they had a good cross-force overview of the casework combined with details of behaviours of offenders as well as forensics from legacy data. The FSS service also worked with the client police services to improve the quality of their submitted casework, thus saving costs whilst improving the detection rate. By the time this book is published in 2012, the sexual assault service may be scrapped with the government cost-cutting exercise in progress in the UK or the service may find a private company to take it on.

Improving the Potential of Legacy Data Use

In reviewing the potential for legacy data to be available, the following actions can improve the situation and the way in which policing organisations do business by obtaining the data they require through the following actions, which can be very productive:

- Review internal and external working practices.
- Examine business plans and forensic science provider contracts or service-level agreements.
- Is legacy data provided in some form?
- Are the data supplied fit for use?
- Hold workshops with forensic science providers and stakeholders (i.e., contract managers etc.).
- Recommend the best options for stakeholders to minimise knowledge, systems, and intelligence gaps.
- Give forensic science providers insight into the needs of the customer to improve business on behalf of the customer.

The Importance of Regular Meetings

Most police force intelligence bureaus (FIBs) hold daily intelligence meetings (DIMs) or weekly intelligence meetings (WIMs). New issues are raised and progress charted at the DIM as to the position of ongoing investigations. In police divisions, lower key versions of the DIM are held (usually referred to as 'morning prayers'). CSIs should attend intelligence meetings or send a briefed representative from the forensic support team on a regular basis—and certainly when fresh casework is to be introduced. The attendance at these meetings raises awareness of the contribution of forensics and also awareness of issues where the forensic support team can provide input from their intrinsic knowledge of crime in the division. This process also gives police management the opportunity to ask questions about the forensic support and task that support in support of operations.

Further, crime management has the opportunity to provide forensic strategies around developing crime problems to make best use of resources as they present themselves. It is all part of improving teamwork in pulling together the assets of the policing team. Attending the intelligence meetings and tasking meetings can provide valuable insight into the work and offers a briefing for suitable material to be cascaded in other forums such as cross-divisional meetings, which are held less frequently. Each section contributes to the meeting process, so the forensic support is represented and management is made aware of the contributions made. Management is also offered the opportunity to involve the forensic support staff in operations offering timely and quality support to the policing team.

Outputs from meetings take the form of briefing and tasking reports for dissemination to police manpower. The tasking of intelligence and analytical assets can also result from the meetings, which are a very good means of raising new series and emerging threats.

The Different Experiences of CSIs and Analysts

This is one of the most important sections in this book and should be noted well. It is worth remembering that crime analysts in many business groups only look at those issues at which they are tasked to look. The CSI, on the other hand, has a brief to visit most or nearly all major crime and is working through the activities and living spaces of criminals in the area, whilst witnessing the types of victims by dealing with them directly; management does not dictate what the CSI should and should not look at. Often the CSI does not need a complex crime mapping program or have to look up records secondhand to establish facts because they are actually there in a working, living experience. The CSI is therefore a valuable member of the team who can greatly assist crime analysts and not just someone paid to put evidence in bags. It is all about injecting elements of firsthand truth into secondhand analytical data to reinforce the quality of the intelligence products.

In this chapter, the concepts of the values of forensics in intelligence are covered, although many readers will work in situations where forensic services are not so well developed, or where crime analysts are not available owing to pressure on resources. At a local level, it is still a practical proposition to look at how the problems of the provision of forensic evidence and crime analysis can be resolved within resources. In the subsequent chapters, each main forensic evidence type and best practice in recovery is covered, as well as a practical routine for officers to carry out forensic intelligence research whilst carrying out a useful job in basic crime analysis. For those wishing to develop intelligence and crime analyst skills, the International Associations of Intelligence and Crime Analysts offer training. What they do not offer at this time, although that may change, is useful awareness on forensics in crime intelligence and analysis, which is offered in this text.

Summary

This chapter included the following:

- The potential intelligence features of forensic evidence types, with some examples
- What is meant by crime linking and the various forms of linking
- Receiver operator characteristics (ROCs) enabling a value to put to the strength of links with the area under curve (AUC) method
- Truth and probability: Are we getting to the truth or just a perception model of it?
- The concept and definition of what intelligence is opposed to performance management analysis
- The 'crime triangle' model and the concept of the fourth factor 'evidence' to secure detection and prosecution
- The value of forensics in case linking
- Case examples of persistence and swift resolutions though forensic intelligence
- Dealing with forensic crime links and clusters
- The properties of forensic evidence types, with respect to their intelligence potential, covering the features of the evidence types in collections or databases
- The concept of the use of forensic legacy data and what these are
- Methods to improve the use of legacy data
- The importance of regular meetings to advance casework and intelligence products
- The different work experiences of CSIs and analysts

Research and Analytical Processes

3

Introduction

From a practical point of view, the process of dealing with forensic intelligence mirrors many of the features of the approaches used by police intelligence units in research and crime analysis. The focus, however, in dealing with forensics is to focus on crime and evidence types as well as the traditional tasks of researching methods, locations, victim profiles, behaviours, types of property taken, etc. That is not to say that activity defines the limits for forensic intelligence. It has applications in market analysis and, in dealing with illegal commodities, offers opportunities to upstream casework with considerable impact, as is the case with drug markets in Operation Endorse created by the UK Serious and Organised Crime Agency (SOCA) (see Chapter 1). At any stage in an intelligence-led operation, what seems to be reactive forensic evidence at the outset can be used to create a proactive intelligence product or assist in the creation of one.

Forensic intelligence can and does have an impact on applications of the nine main analytical techniques used to support the UK National Intelligence Model (NIM), which are used to create the four main intelligence products in the form of strategic assessments, tactical assessments, problem profiles, and subject profiles. For this reason, forensic intelligence should be viewed as the tenth standard analytical technique because, if it is ignored, then an intelligence product cannot be viewed as complete.

The Nine Analytical Techniques

It should be stressed that the different analytical techniques described next are not stand-alone items. Rather, techniques from each are borrowed to construct intelligence products as required, although discreet outputs from each of the nine techniques should form as required the basis for quality presentations for the purposes of police coordination and tasking:

1. Crime pattern analysis
2. Market profiles
3. Demographic and social trend analysis
4. Criminal business profiles
5. Network analysis
6. Profile or target (subject) profile analysis
7. Results analysis
8. Risk analysis
9. Operational intelligence assessments

Crime Pattern Analysis

Crime pattern analysis looks for links between crimes and offending to seek similarities or differences. Some of the techniques of crime pattern analysis are intended to resolve the problems of crime linking as defined in Chapter 2. The forensic intelligence input is a potentially powerful tool to help resolve the problems of linking crime, particularly where normal techniques have difficulty in sorting out linked series from common-method crimes. Forensics offers the facilities to link over great spans of time and space and the opportunities to develop casework from intelligence sources, which would be difficult without the facility.

Forensic intelligence can provide the evidence of emerging threats and risks within linked cases hidden amongst many that would not be perceived so easily without its help. Crime pattern analysis offers the police business group the research to enable the efficient deployment of police resources in prevention and diversion initiatives. Through joined research and analysis, forensic intelligence problem profiles, recorded in the force crime intelligence system, offer police the opportunities to seek evidence from suspected persons whilst employed in prevention and diversion exercises. From personal experience, all too often analysts do not make best use of the forensic component in establishing and resolving crime problems and, because they have no proper grounding in forensics, do not make best use of the specialities in this area provided outside their section. To make things happen requires the awareness of forensic services management and some active participation by intelligence units to work through processes for best delivery. Managing the whole business requires management as an active trade.

Crime pattern analysis also includes identifying crime hot spots, finding trends or otherwise in crime, which may be increasing or decreasing, and establishing crime series and the profiles of offenders with some confidence level. Without the acquisition of an element of established truths and evidence, the inclusion of individuals as targets in analytical reports can result in individuals being spotted by briefed police wherever they happen to be and these locations being entered in intelligence logs—thus providing an almost self-fulfilling prophecy in a situation where the 'suspect' is just hanging around or going about his or her daily business. Using crime pattern analysis to drive research into individuals associated with crime hot spots is a laudable objective, but without a real surveillance effort (which is expensive), only forensics offers the practical cost-effective solution to prove cases—but only if that option is recognised, involved, and enabled.

In forensic intelligence, crime pattern analysis is of interest because of the potential in relating offenders interactively to the crimes and evidence found in the offenders' living spaces. Interactive offender profiling is a developing technique with which I have personal experience. Through associate membership of the International Academy of Investigative Psychologists (IA-IP), in which I am a full associate, I have some insight into current research and developments.

The Radex and Smallest-Space Analysis in Crime Analysis

The Metropolitan Police, working with Prof David Canter's IA-IP group, produced the Interactive Offender Profiling System (IOPs) used in development work in this area by the Metropolitan Police. The system uses a technique called smallest-space analysis (SSA) that, within a crime mapping, enables profiling to integrate crime, forensics, location, time, and other intelligence in a multivectored SSA environment. Using SSA, the locations and anchor points of offenders are related to the other intelligence and data. The power of the technique is that it enables research that would otherwise be on complex spreadsheets with which it would be difficult to work. When combined with accurate forensic and method data, SSA reveals patterns of offending relating to offenders, which would be more difficult to deal with or even perceive in some cases.

The concept of using smallest-space analysis techniques came from the empirical discovery of the Radex of criminality.[11] The Radex enables the use of the combination of qualitative and quantitative facets of data in which the quantitative modify the qualitative facets in the crime type data sets. Different sets of data such as behaviours or a crime type can be the 'subject' of the Radex. (See the diagram in Figure 3.1.)

The term 'facet' in this context refers to mutually exclusive components of an exhaustive classification system. In mathematical terms, a facet is a subset of nonoverlapping sets; for example, gender, build, forensic mark descriptor, and method are all facets. The facets can play a role in modifying other facets and are termed as modulating facets. Modulating facets have often been found to relate empirically to the frequency of occurrence of variables.

The concept of the Radex is enabling new directions in the production of analytical software enabling the handling of multiple data sets and the best fits or correlations between them in SSA. This takes the process out of the Excel spreadsheet environment and moves it toward true crime intelligence

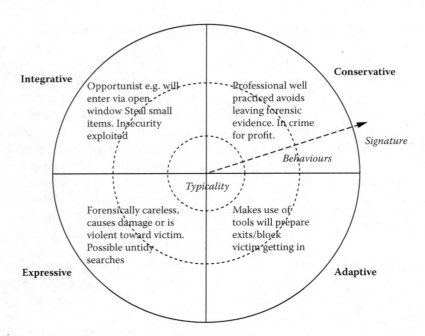

Figure 3.1 A generic simplified diagram of the Radex in burglary. (Drawing by R Milne.) Offenders exhibit behaviours that are facets. Abilities in one area can enable other facets. Offenders in real cases exhibit a mix of facets of behaviours and methods, possibly creating their average signature.

techniques other than processes akin to performance management systems. The interest in this approach is in its applications in dealing with analysis around the concepts of real entities and in merging the main areas of intelligence and crime research into ergonomic working systems, which will make best use of forensic intelligence.

To describe the process simply, if the full range of behaviours, methods, victim types, and locations can be expressed in a circular model where the sections radiating from the centre can be ascribed to the full range of behaviours and activities, then a basic descriptor for that arc of the radix can have inside it the range of facets ascribed to an individual person as an entity. Here, in smallest-space analysis, the best correlations between the data, evidence, and intelligence can be found. This applies to the neighbourhood burglar as well as to serious criminality involving sex crimes and serial homicides.

The SSA techniques were successfully used in development work by my unit in sex crime, burglary, robbery, arson, and drug distribution cases and, if adopted, fully enable forensic intelligence to become a powerful tool in problem solving and crime analysis. The work in developing SSA is ongoing at Huddersfield University.[11]

Descriptions of Terms in Figure 3.1

Psychologists have used the four terms in Figure 3.1 to describe facets of behaviour that can be attached to criminal activities. In a sensible pragmatic approach, David Canter and the IA-IP (based in the University of Huddersfield, England) have embraced other disciplines, such as geographical profiling, crime analysis, and forensics to reinforce investigative psychology toward developing useful models in criminal investigation. They recognise the need for evidence alongside probability assessments and opinion in the production of robust, useful investigative support intelligence products. Following are brief descriptions of each term, but readers are advised to refer to Canter and Youngs' book, *Investigative Psychology*.[11] To further appreciate the context within which Canter and Youngs place these concepts against different crime types and criminal behaviours is beyond the range of this book. It is my view that the concepts explored in their work offer ideas and opportunities for a whole new generation of analytical practices, improvements in police terminology, and software. The following descriptions of terms are from Canter and Youngs' definitions:

- *Conservative tragedy.* Offenders exhibiting this offending style will be highly focussed on the job, yet unaware consciously of the owners/occupants of the property. The offences will be efficiently carried out in a streamlined manner relying on technical competency rather than any other broader strategy. The focus is on material gain with no regard to the emotional response from the victim(s) losing items accrued throughout their lives and precious to them. The term 'conservative' relates to what is more like a commercial approach to burglary in acquiring external resources and may be part of a broader organised criminal activity. It is thought that this type of activity may be an adaptive one in active avenging, where offenders may target wealthier homes because of a sense of deprivation.
- *Adaptive adventure.* In this style of offending, the offender will be fully aware of the intrusion into someone else's home, and the behaviours expressed are characterised by planning and precautionary activities. In gaining entry, these offenders avoid where possible leaving forensic evidence and prepare escape routes whilst at the same time locking or blockading the normal means of entrance to the property to avoid the occupants should they return. Items are taken for gain in a more business-like manner.
- *Integrative irony.* The offender exhibits a lack of awareness of the entered property as someone's home and at the same time lacks focus on the task. This can result in bizarre offences neither about

illicit gain nor any sensible motive being understood as the point
of the intrusion. The actions may be just focussed on the individual
feeling better from the excitement of the commission of the offence.
There may be failure to take into account the possibilities of detection by taking easily identified items.

- *Expressive quest.* This style of offending shows an awareness of the
  dwelling being someone's home, but there is a lack of focus on the
  process of actually committing the burglary. Carelessness in leaving forensic evidence can be accompanied by offenders expressing
  themselves by a desire to cause damage, write graffiti, and victimise
  the loser. In basic terms, those who attack victims and property are
  viewed as 'expressive' and those who use tools and devices are viewed
  as 'adaptive'. Note that the types of offenders can often be associated
  with the ease or not of opportunities they create at the crime scenes
  for CSIs to find hard evidence, as those who are adaptive and conservative try to avoid their business being ruined by being detected.
  The expressive types can be very problematic in that they can be
  expressive in being violent toward victims. In real casework, there
  is a blend of these combinations of behaviours and methods, which,
  collectively, can help sort one series from another.

The Value of Improving Forensic Support in Problem-Oriented Policing and Crime Pattern Analysis

Inhibiting factors to forensic intelligence are in the area of under-resourced
forensic support services where, owing to short-sightedness and poor business models, forensics is not properly supported. In dealing with this problem, the Metropolitan Police improved its capabilities by recruiting staff to
increase its field force to over 400 CSIs, servicing a 35,000 strong police service at a ratio of one CSI per 70 police officers. The business model enabled
was one of CSI sole response for burglary cases, where if there is no suspect,
then the scene is visited by a CSI, who examines the scene and updates the
crime report. If a suspect is generated by the forensic activity or other source,
then a police officer is assigned to the case. The obvious savings in police
time, combined with the real fact that most of the volume crime scenes had
been dealt with by the CSIs in the first place, more than made up for the business change.

To support the CSI field force, the Met Police also installed four fast-track
volume crime fingerprint laboratories with a same-day to 90-hour turnaround time for casework. DNA profiling was contracted to be dealt with
in 4 working days and all fingerprint lifts to be on the National Automatic
Fingerprint Identification System (NAFIS) in the same 24-hour period as
the scene examination. This makes such a forensic field force a vital link in

intelligence-led policing and a valuable real-time operational resource, very much on the front line and not in the back room. Not to capitalise on such a resource in crime analysis and intelligence-led policing offered by this business model would be a travesty.

In developing forensic intelligence, one weakness was that the CSI field force operated on shifts and individuals were often not available in the core time to deal with divisional intelligence units in office hours. Therefore, as a development issue, I assigned a forensic intelligence researcher to Enfield Borough in North London. The researcher prepared problem profiles from the CSIs' input and looked after footwear and tool mark screening, digital footwear mark imaging, and processing research on fresh daily identifications from DNA and fingerprints. The intelligence products generated were taken daily to the morning meeting for action and updating of the police team, with good results. The cost incurred in using the forensic intelligence researcher was not supported unfortunately, despite the success; therefore an alternative would be to increase awareness of the existing crime analysts so that they could manage the resource in partnership with their local CSIs. Not to adopt this approach is really to misuse the opportunities modern forensic science offers policing.

Up-to-date forensic coded data of the softer forms of evidence from crime scenes combined with a daily input of the latest DNA matches and fingerprint identifications provide a wealth of material to introduce into crime pattern analysis. Once briefed, crime analysts or investigators can merge the forensic intelligence data into their research and analytical products. It is important to stress that the evidence recovery rates for each evidence type have to be kept at the high end. Management allowing CSIs not to bother about recovering footwear marks or tool marks because they say they never get a result is just not good enough. The reason that they would not obtain the levels of results are usually because of bad evidence recovery techniques, combined with a low recovery rate compromising the ability to see a complete picture of what is going on.

All this combined in some organisations with a failure to supply information technology systems with the capability to handle the various evidence types quickly and easily (Treadmark or SICAR [Shoeprint Image Capture and Retrieval] being an obvious example) can transform the capabilities of a police service to deal with footwear evidence linking the crime scene, custody suite, scenes of crime office, and forensic science expert examiners. Through developments like Treadmark and SICAR, forensics can provide better real-time support to crime analysis.

Refresher training and workshops for staff are part of the answer, but organisational changes with proper information technology support are needed to take some of the forensic processes out of the cottage industry stage. Details of best practices around various evidence types and the efficiency of forensic systems are covered in later chapters; these can enable police managers to create their own reforms to improve their performance in the forensics arena whilst achieving the maximum use of forensics and crime analysis within their resources.

Market Profiles

Intelligence units carry out assessments that are updated around markets in commodities marketed by criminals, such as illegal drugs, counterfeit goods, etc., or types of property targeted by thieves, such as high-value cars. Prostitution or other services offered by criminals are also profiled. This research establishes the states of the markets: whether or not problems are increasing or decreasing. The criminal networks engaged in the markets are researched and various techniques such as test purchases, surveillance, and lifestyle research into suspected persons are all part of the armoury of techniques employed. With respect to criminal networks, analysis of the market is a useful technique to identify individuals as targets and for the production of subject profiles to deal with them under the UK NIM. COMPSTAT makes use of market profiles in addressing crime problems, targeting surveillance and test purchase operations. The relentless follow-up activity is a major component of COMPSTAT.

Forensic intelligence has had some spectacular successes in recent years—for example, in forensically linking nearly 2,000 Far East nationals between UK cities involved in the illegal production of cannabis. This work enabled an estimated range of the total number of illegal nationals trafficked into the UK in a ballpark figure of around 10,000 persons, based on the actual 2,000 offenders' hard evidence (fingerprint and DNA) hits. This work providing links within the illegal cannabis market offered the opportunity to single out individuals for surveillance to lead back to the criminal networks financing the production—all backed by A1 intelligence grade biometric matches (see Figures 3.2 and 3.3).

Success was had in tracking the links between suppliers and manufacturers of illegal converted firearms, across Europe, down to street dealers in London, with links in the tooling of the weapons, etc. from the forensic domain. Note that the private ownership of handguns is outlawed in the UK, so criminals have to resort to converting gas guns and old decommissioned weapons for the illicit market in firearms. This understanding of the illicit guns market combined with criminal networks and research on gangs led to a reduction in the availability of illegal handguns caused by upstreaming forensic intelligence casework; this resulted in shutting down the converter workshops in Lithuania. The linking of larger consignments of hard drugs across police and customs services enables upstreaming

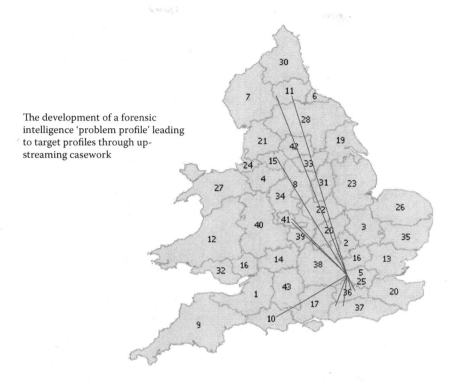

The development of a forensic intelligence 'problem profile' leading to target profiles through up-streaming casework

Figure 3.2 Forensic intelligence in between illicit cannabis factories in England, mid-2006.

casework back to countries of origin and shutting down the drug networks at the sources. Counterfeit goods cases have had success with forensic links, showing common sources and leading to the detection and arrest of networks of criminals.

In forensic intelligence terms, I made use of this technique in the mid-1980s in using information about a local drug market where a popular public house in Canning Town in East London staged weekend entertainment events that were frequented by travelling criminals seeking recreational drugs. The burglary rate in the commercial premises surrounding the public house was considerably higher over weekends when events were staged. Finger marks and other forensic evidence were recovered from these scenes, but because the criminals were travelling considerable distances, no identifications were being made because of the need to search for fingerprints manually in the geographical area during this time before computerisation.

I secured 10 police covert radio burglar alarms and set these in the most attacked premises; within the following year 17 burglars were arrested through activations of these alarms. From the fingerprinting, blood sampling, swabbing (before use of DNA) of these persons and seizure of their footwear and tools, I then had considerably more matches at other scenes in the area.

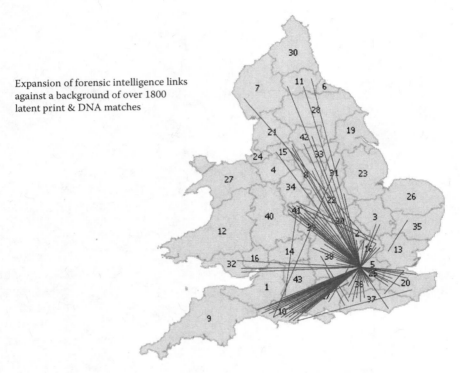

Expansion of forensic intelligence links
against a background of over 1800
latent print & DNA matches

Figure 3.3 Forensic intelligence links DNA and fingerprints between illicit cannabis factories in early 2007 revealing 'movers and shakers'.

The intelligence gleaned from these individuals impacted shutting down the drug dealers using the public house; other source information outside my focus of activity was handled by officers to secure and detect more casework.

Here was an example of proper teamwork: policing, technology, forensics, analysis, and full-blown crime intelligence application operating in a multilevel, joint way, leading to the closure of the public house. At the time, I was managing the forensic team in Newham Borough and we were the top team in Metropolitan London for results, purely because of the forensic intelligence methods employed. Indeed, the subsequent setting up of forensic intelligence in the Northeast London Forensic Science Support Unit in 1997 predated the UK NIM implementation by 7 years.

Demographic and Social Trend Analysis

This type of analysis centres on the social demographics of neighbourhoods and areas, focussing on the change factors, which can act as crime drivers or inhibitors. Here the relationships between offenders in their activity spaces and the research into these factors can drive policy making and restructuring of areas. The products of this analysis can be used in police deployment and manpower assessments according to calculations of the rate of growing populations and changes in the population density, etc.

At the high end, demographic and social trend analysis has implications for strategic planning with a view to future decision making and planning. Knowing where there are concentrations of offenders in locations acts as a focus for intelligence gathering. Seasonal factors such as school holidays can affect robbery and burglary levels and give opportunities for diversion or crime reduction opportunities.

Criminal Business Profiles

Criminal networks are like legitimate businesses: They have customers, staff, target markets, research, money laundering, security, enforcement, and areas of business. Unlike legitimate businesses, however, they have victims who either complain about losses or who are damaged by the criminal activity.

In criminal business profiles, various factors need to be researched, such as victim profiles, geographical area of operations, criminal methods, and the journey to crime (even in cyberspace through networks, etc.). This form of analysis enables key issues to be dealt with in partnership, working to deal with crime problems—for example, drug markets where police, cross-forces, customs, and multiple forensic science laboratories are involved. From the forensic intelligence point of view, however, questions have to be asked around the working practices of the various partners.

For example, when I was running the Met Police Forensic Intelligence Desk in 2005, the issue of evidential drug testing kits was raised and there was a cost-reduction issue associated with their use. As far as dealing with drug users with small amounts of drugs, the kits were cost effective, leading to minor prosecutions. With respect to criminal networks in the supply business, relying solely on kits to save money on analysis would completely compromise the ability to establish forensic links across agencies. Worse still, the opportunities to submit the packaging materials for full sequential fingerprint and DNA recoveries were lost and the drug teams reduced to being fast parcel interception services. When cases were tested in the multiagency approach, finger marks and DNA recoveries from materials enclosing drugs smuggled from other countries in some cases identified criminal network organisers who were from the UK and already in our own systems. The businesses were often organised by UK criminals who travelled to other countries to set up purchase and export facilities, rather than by unknown foreign nationals. By getting involved in this type of analysis, upstreaming of casework was achieved by using the forensic services facilities properly.

This illustrated the weaknesses in business groups using crime analysis and intelligence facilities in short-sighted working practices to attain short-term localised objectives. At UK NIM levels 1 and 2, linking and solving

commercial burglaries across police boundaries can be facilitated by forensic intelligence techniques leading to the detections of persons involved
in criminal enterprises involving millions of pounds worth of goods. For
example, in North London, schools were subjected to burglaries where computer projectors and laptop computers were stolen. It was assumed by local
police that, because these items were popular, many local thieves would target the schools, but that was not the case. In researching the forensics around
the burglaries, it was discovered that there were a limited number of shoe
mark patterns and, in combination with one another, these indicated a small
number of travelling offenders in a criminal network.

Upon inspection of the crime report systems and Metropolitan Police
Stops Database, it was discovered that the same individuals in separate jurisdictions had been stopped or mentioned in crime reports in different jurisdictions. A forensic intelligence problem profile with unknown offenders
revealing their presence by their actions and evidence left at crime scenes
became a proactive subject profile naming suspects for targeting by police. Here,
the victim profiles combined with research into a criminal network combined with forensics led to the resolution of a crime problem not seen by
local analysts, because the perpetrators attacked premises in one division and
then moved to another, returning to the same divisions a few weeks later. The
short-sighted business-tasking model used by each division failed to notice
or deal with the series until it had become a serious level 2 crime problem.

Network Analysis

In network analysis, the links between the people involved in criminal enterprises are looked at with a view to establishing the importance or otherwise
of those involved in the functioning of the criminal network. It is important
to visualise the nodes in networks where the key players interact. Software
for visualising networks can be employed to achieve a very good visualisation
of networks and links. Typical software ranges from programs such as i2, Tec
Flow, NodeXL, and others for development into social networking software
for phone and computer network analysis. Social networking software such
as Tec Flow and NodeXL are available free on the Internet and NodeXL is
offered by Microsoft with development tools, etc.[18] These programs can be
loaded with large numbers of telephone numbers or e-mail links and can
unravel quite complex networks of communication between persons and
locations, leading to nodes of interest. Police services can make big savings
by getting their IT professionals to adapt NodeXL or TecFlow to produce
really useful networking programs to deal with phone and computer links.

A criminal network generally is defined as three or more persons engaged
in persistent or prolonged criminal activity for the motives of profit, power,

or self-gratification. In the preceding drugs-linking scenario dealing with linked substances and the journey to crime, in unravelling the test purchases in a whole quarter of a major UK city, suspects would travel miles from different directions to areas quite close to one another to sell linked substances. The question then is, 'Who is looking at the mobile phone data of those found with linked substances, in order to ascertain whom they have in common?' After all, even if the mobile phones are unregistered or pay as you go, someone will call his or her mother, or a mobile, or a location on a contract or landline, thus revealing a way into the problem and upstreaming of the case into the drug supply network locally, nationally, and even internationally.

The other option is to ignore forensic intelligence, not to pay for it and operate instead a police fast parcel interception service that typically arrests unmarried mothers, who are threatened by criminals and paid by them to sign for the packages. This leaves law enforcement officers to deal with a small army of intercepted drug mules and minor players looking after mail drops—with no forensic input to enable tactical intelligence products aimed at removing the criminal organisers at the point of origin.

In the case of Vietnamese cannabis growers in the UK, a vast forensic intelligence hard-evidence-linked database gave police the opportunity to terminate the problem early on. However, because under the NIM cannabis was graded as a level 1 minor crime class 'C' drug, the opportunity was deferred because it did not progress through the intelligence model to become a strategic issue. This was despite the fact that the criminal networks involved were found to be involved in homicide, drug production on a vast scale, kidnapping, money laundering, illegal trafficking of thousands of workers, destruction of properties, etc.

For example, in 2005, the London Fire Brigade estimated the number of dwellings burned down in London by organised crime cannabis growers cutting into the main electricity with no fuses and bypassing gas meters was in the region of 40 houses. Often the joists were removed in these properties to make room for more plants, leading to structural weaknesses exacerbated by fire damage, where the structure would be unable to support the dead weight of the building much sooner than expected in a normal house fire. This factor could have led to the deaths or injuries of fire fighters.

Between 2004 and late 2006 management asked, 'Why are you doing this research? It's only a class C drug'. In this case, the interpretation of the NIM, grading the cannabis production problem as level 1 crime, led to cross-force inactivity, allowing the criminal networks to flourish unchecked. Individual operation command units had no will to take the problem to level 2 and deal with it across forces. The forensic intelligence research from the Met Forensic Intelligence Desk was used to support the Met Police national presentation on the problem held at the London Guildhall in 2008. This conference led, belatedly, to serious operations to try to tackle the cannabis production problem, which by that time had become a national problem and was somewhat out of control.

The network analysis supporting forensic intelligence in the Vietnamese organised crime problem also led to the reopening of a homicide case because the original investigation had no intelligence about the large criminal network in which the cannabis growers at the murder location were involved. During the first major UK operation against the cannabis-growing criminal networks, the murderer was arrested in a city 100 miles away from the homicide scene and successfully prosecuted.

Profile or Target (Subject) Profile Analysis

Analysts use a range of techniques to ascertain the lifestyle and forms of crime and disorder in which suspected criminal subjects are engaged. With this technique, some prioritisation of subjects can be arrived at. Analyses of the risks posed to partners in investigations are also made. The focus on subjects also acts as an enabler in assisting the process of network analysis; indeed, subject analysis can lead to the discovery of hitherto unseen criminal networks or associations between networks.

Through targeted use of forensic resources, as described later in this book, resolutions of problems can be achieved with savings in the area of specialist staff having to work in a risk environment by reactively reviewing the forensics and working practices and proactively creating a forensic strategy to close potential intelligence gaps as the case progresses. Through quality forensic work, the case can be proven and successful prosecutions achieved.

Results Analysis

Results analysis is used to evaluate the effectiveness or otherwise of operations. In a prequel to the use of this technique in the 1990s, the Metropolitan Police tried to organise an operational response database because it had been noticed that hardly any police operations appeared to fail! Recording accurately the facts about operations and the results achieved was thought to be a way to improve the results using the techniques in problem oriented policing (POP). The operational response database did not, however, seem to get the support it deserved, although the policing models under the NIM and COMPSTAT are supposed to meet the aims of the operational response database exercise.

Results analysis is a useful technique for some forms of operation, and tactics may work well, say, in an inner city environment but not so well in a more rural setting; therefore, having the reference should be useful. Access to results analysis can be useful in planning new operations and in researching the status of current operations. The decision-making processes whereby operations are continued, put on hold, or stopped are supported by this technique. In the review process and in the original planning stages, forensic strategies should be examined because forensics can start a case, stop a case, or solve a case. Ineffective use of forensic facilities and a lack of understanding of what is significant in the forensic and behavioural areas can lead to failures in operational casework. For examples, see Chapter 7 ('The Oxford Street Department Store Arsonist') and 'Network Analysis' in this chapter regarding organised crime cannabis growers.

Risk Analysis

Risk analysis is a technique that arose as far as the UK is concerned from the changes caused by the UK Human Rights Act 1998 and case law covering the duties of care organisations to their members and the public generally. The scale of risks presented to potential victims by offenders, the public at large, and stakeholders in detection and law enforcement are covered by this technique. The realisation that apparently isolated events are in fact part of a larger, possibly linked problem is a product of risk analysis. Under the UK Human Rights Act, there is a rule of proportionality in dealing with the solutions of problems whereby any restriction of rights must be balanced to achieve the protection of individuals' rights against the general interests of society.

An interesting risk assessment was held in a UK police force following the installation of a new crime intelligence system. In an attempt to reduce the amount of intelligence logs in the system, the 'intelligence hawks' charged with implementing the system decided to try to define what was 'intelligence' and what was not 'intelligence'. The new rules led to a nearly 60% drop in intelligence logs being placed on the system by operational police as well as CSIs. The tasking for the force intelligence bureau was to assess the risks to the organisation posed by this dramatic drop in input to the intelligence system, leading to review of the rules created by the hawks. An intelligence miss can be a totally catastrophic event that can be avoided; after all, computers handle vast amounts of data quickly and those data are easily graded.

The key area here for forensic intelligence is in proving or ascertaining with a good confidence level that isolated events may be linked or confidently unlinked, thus improving the analysis product.

Operational Intelligence Assessments

This analysis product provides an evaluation of information collection to inform decision makers about existing operations. Operational intelligence assessments are often the meat and drink of daily or weekly intelligence meetings where fresh operations are introduced and existing ones updated, terminated, or put on hold. The current position of the forensic effort is often reviewed in this form of assessment as to what stage the laboratory results are at or fingerprint bureau laboratory work being carried out. The quality of the offenders data in AFIS (Automatic Fingerprint Identification System) can be reviewed (see Chapter 4) as well as opportunities to improve foren- sic support response times, etc. to meet the requirements of the operation(s). If no consideration is given to the forensics aspect of the investigation and assumptions are made that everything is fine and on 'autopilot', then time and resources of policing assets can be wasted in light of a forensic resolution of the case. This may not happen so quickly if forensics is out of the intelligence loop.

The Daily Work of the Crime Analyst

Most textbooks on the topics of intelligence-led policing, problem-oriented policing, and crime analysis concentrate on the big picture with the focus on the benefits for the whole organisation in achieving performance targets. Most of these references have to do with performance statistics and manage- ment objectives, rather than detection and actual intelligence work. Indeed, the very words **detection**, **prosecution**, and **forensic science** are virtually totally missing from these texts.

One well-written text on intelligence-led policing, which gives an excel- lent account of the introduction of COMPSTAT,[19] cites the attempt at imple- menting COMPSTAT by New South Wales and Queensland Australian police forces, where the project was deemed to produce results that were assessed as cost effective. In contacting Victoria State Police, it appeared that part of their experience to improve results involved tasking their forensic support to visit more scenes; however, forensics was under-resourced to cope with the scenes and the laboratory backup was not there either in real time.

The possibility of business development to put matters right, by per- haps civilianising forensic services to bring qualified people straight into the workplace, was potentially an option. I understand, for example, that in 2010/2011 the state of Victoria was considering civilianisation of its CSI field force, so they are possibly taking positive steps in advancing their forensic business model.

In most of the current intelligence models, the total focus is on managing a performance model where intelligence work is tasked only on perceived pri- orities, whereas with the resources made available, the whole model should include a daily trawl of everything coming onto the police radar across the intelligence assets (knowledge, systems, and intelligence assets). Then, to deal more effectively across the business, proper business route maps should be in place, enabling the steering of the intelligence to the right departments in real time. Typical 2-week tasking cycles are too long in many cases and, in my experience working under the UK NIM, the processes too bureaucratically slow to be effective in many instances. The route maps would be created in a flexible structure to service operations and monitor the current strategic crime types.

The test for an intelligence function is within the dictionary definition of intelligence, and I make no apologies for returning to this definition: **'Intelligence is a capability to produce solutions to problems in new and novel situations'.** Clearly, a model that focuses the work of analysts on only known problems and priorities cannot by definition be in a position to explore new and novel situations. In moving away from the big picture, of what does the daily work of a crime analyst in level 1 and level 2 crime really consist?

The Daily Work of an Analyst

At UK NIM basic crime levels 1 and 2, the work of intelligence unit staff is focussed on the tasks in the following bulleted points. At NIM crime level 3, the work has more of a confidential and secret nature, with use of the Home Office Large Major Enquiry System (HOLMES), but still has the same basics to cover as in the lower crime levels. HOLMES is used by lower crime level business groups but not on normal day-to-day levels 1 and 2 crime analysis as it is at level 3. A recent development in the UK has been the HOLMES2 system, which is intended to be used more by NIM level 1 and level 2 command units.

It has to be said that some police services will have superior geographical information systems (GIS) and possibly better interagency partnerships than others, but in reality the bulleted points cover the work that average jobbing analysts carry out from day to day. In under-resourced smaller police services without much analytical support, there is nothing in these points that officers could not cover themselves—hence the approach in this book. After all, there is a bigger picture covering the grand scheme of things, although, in reality, for things to work, this is what it largely boils down to. At precinct level in the COMPSTAT model, which is statistically driven, these basic functions (taken from picking from the nine basic analytical products) have to be performed; otherwise, the operational manager will not know where the precinct stands with respect to results or current taskings. Notice that a lot of the work is in Microsoft Excel from data extracts taken from systems assets, with inputs from intelligence sources.

The following points cover the typical work of an analyst researcher in assembling briefings and statistical work (Figure 3.4)—rather than the work

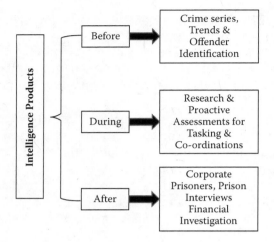

Figure 3.4 Crime analysis processes.

of an analyst aware of forensic intelligence who is seeking fresh intelligence links from forensic sources:

- Maintain problem profiles for current strategic crime types under the strategic assessment by trawling crime reports and intelligence logs for new information and intelligence around defined strategic crimes. Closed-circuit analysis is used to research submethods, etc. to try to differentiate crimes in the strategic categories to try to gain confidence around potential links. In reality, the closed-circuit analysis usually consists of counting submethods and behaviours in a section of the spreadsheet and counting which have a higher count in an attempt to sort one common crime from another. Spreadsheets are maintained and developed for research and analysis purposes. Performance statistics are produced through this exercise to establish the current position with regard to the strategic casework for tasking and coordination review purposes, so graphs, pivot tables, and simple maps are produced.
- Research current prison intelligence around the release of persistent and prolific offenders. Monitor crime in the offenders' locations, with respect to increase in reported crimes, with the offenders' methods and behaviours. Subject profiles are created as required and liaisons with the prison intelligence units are maintained.
- Review current status of live operations updating intelligence products (spreadsheets) as required. This crosses over the work in maintaining profiles around strategic crime types.
- Search intelligence logs containing source intelligence on the force intelligence system. This is usually a text searcher type of program

searched by Boolean operators to establish possible links to other intelligence logs and links into reported crime. The results of these searches are entered into spreadsheets or placed into reports, assessments, or briefing slides for dissemination.

- Check automatic number plate reader (ANPR) data for offenders (if the country or police service has these) of interest's motor vehicles and speed camera (GATSO) data. ANPR and GATSO data can reveal times and places where stolen or unregistered vehicles or vehicles belonging to people of interest were thus establishing part of the journey to and from crime.
- Prepare simple crime maps and graph displays in Excel for management briefings at the daily or weekly meeting.
- Prepare comparison graphs and maps for crime types showing increases or decreases in the current period against 2 and 12 weeks before, and the position in the same period the previous year.
- Research and disseminate the content of briefing slides from the Briefing and Tasking System (BATS) and prepare slides for dissemination of the output from the intelligence unit. Prepare and disseminate slides detailing wanted offenders.
- Provide in-camera confidential debriefs from surveillance officers and handlers of sensitive confidential information with the intelligence manager.
- Collect CCTV and memo cam stills for dissemination on the briefing system.

The Daily Work of a Forensically Aware Forensic Intelligence Analyst

The focus of this section is shifted somewhat from the performance management framework associated with what has become thought to be the daily work of an intelligence unit. The NIM and, to a certain extent, COMPSTAT place the analyst in the position indicated in Figure 3.5. Within the NIM, the alignment of the placing of the analyst is not quite where it should be with respect to the pure objective of driving the police business by intelligence found by research, but rather by taskings from police management dealing with problems already perceived and prioritised. The statistical drivers in COMPSTAT must surely place the analysts in that business model in a similar position as in the UK NIM. Perhaps to raise awareness of this problem in logistics around the positioning of the analysts in the police business model with respect to intelligence research, descriptors of 'position 1 analyst' and 'position 2 analyst' could be used to define the role as being performance or intelligence based?

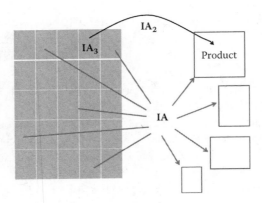

Figure 3.5 Position of analyst in the NIM and COMPSTAT models (position IA3: left of field). Position of analyst reviewing everything coming in for fresh leads across the business as in checking for forensic features (position IA) (Source: International Association of Intelligence Analysts. Copyright notice: Source IntelligenceAnalysis.net http://www.intelligenceanalysis.net/index.)

The Aims and Objectives of Incorporating Forensics into Crime Analysis

- To improve the impact of forensic intelligence within the police service by effective use of analysis techniques around all forensic recoveries
- To make best use of forensic evidence in the intelligence arena by creating intelligence products and research from forensic recoveries
- To liaise with forensic science providers in providing scientific support to intelligence casework where research of forensic recoveries has indicated that a benefit would possibly be achieved in providing scientific links to support the forensic intelligence products and research
- To promote the best practice and management of forensic evidence recoveries
- To support the police service in the disruption of organised criminal networks and the reduction of crime across the police service's business groups through forensic intelligence and the increased detection rate accrued
- To increase the detection rate of the police service through the creation of forensic intelligence packages around each operation and planned arrest
- To provide evidence for prosecutions backed by complete audit trails of the intelligence activity leading to the operational actions of police and subsequent arrests

In achieving the aims and objectives, quite an amount of progress can be made by incorporating the processes and methods described later to achieve value for money and, at the same time, actually inject a fresh view of linking crimes and finding new patterns of criminal activity. Where this approach has been adopted, police services have created their own models and business changes to make best use of the forensic intelligence approach. West Yorkshire Police created 'Operation Converter', where forensic intelligence packages are created within 24 hours of each fingerprint or DNA scene match, leading to a high detection rate of up to 40% more sanctioned detections. To enforce Operation Converter, a detective sergeant has to visit and liaise with each operational command unit to ensure that the converter staff have not been switched to other duties, thus stopping the ability to secure detections. Converter teams are also trained in interview techniques to deliver the benefits of the forensic intelligence products by dealing effectively with offenders.

It is expected that CSIs in most UK police services deliver some level of forensic intelligence input into the police business; in US police services, there are quite a range of operating practices, but most officers would agree that a latent print identification or DNA match is seized for action with relish. The question is, however, **'What other evidence is collected to enable expansion of the hard-evidence matches into a higher level of detections?'**

From a 2005 visit to the United States to the National Institute of Justice (NIJ) 8th Crime Mapping Conference, where I presented 'The Mapping of Forensic Evidence and the Mathematics of Scene Linking', the picture from American colleagues was that in the volume crime area in level 1 and level 2, crime investigation was not well developed forensically in many police services. There is, however, a real interest in reviewing working practices and in bringing in new techniques where resources allow. The US NIJ provides a pivotal role in promoting best practice and in funding research and operations related to that research. US readers are advised to look at what the NIJ has to offer and can find support from the NIJ if they submit a quality business case.[21]

A Structure for Dealing with Forensic Intelligence

Forensic evidence is by its nature split into two main categories as the biometric forms of evidence, fingerprints, and DNA are viewed as harder forms of evidence because they are for practical reasons almost infallible, specific to individuals, and can conclusively link crime scenes. The other forms of forensic evidence, such as marks, ballistics, mechanical fits, impressions, paint, glass, fibres, etc. are viewed as softer forms of evidence but even they can range from various forms of significance in analysis to providing conclusive evidence. **What is certain is that, if no one collects the evidence or records in a format fit for retrieval and analysis, then the use of the forensic evidence for intelligence and crime analysis purposes is compromised.**

Forensic intelligence work is therefore resolvable into two main areas

- Hard-evidence research and analysis enabling mainly the creation of intelligence subject (target) profiles, although hard-evidence-linked scenes offer the opportunities for creating quality problem profiles with the truths that hard links provide
- Softer forms of evidence research and analysis enabling mainly the creation of intelligence problem profiles

These two areas lend themselves to the creation of the two main intelligence tasking products in that hard evidence is specific to individuals and softer evidence forms are specific to the items creating them. This helps to identify clearly the tasks to be carried out by forensic intelligence analysts in the production of either subject or problem profiles. The following table defines these two main areas of 'soft' and 'hard' evidence in dealing with forensic intelligence, together with the main activities and intelligence products accruing from organising research and analysis in an intelligence-led system:

Hard-Evidence Research and Analysis: Creating Subject Profiles	Other Softer Forms of Evidence Research and Analysis: Creating Problem Profiles
• Every fingerprint (latent print) and DNA match is researched daily. • Cases are examined, particularly those with linked cases, to determine the potential scale of offending. • Cases with 10 or more detections can result and should be referred for fast-track development and action. • Hard evidence matches are compared against live and archived problem profiles. • Forensic intelligence is used to identify real persistent and prolific offenders (PPOs). • Subject profiles are disseminated via the US COMPSTAT system or via the proactive assessment process under the NIM.	• Forensic retrievals and CSI intelligence logs are daily checked for links, clusters, unusual methods, behaviours against crime types, and other intelligence • Forensic intelligence analytical data derived from crime scenes and partnership data with other stakeholders across forces and with government and rescue services is maintained daily. • Input to forensic crime mapping products for analytical use is created. • Problem profiles are disseminated for action or tasking via the US COMPSTAT system or via the proactive assessment process under the NIM. • Problem profiles are constantly checked against the hard evidence matches to maximise detections and expand linked crime series.

With respect to the table covering the routine work of the forensic intelligence analyst, setting up a clearly defined forensic intelligence capability opens the door to the development of new forensic intelligence products more aligned to the improvements in information technology. The police business should allow enough flexibility for development to happen and not cast everything in stone once it is set up under a framework of due process.

A Forensic Intelligence Process Route Map

The process map in Figure 3.6 indicates the position of a forensically aware crime analyst and fits well with the position **IA** analyst diagram earlier in this chapter in Figure 3.5. In this process, the analyst is well positioned to see the inputs of knowledge, system and intelligence assets with a focus on forensic intelligence and is not restricted by being only tasked to look at specific issues. This work, of course, can be woven into the regular work of an analyst as perceived without the forensic dimension. In this diagram is the key to why analysts not using forensics properly are found to have poor performance in distilling crime series from reported crime data and only producing a product if someone as a source tells them what is going on.

The analyst is at the focus of the inputs producing analytical and intelligence products through the two main routes: the problem profile route, where no exactly confirmed suspect is defined, and the subject (target) profile route, where suspects are positively identified (see Figure 3.6). There is,

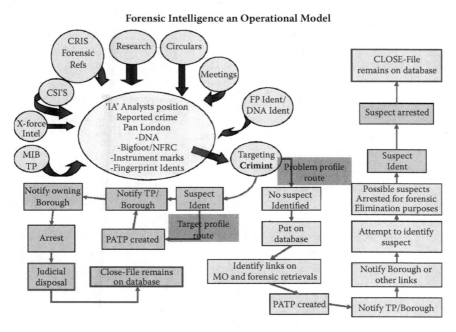

Figure 3.6 A practical forensic intelligence route map.

in the main, one process for the problem profile route map, and a forensic intelligence package in the form of a proactive assessment is made to notify the tasking and coordination forum. This proactive assessment presents the results of the analysis together with the business case for resources to deal with it.

In the subject profile route, two choices can be made. If the identification is researched and there is confidence that the case is a single one, the owning division is notified directly. If there is a possibility that more detections can be accrued through preparing a forensic intelligence package, then a subject profile is used to present the analysis and the business case for the allocation of resources to deal with it. In reality, as crime series develop, problem profiles will be created with unknown offenders. When a hard evidence biometric hit potentially related to the series is received, this should be checked against the existing problem profiles as well as consideration given to the creation of new problem or subject profiles.

The Input of Forensic Intelligence into Intelligence-Led Policing

The actual subject of using forensics in intelligence is really wide in scope and requires the right mind-set to treat forensics as a critical tool in problem-oriented policing; otherwise, errors will occur in quite serious cases because of the lack of joint thinking and awareness. A lack of performance in expanding detections can also cause problems leading to diversions of resources in order to rectify matters. It should be pointed out that police systems such as crime reporting and intelligence systems have complete audit trails and procedures used by CSIs to cover complete chains of custody for evidence and fully traceable audit trails to account for each action in order to meet the requirements of criminal justice.

A quite salient example occurred in London in 2005 and 2006 against the backdrop of the Metropolitan Police declaring itself to be intelligence led since 2004 with the adoption of the Metropolitan Police Model as their implemented version of the UK NIM. Two main force intelligence units were administering the Metropolitan Police Model under the UK NIM—one covering territorial policing at crime levels 1 and 2 dealing in the main volume and more serious cross-divisional crime. The other, prior to the creation of the Met Intelligence Bureau, was based in the old Service Intelligence Bureau (SIB) and covered mainly level 3 and level 2 crimes. All appeared to be going well with the production of the new NIM products and these were fed into a 2 weekly tasking and coordination forum at the assistant commissioner/commander level for resources to be allocated to enable operations and decisions to be made about the status of the larger police operations.

This forum considered whether to open or close operations or to perform more research—the main forms of decision making at the forum. The forum also made decisions about allocations of resources in pursuit of strategic and tactical objectives. Forensic intelligence problem profiles, subject profiles, strategies, and tactics were fed into the Met Model system and action was taken on some through the tasking and coordination forum. However, when the developers of forensic intelligence tried to present what they were doing to the two main intelligence units, they were advised that the units were busy and consequently the attitude with the Territorial Police Intelligence Unit was that, yes, forensic intelligence was there and they would respond to products as appropriate.

On the other hand, the Service Intelligence Bureau Specialist Crime Directorate Unit did not like original forensic intelligence research performed without specific taskings from it because of the sensitivity of the work. Thus, it placed forensic intelligence researchers very much in the **IA3** position (Figure 3.6), although it did regularly task its forensic intelligence desk to try to add value to existing cases. During 2004 into 2006 the forensic intelligence units placed hundreds of problem and subject profiles on the intelligence system. In addition, thousands of hard-evidence latent print and DNA matches were also put on the intelligence system. This was to cover the possibility that within those forensically identified cases there may be the methods, behaviours, or other facets of the identified person sought by investigators or analysts searching the intelligence system. The other option being not to input these forensic matches into the intelligence system and just notify each officer dealing recording the forensic identifications just on the crime report system. The forensic identifications, however, in restricting their inputs to the latter scenario, would be held in record fields in the crime report system and some data would not be shared with others on the intelligence system leading to the possibility of a serious intelligence miss from time to time. In the latter scenario divisions dealing with local 'level 1', volume crime had an inbuilt resistance to taking on cross divisional or cross border work and as it transpired stored volume crime forensic match cases to be dealt with in batches. The NIM based Met Intelligence Model continued to develop covering everything efficiently—or so they thought.

In December 2005, the UK Home Office informed the Metropolitan Police that extra money in the eight million pounds range would not be available for the new financial year unless the Met hit its burglary detection and reduction target. At that time, domestic burglary was not regarded as a strategic crime type in the Met's strategic assessment because of a drop in the burglary rate over a few years. I thought that even with the drop to over 100,000 reported cases per annum, burglary was really still a strategic problem and not to regard it as such was an error of judgement. The effect of this thinking was to defer burglary problem and subject profiles around biometric forensic matches and to leave level 1 units to deal with them.

The territorial policing group discovered a problem in that they had to deliver their Home Office burglary detection target in 3 months, so the forensic intelligence desk was asked for an assessment of the situation. Research was carried out by the forensic intelligence desk and it was found that some 6,000 fingerprint and DNA hard-evidence matches had been on the crime report system, which had no detection results entered against the matched cases. This meant that none of those forensically identified persons had been dealt with and prosecuted for the offences. These forensic identification cases had actually been farmed out directly to level 1 divisions; no notice had been taken of the possible 'converter' option of researching the identifications in order to maximise detections. The cases were left to pile up by level 1 divisional units, possibly for overtime-claiming purposes when they were saved to be cleared in bulk.

An NIM tactical assessment was written covering the details of a force-wide operation for all operational command units across the city to clear the backlog of forensic identifications. There were also thousands of other potential suspects to be eliminated from the 6,000 crime cases, so it took over eight operations into 2006 and 2007 to clear the backlog.

The total focus on operating a performance management-oriented intelligence system focussing only on strategic issues was responsible for ignoring the forensic intelligence option. Even when we wished to present what we were doing to set the forensic identification problem in context, we were only allowed to present the material backing up threats of discipline to the operational unit superintendents over the failure to take action on the forensic matches.

The situation was resolved through Operation Halifax, clearing the arrest backlog and enabling the achievement of targets; forensic docket units were set up in each London borough to ensure the forensic matches were in fact translated into arrests and prosecutions in more like real time. In an attempt to encourage level 1 divisional units to deal with volume cross-divisional cases, a policy of declaring offenders as 'corporate prisoners' if research indicated that more than 10 detections would accrue was implemented, whereby level 1 units could receive funding to deal with such level 2 cases. Here was evidence of a change in Met Police working practices being caused by the resolution of a problem that would not have developed if the concept of forensic intelligence in expanding detections had been embedded in the working intelligence model and not treated as an experimental development.

Common Policing Problems Inhibiting Forensic Intelligence

Evidence of the problems in policing cited in the UK Audit Commission report of 1993[19] concerning focussing on crime and not criminals were evident in this 2006/2007 exercise, bearing in mind the lack of interest by Met management to adopt an Operation Converter West Yorkshire Police approach to increasing detections from forensics in London. The UK Audit Commission report listed the following areas where matters could progress in making policing more effective. The comments in italics are the author's views:

- Insufficient police offender interview training (*leading to a lower clearing-up of cases at the interview stage*)
- Forensic potential not utilised (*lack of awareness of forensics potential and older restrictive practices by analysts and intelligence managers failing to support forensic intelligence operationally and to provide the technical support to make it happen*)
- Scientific support under-resourced (*true in 1993, but not in London in 2006*)
- Pattern of activity highly reactive
- Intelligence work having low status and being under-resourced (*not after 2004 in some policing areas following the adoption of the NIM, but little thought by the original planners about forensics as a true intelligence tool*)
- Failure to exploit crime pattern analysis and informants (*lack of consistency in approach to research and analysis techniques between intelligence units is a very real feature after several years of working the NIM*)[11,22]

The CSI's Role in Forensic Intelligence

As the eyes and ears of the policing organisation in dealing with detailed forensic examinations of crime scenes, suspects, and victims, CSIs have a key role in forensic intelligence. The quality of CSI training, career development, and accreditation cannot be overemphasised in achieving the level of recoveries and results required to support problem-oriented policing models.

The following example of the CSI's role in forensic intelligence is taken from the Metropolitan Police; however, elements of this approach can be used in any police service according to the resources available. It is included for those in other jurisdictions who may wish to compare and contrast their own methods and practices:

- Conduct full quality work of as many crime scenes as are practical to maximise the recovery of evidence.
- Attend *all serious crime scenes* within 'the golden hour' if possible.
- Examine burglary scenes within 4 hours of reporting with a 100% attendance target. In reality, because of the nature of the work and logistical problems, a typical 85% attendance rate is achieved in London.
- Prepare all latent print and DNA exhibits for submission to the Fingerprint Bureau and laboratory by the end of each shift.
- Search latent prints in the same 24-hour period as the recovery from the scene.
- Process DNA profiles in the laboratory to input to the National DNA Database in 4 working days. Weekend days are not counted, in the same way that banks count working days.
- Strive to recover or digitally image forensic marks with fine, third-level detail. First-level detail means there is a mark of a type with little clear detail, level 2 detail means that wear and larger features are visible (e.g., wear pattern on a shoe sole), and third level means fine up to microscopic detail is present, enabling conclusive matches.
- Accurately record forensic retrieval and useful intelligence from crime scenes and victims in police recording and intelligence systems.
- Adhere to data standards as defined by the police service in crime reporting, briefing, and intelligence systems.
- Maintain accurate and timely records of forensic retrievals, enabling evidence types to be databased and researched.
- Participate in the intelligence processes within the police service via input and meetings. Use initiative and bring evidence of new intelligence, emerging threats, and risk items to the intelligence unit links to tasking and coordination of the police service.

Obviously, this form of service-level agreement is only achievable if a police service is very well resourced, but the points raised indicate areas where any police service can look at its current working practices and produce some improvements within resources. One obvious tactic in a restricted resources situation is to produce a forensic strategy and tactical assessments around certain crime types or identified series to prioritise examinations to provide a clearer forensic picture around those strategic cases. A better approach is to ensure that at least 1% of the police service is competently trained to deal with routine scenes of crime examinations to an accredited standard.

The Forensic Services Team

Although vital, CSIs are part of the forensics team in a police service that will rely on a dedicated team of specialists in processing and matching the forensic exhibits recovered from the crime scenes. These specialists rely on quality submissions from the CSIs to enable a high quality and quantity of results to feed into the police business as performance enablers.

In addition to CSIs both inside and outside the police service (private laboratories), the forensic team consists mainly of

- Latent print experts
- Fingerprint laboratory staff
- Photographers
- Forensic scientists across a range of scientific disciplines
- Medical examiners
- Pathologists
- Psychologists
- Systems specialists (e.g., AFIS systems, DNA database, etc.)
- Computer and mobile phone analysis experts
- CCTV analysts

Clearly, there is a significant resource investment in those who process forensic material recovered from crime scenes. Likewise, care should be taken in ensuring that the results achieved by these specialists are recorded and proper action taken. In addition, care should be taken in managing the information and intelligence produced in order to maximise results.

Many forensic exhibits recovered from scenes where there are no immediate suspects are stored, usually at the same premises from which the respective investigating officers operate. This forensic material can represent 80% to 90% of forensic recoveries stored for possible future use. Unless the case is a serious crime case, forensic exhibits taken from scenes where there is a suspect are only submitted for expert examination and possible matching purposes if there is a suspect and usually only if that suspect will not admit to committing the offence. In serious crime cases, expert examination is usually sought regardless of the willingness of the suspect to admit committing the offence.

To resolve the resource implications around dealing with forensic casework by experts in the UK, the principle of staged evidence is used. In this instance, extra work—for example, the creation of marked-up fingerprint enlargements, is only done if the identification itself is going to be challenged in court.

Intelligence Features of Forensic Evidence Types

The stored exhibits represent a significant forensic intelligence resource because, in the case of ballistic items, shoe marks, and tool marks, they lend themselves to coding, scanning, and measurement, thus enabling searchable collections and the creation of data for input into casework and crime analysis data. In some countries, ballistic items are now dealt with by ballistics intelligence units utilising Integrated Ballistics Intelligence Systems (IBISs) and are examples of how to deal with forensic intelligence.

The ability to produce data from forensic evidence enables the identification of links and clusters from softer forms of forensic evidence so that two concepts—'known' and 'unknown' offenders—can be of immediate use. In the cases of forensic scene links with no suspect, we know that a problem is created by an unknown offender who is causing a subset of crimes in a larger set within an area or crime type with crimes of similar features. In the case of ballistics, the concept of the unknown gun being involved in linked crime is a product of the same concept. The scenes with useful linked ballistics material feed into other crime analysis work.

In the known-offender scenario, there may be intelligence to imply that an offender is involved, but more work has to be done to firm up the evidential links between the offender and the set of crimes under consideration. A typical example is a latent print or DNA match against one case in many; then, through follow-up by seizing other forensic exhibits from the suspect, further cases can be solved. Through proper use of forensic intelligence, the door could be opened into other areas and even more serious crimes in which the offender is involved. A common scenario of linking a known offender to other cases is a very useful tool for skilled police interviewers to use in maximising detections.

The terms 'subsets of crimes in a geographical area', 'crime type', and 'evidence type for forensic intelligence collections of coded data' enable searches to be carried out against sets of data under these three terms, for forensics can link cases over considerable time spans and distances. For example, analysts should not be put off at looking at a common evidence type, for in filtering the common evidence type data, there will be geographical, method, and behavioural subsets of that evidence type data, enabling intelligence products to be produced in the form of problem profiles by establishing links between and clusters of cases. The strength of dealing with data in this way is that it is not always the unusual features that lead to scene linkages. The other advantage of forensics is that the use of forensic evidence with a proper process for the positive screening of evidence from potential suspects takes the analytical process out of the area of probability and into the area of truth, a fundamental feature, which geographical profiling and analysis of method, times, etc. cannot do.

The proper application of the forensic support team and a willing awareness of those involved in crime analysis are required to make forensic intelligence happen. In the Metropolitan Police forensic intelligence development project, the lack of digital images was a major obstacle caused by the photographic department lagging behind the times in using chemical film and then finally abandoning the medium in 2007, when the film was no longer manufactured. The methods used by the photographers to retain old materials and working practices had to be admired, unless of course such practices made it impossible for certain processes to work properly in real time.

What was required was a digital system from the crime scene to the courtroom, with a professional digital image management system such as the Digital Image Management System (DIMS) produced by Linear Systems in California. For dealing with forensic softer evidence type marks, Treadmark or SICAR software is available off the shelf; however, many police services seem to show no interest in moving on, preferring to sit in an old-fashioned comfort zone. The forensic intelligence project was born when the lack of suitable systems providing images forced using Bayesian probability techniques with respect to footwear intelligence evidence. This, combined with a lack of information technology support around footwear evidence blocking the efficient use of scanning and screening software, created a major obstacle to realising the 'truth' dimension to specific matches in linked scene casework.

Software such as Treadmark or SICAR makes lighter work of managing footwear evidence, enabling measurements, overlay comparisons, enlargement, etc. To assist readers in sampling this technology, the CD ROM enclosed with this book has a full stand-alone version of Treadmark ready to use on a free 30-day licence. This version has sample offender footwear scans and scene marks made with the footwear to enable test searches and screening comparisons with measurements, etc. Treadmark has a glove mark storage and comparison section available and SICAR has a tire mark database as well as a shoe pattern one.

Tool marks have also been used for forensic intelligence purposes in the Bayesian probability area because of costs incurred through using private sector laboratories in the UK. Yet, prior to 1988 when the Metropolitan Police had its own in-house laboratory, tool mark links were often received linking scenes across London and the surrounding Home Counties' police services. A paper was written by the Met Lab (MPFSL) team about the work carried out.[23]

If more is to be made in a police service with respect to forensic intelligence, then the key area is to look at the entire police business and the forensic support team with a view to reviewing the working practices and service level agreements. This is the only way to progress, for outdated, unimaginative, restrictive practices will merely maintain an inadequate state of affairs and waste of effort. If privatised laboratory costs are too high, then forensic intelligence products will not be bought, so the forensic science provider facility might just as well not be there.

Summary

This chapter included the following:

- The basics of crime research and analytical processes
- Outlines of the nine analytical techniques with examples of how forensic intelligence can support those techniques
- A realistic discussion of what should be covered in the daily work of a crime analyst section contrasted with the work of a forensically aware forensic intelligence analyst
- A structure for dealing with forensic intelligence
- The input of forensic intelligence into intelligence-led policing, including the main uses of harder and softer forms of forensic evidence
- Common problems inhibiting the use of forensic intelligence
- The CSI's role in forensic intelligence
- The main intelligence features of the two main categories of forensic evidence

Forensic Evidence Recovery, Processing, and Best Practice

4

Purposes and Objectives of Crime Scene Examinations

The purpose of crime scene examinations is to extract *accurate information* from the crime scenes as to methods, locations, types of property stolen, and the recovery of forensic evidence with these main objectives:

- To provide evidence that a crime has actually been committed
- To identify offenders
- To link other scenes and potential suspects to crime scenes either at the time of the examination or at a later date
- To establish through accurate examination the key elements of the crime
- To corroborate or not corroborate witnesses and/or confirm or disconfirm information from sources
- To eliminate persons from the enquiry
- To find investigative and intelligence leads for the case and forensic intelligence links into other cases past, present, and future

Experienced crime scene examiners can provide valuable insight into sorting one series of similar crimes from another. This gives rise to different forms of record keeping by the examiners. The first is the totally factual process of recording details accurately about the physical crime scene and the recording of times and precise locations of forensic evidence recovered from the scene. The second set of record keeping is about the opinions of the examiners in the areas of assisting in the crime scene linking process, which by its nature has a range of outcomes from opinion based on observation and or probability right through to positive links, with physical or corroborated witness evidence. This second set of record keeping is within the context of problem-oriented policing and intelligence-led policing. For example, it could take the form of an intelligence problem profile, citing a particular shoeprint pattern in combination with a particular tool mark descriptor present at burglaries across a defined area, where there was a similar method and property types taken.

Clearly, the process of investigation has to start somewhere, and forming an intelligence product starts from a suspicion that something could be linked or that an event could be part of a crime series or, for example, form part of the activities of a criminal network creating a problem. It is all about creating confidence factors and evidence that the product has foundation and is fit for police tasking.

In the processes of recording perceived or believed provable truths and the process of recording other legacy data to aid in crime analysis, it is obvious that the more complete the picture gleaned from forensic examinations is, the easier it will be to provide accurate, timely crime analysis intelligence products for action. The processes actually follow the principles of scientific method in that hypotheses are made and tested to find the best outcome.

Inhibitors to Effective Uses of Crime Scene Examinations, Forensic Recoveries in Linking Crimes, and in Contributing to the Production of Intelligence Products

Inhibitors to the effective use of these processes arise in the working practices, legal framework, and business models practised in different jurisdictions. These inhibiting factors can be

- Financial, where forensic resources are not made available to cope with providing a fuller and bigger picture
- Restrictive working practices, where, for example, a service clings to the old ways of using sworn officers only, which contributes to the financial resource problem because sworn officers usually have larger salaries and a range of equipment issue considerations beyond that of a civilian counterpart
- Restrictions on experienced (usually civilian) scientific support workers on what they are allowed to examine, thus capping the effectiveness of the service in order to extend the grasp on the more interesting work by the older, established sworn officers
- Legal powers of police that are inadequate to deal with new evidence types and emerging technologies in detection by not tackling head on those who procrastinate in changing the law to accommodate, for example, the taking of DNA buckle cell swabs from offenders in custody or in not prioritising passing legislation to make way for a regional or national DNA database or allowing police to seize footwear of offenders for search against databases of crime scene marks
- Technological in restrictions caused by out-of-date information technology facilities and a resistance to any form of change allowing new technologies into the workplace

In the United Kingdom, as in most countries, by law, fingerprints are required to be taken from those who are charged with recordable offences, fingerprints being a traditionally entrenched method of identifying offenders because of the requirement to associate persons in custody to their correct criminal records. In fact, in the UK and in many countries, it is the law that fingerprints will be taken by police in the preceding scenario. This is also the case with respect to DNA in the UK, although in many countries this legal requirement to DNA sample those charged with recordable offences is not on the statutes. The reason the UK made it compulsory for police to fingerprint and DNA sample offenders was because if it was not law, then some officers would not fingerprint or DNA buckle cell swab the offenders and the system would then have inbuilt possibilities to fail in its purpose.

Rights or Not to Obtain or Seize Forensic Material from Offenders

What about the nonbiometric forms of evidence in the rights area to seize, for example, footwear from offenders? In the UK, the police are given rights, as are those in custody, under the Police and Criminal Evidence Act 1984 (PACE). The police have the right to take fingerprints, DNA, or personal property such as shoes, clothing, etc. if it can be established that those seizures are believed to be able to prove involvement in a criminal act. In 2006, PACE was amended to include the seizure of footwear from offenders to elevate the right to take footwear to the same position as the rights to take fingerprints and DNA. Thus, if PACE allows the taking of fingerprints and DNA, then officers can take footwear for speculative search.

The ways in which the harder biometric forms of evidence were dealt with differ from other softer forms of evidence and have, without a doubt, had a negative impact on the management of the softer forms of evidence, thus contributing to a much slower development of technologies to deal with these softer forms of evidence efficiently.

An Example of Volume Crime Practices Inhibiting a Serious Investigation

An unfortunate case occurred in the UK where a night stalker rapist broke into senior citizens' homes over a period of 17 years and evaded detection owing partly to a failure to provide volume crime footwear and tool mark evidence to set the volume picture against the major crime sex attack burglaries. The focus with South London management was on fingerprint and DNA recoveries. In contrast, North London management had a broader approach in these areas and developed forensic intelligence as a concept using shoe and tool marks. Even the Metropolitan Police had, in some areas, a parochial attitude to other jurisdictions within its own business practices.

When the court case was completed and the case reviewed in 2011, it was estimated that, over the 17-year period, the offender had committed around

1,000 burglaries plus the 29 reported sex attack burglaries. Those 1,000 burglaries represent hundreds of possibly missed opportunities to detect the offender by linking in the softer forms of evidence, for even the shoes he wore were a rare pattern and would have been a potentially significant linking factor into burglaries in the area. The working practices of the investigative team also caused a failure to detect the offender, who was found within 2 weeks when the case was given to a specialist murder investigation team, who reviewed the forensics effectively, finding that, early on in the investigation, the suspect had not had the taking of his DNA properly confirmed, leading to his profile not being on the system. Sadly, there are other parts of the world where police facilities are so inadequate that the crime series would not even have been perceived and other parts where under-resourced services struggle even to look at any volume crime properly.

The Advantages of Databasing and Managing Collections of Forensic Evidence

A major lesson learned from working on the development of forensic intelligence reflected the ways in which different forensic evidence types were managed in that CSIs in most police services focus on fingerprint and DNA quality submissions for three main reasons:

- The quality and quantity of submissions to structured regional or national systems carry a high investment, such as AFIS (Automatic Fingerprint Identification System) or DNA databases (e.g., UK National DNA Database, NDNAD), and are inspected for quality, quantity, and performance managed.
- The result of poor performance in submissions to these systems carries a high element of investment that will reflect on the career opportunities of the CSIs.
- A biometric match is the quickest and easiest way to identify an offender.

What about the other forms of evidence, which are packaged for storage or submission to a laboratory at a later date because there is no immediate suspect? In the majority of police services, these other exhibits are only scrutinised in detail when they are submitted to a laboratory; otherwise, after a term of storage, the exhibits are sent for destruction. Make no mistake: The destruction after a term of storage route is the fate of the majority of forensic exhibits recovered from crime scenes. Yet this material forms a vast resource of material that can be imaged, measured, and coded and should form databases for use by analysts from the majority of crime scenes.

It is worth remembering that finger marks are found in a best performing police service at 25% and DNA at 7% of burglaries, which means finger marks are not found at 75% and DNA at 93% of burglaries. In services with under-resourced forensic capabilities, the picture is worse. There are many offenders escaping detection because they take basic precautions not to leave the biometric forms of evidence, but with respect to footwear, for example, they cannot fly and in using tools they cannot avoid leaving marks or random transfers of trace material.

A Scenes of Crime Field Force Checklist for Effective Management of Forensics

Often fingerprint or DNA evidence will place a person in a crime scene at 'some time', but will not always prove that he or she actually did anything inside the crime scene; thus, ignoring the other evidence at crime scenes runs the risk of an offender accounting for the biometric evidence and walking away from court with a not guilty or unproven verdict. It is therefore wise for police services to review the working practices of their forensic field forces and to check on the following features of their work:

- The intervention rate of the field force related to different crime types (e.g., the percentages of scenes of each crime type actually visited and examined; to be effective, the intervention rate should be high)
- The evidence recovery rates for the main types of forensic evidence recovered for each crime type
- The result rates from forensic submissions for those evidence and crime types
- The intervention rates for cases where the field force has actually dealt with material from offenders (e.g., screening offenders either in custody or during execution of search warrants)

From this performance data, logical decisions can be made about the strengths and weaknesses of the service provided within the context of its quality, quantity, and propensity to provide useful forensic data in the production of analytical forensic intelligence products for action, as well as the capacity to relate softer forms of evidence to suspects.

Using Intervention Rates and Forensic Recovery Frequencies in Crime Analysis

In estimating the range of the size of crime-linked clusters established by forensic features, the evidence recovery rate combined with intervention rate enables calculation of the total number of crime scenes in a linked cluster.

For example, with five scenes linked with a forensic evidence feature and an evidence recovery rate for the evidence type of 1 in 4, the total range for scenes with the forensic feature and without it, within the same time frame, is in the range of 5 to 20 scenes. Further research into method, behaviours, times, victim type, and property stolen can establish how many other scenes within that range are potentially linked. A high intervention rate gives confidence that the whole picture is being seen. The result rates for the various evidence types can result in the following:

- Good results from a good recovery rate with quality recoveries and a good system for dealing with material from suspects give quality products and minimises intelligence gaps.
- A healthy volume forensic examination rate gives the opportunity to increase sanctioned detections around subjects of direct police arrests as well as extra detections around those found by fingerprint or DNA searches.
- Having systems such as Treadmark or SICAR (Shoeprint Index Capture and Retrieval) in place to inspect, screen against offenders, and code forensic marks such as footwear marks enables proper management with quality control of those evidential recoveries. Better still, if the CSIs have to search and screen footwear marks, they will be keen to deal with good quality marks carefully recovered from scenes. (See Chapter 5 on best practice in footwear marks recovery.)
- Real positive management techniques in quality and results are achieved instead of the practice of negative management techniques, which restrict, prevent, and minimise the output of the forensic team, funnelling it only in certain directions.
- The greater use of forensic recoveries is enabled. This would not be the case if restrictive practices were used, limiting the scope of examinations, screening, and submission of cases for evidential purposes.

Issues around Positive and Negative Management Techniques of Forensic Support

There is an issue with regard to forensic examinations of crime scenes around the perception of managing a forensic service on a budget. The idea of creating a 'manager' to decide about doing anything with certain cases and cherry picking what and what is not collected from crime scenes or submitted for examination arose in the UK from the introduction of privatised forensic science laboratories. The costs incurred from privatised laboratories led to a dramatic increase in forensic budgets to service the requirement to process certain types of forensic exhibits pivotal in delivery of certain criminal justice products—for example, criminal justice DNA buckle cell swabs required for DNA database search and blood/urine samples for toxicology cases. Under the preprivatisation system, cases were screened at laboratory reception by laboratory liaison staff tasked with rejecting badly packaged exhibits or cases where the business of analysis would not contribute any useful outcome. Under the privatised system, almost any properly packaged and documented exhibits will be accepted with the objective of billing the customer.

To put some figures around this business change, prior to selling the Metropolitan Police Forensic Science Laboratory in 1988 to the then newly created Forensic Science Service, the Metropolitan Police ran their laboratory for £11 million per annum. At the end of the first year of privatisation, the newly privatised laboratory invoiced the Metropolitan Police for £15 million, and by the year 2007–2008, the bill for laboratory examinations across different privatised forensic science providers had increased to £45 million per annum. This expenditure covered the core business, and improvements in DNA and latent prints casework were driven not by privatisation but rather by improved technologies also enjoyed elsewhere in the world under different forensic science funding regimes.

With the introduction of privatised laboratories, in-laboratory volume crime shoe mark and tool mark scene linking facilities went on the back burner and even certain types of exhibits in volume crime cases were prevented or restricted in submission for examination. Although there must always be an element of management in dealing with forensic examinations, it has to be acknowledged that in many police services, forensics has been viewed as something that came along later after the basic concept of policing; there is a lack of perception that the full and proper forensic examination of all potentially useful crime scenes within a jurisdiction is just as important as having regular police car and foot patrols.

Creating a forensic intelligence capability can increase management's perception of the quality or otherwise of the business model, and a view from outside police services—even across national boundaries—can be useful in broadening the view of where police services should be moving in this area. Practising forensic intelligence techniques encourages positive management of forensic services, for, in so doing, staff are encouraged to make use of everything they recover and record. This is irrespective of cases being screened in or out for police investigation in crime report systems. If each case has a basic minimum standard of reporting and examination, then each case, whether screened in or not, has the potential to be of future use in light of fresh intelligence or forensic identifications or in forming part of the complete picture necessary to achieve strategic and tactical objectives.

The majority of forensic intelligence research and screening is carried out in house free of billing by commercial organisations, and the ability to manage forensic recoveries more effectively is realised by having the right business model and practices in place to empower better management of forensic recoveries and submitted casework to laboratories.

For example, in 2005 I was invited to visit a small police service in the United States and, with my background in forensic services at New Scotland Yard, I found the visit interesting from the point of view that what I saw I considered to be requiring some investment and development. The officers were, however, keen and knew that 'things needed doing', which was an understatement. The service had sworn officers only and forensic exhibits were left for examination in a small block of lockers each about 1 foot tall and 8 inches wide, with a sign on the lockers warning that nothing should be left for over 2 weeks. The bloodstained drying room was a terracotta tiled room with a clothesline, tap, rubber hose, and drain in the middle of the floor, with no air filtration. I noticed that the ninhydrin fingerprint exhibit treatment cabinet was on the side of a vehicle examination bay and had articles lying in it with cobwebs on them.

They did have a very good computer drive examination facility; however, the perception I had was that the chief was right that some things did need doing and I wished I had the time to spend on those things. I mention this experience because the best practice I include in this book is not expensive and really is not out of the reach of even the smallest of police services. It just requires some changes to attitudes, planning, and basic training to start to achieve positive results.

Questions That Police and Forensic Managers Need to Ask Themselves

- Is there in my organisation the provision of an adequate forensic examination and recovery service covering useful applications of most common evidence types?
- With the softer forms of evidence, is there a situation created through inactivity and a poor set of processes—a prestorage facility for the dumpster awaiting the majority of forensic exhibits at the end of their storage time instead of making those recoveries useful?
- Does the policing organisation management know what it is doing with the forensic teams' biometric (DNA and fingerprint) identifications and matches?
- Does the police service forensic department contribute positively to intelligence-led problem-solving policing within the business group?

- Can forensics management enter the debate within police service business groups toward developing a better policing model where forensics is used more effectively?
- Are those providing forensic services in a position to workshop with other stakeholders to improve the service and influence contracts, which may otherwise inhibit overall forensic services performance?
- Is the forensic services department causing backlogs and delays in processing forensics though inadequate resources and restrictive working practices?

I make no apologies for covering best practice in retrieval and packaging of the main forensic evidence types in this book for the simple reason that, from real personal experience, once those evidence types were scrutinised for scene linking, it was found that there were issues with the quality and quantities of forensic exhibits. These quality issues led in my service to refresher training of CSI staff in order that best use could be made of the forensic retrievals. For example, use of the Treadmark software supplied with this book easily illustrates the advantages of correct shoe mark recovery and development techniques, for without quality management of the evidence, the quality and levels of detail required for positive use will not be there.

The Issue of Areas Disclosed in Forensic Marks as an Enabler of Forensic Intelligence

An important issue around forensic marks is the fact that marks found at crime scenes—whether they are latent prints, footwear, or tool marks—leave limited disclosed areas of the items that made the marks. Scenes can be linked on probability if the same types of features are found and, more rarely, the same areas will be disclosed from the same sources at different scenes, enabling positive forensic linking support. Unless, however, a system like Treadmark or SICAR is in place to scan offenders' footwear, the whole area of each item from which scene marks were made will not be in the evidence system and then only limited use will be made of those forensic recoveries.

In UK Home Office report 43/05,[24] this problem of low results was examined and reported on by eminent academics. It was professionally researched, but the whole point raised regarding areas of forensic marks disclosed was not mentioned and the opportunity to relate solutions to the problem missed. It is a bit like wondering why there would be hardly any latent print crime scene matches if no one took 10-print sets from offenders for search purposes! It is all about areas disclosed in the area of forensic marks.

With that in mind, the following sections in this chapter cover the best practice on the main evidence types found at crime scenes with some advice about the best use of systems such as AFIS.

Best Practice in Using the Main Forensic Evidence Types

Automatic Fingerprint Identification Systems and Their Characteristics

The popular perception of police using a fingerprint computer system, as seen in television fiction, is that all that is needed to be done is to pop a mark in the computer and the screen flickers with quickly changing fingerprint images and then stops with the word 'match' or 'no trace' flashing on the screen. In the case of 10-print exemplar sets, something like that scenario in identifying offenders to find the correct records is delivered by modern AFIS. What, then, is the position with regard to searching scenes of crime latent prints on AFIS?

Fingerprints have the characteristic that scenes of crime marks usually do not disclose the entire areas found on the 10-print and palm sets stored on the system. Areas disclosed in scenes of crime latent prints can be small areas of the friction ridge surface and, to compound matters, the background on which the latent print was found can be textured, irregular, or difficult to read because of damage or particles on the substrate on which the marks are found. Further movement and pressure at the time the mark was deposited can cause distortions or blurring. Therefore, when AFIS deals with scenes of crime latent prints they function by producing a list of responses to scenes of crime searches in a pecking order, with the best possible match response first. In the case of the National Automatic Fingerprint Identification System (NAFIS) in the UK, users check the first 15 responses and, if there is a match, it will usually be found in the first 15. However, I have known cases where matches for difficult marks have been found in the first 50 responses or beyond.

From analysis of the experience with the UK NAFIS (now called Ident One) and from published material by the US National Institute for Justice in 2011, AFIS has a 70% hit rate (or sometimes worse), which means a 30% 'miss' rate with scenes of crime marks.[14,15] That 'miss' figure can be higher as the quality of the mark grows poorer. A human latent print examiner (UK fingerprint expert) manually searching scenes of crime marks has a virtually zero miss rate and could expect disciplinary action and dismissal if he or she had a 30% miss rate. The logistics, however, of dealing with vast fingerprint databases enabling national searches dictate that computerisation is a necessity.

The Four Factors at Work in Existing Miss Rates with AFIS

- Orientation of the fingerprints in the exemplar sets scanned into the system is important; if a digit is recorded several degrees out of the vertical, a miss can result.
- Clarity of or movement in the images of the individual scanned in digits in the exemplar sets can cause misses.
- Some scenes of crime latent prints scanned in for search are relatively poor in quality.
- A regional search may be selected when, with some research, perhaps a national search would have been more appropriate.

How, then, can a CSI with a partner crime analyst make better use of AFIS by creating a forensic strategy within an intelligence tactical assessment to improve results and bring a problem or subject profile, covering a crime problem, to a satisfactory early resolution? Make no mistake: Taking the following actions can save a lot of police time and manpower costs as well as eliminating ongoing crime problems.

The following scenario is an outline of the distraction burglary problem faced in London in 2006 and 2007, where relaxation of the effort to crack down on a then reducing problem of distraction burglary led to a rapid increase in the crime type by travelling burglars. At its peak, London was experiencing some 300 to 600 distraction burglaries a month, resulting in the problem being upgraded as a strategic issue and included in the Metropolitan Police Strategic Assessment under the Metropolitan Police Model, a version of the UK National Intelligence Model (NIM). Crime analysts had to perform the following tasks in order to manage the crime type, feeding into the pan-London crime squad, the Metropolitan Police Coordination and Tasking Group:

- Produce tactical intelligence assessments around individuals and crime series identified
- Keep a daily rolling problem profile for the crime type updated with ongoing crime analysis, results analysis, network analysis, and crime mapping, including reviews of release dates for known prolific offenders with their places of residence on release and known associations; record requests for and updates on surveillance and results whilst ensuring that surveillance issues were raised to maintain permissions, etc.
- Prepare subject profiles around targeted individuals
- Maintain liaison with surrounding police services as well as Operation Liberal, the UK national operation against the crime type

- Update the forensic strategy for the Metropolitan Police around the distraction burglary crime type, containing the following features:
  - All distraction burglaries to be examined promptly by CSIs within 4 hours of reporting and examined as serious crime scenes
  - The suspect list to be maintained and the fingerprint bureau to be updated daily
  - The daily selection of forensically identified offenders as either surveillance targets or for direct arrest following research to establish a forensic intelligence package to maximise detections around each identification
  - The updating of the submissions of scenes of crime footwear marks to Operation Liberal for national search because offenders, in order to avoid detection by divisional policing, travelled across the country; thus, a crime scene footwear mark left in London on one day could be matched to the shoes of an offender arrested in Manchester the next day
  - Analysis of forensically linked cases on DNA, fingerprints, or footwear marks against other intelligence data, including mobile phone data
  - Updating daily the results of surveillance and mobile phone data to liaise with other police services quoting suspects, in areas where the mobile phone data or subjects under surveillance were found to be, for fingerprint and other forensics suspect checks
  - Updating the results and crime analysis to the coordination and tasking group, which is somewhat akin to the presentations for action and results given under COMPSTAT in the United States for follow-up

With all of this activity, it could be assumed that everything would run smoothly with regard to the prompt searching of distraction burglary latent prints. The fact was that, at the start of the strategy to deal with distraction burglary, in the first month there were only a couple of latent print matches. On reviewing the forensic strategy, two issues inhibiting performance were identified. The first was that UK distraction burglars are mainly career criminals, who are very forensically aware and will try to avoid leaving latent prints and DNA at crime scenes. This means that, for example, they will try to nudge things open or place a fingertip on the top of partly open doors to pull them open further. Distraction burglary usually relies on convincing elderly persons that the offender is an official of some sort in order to enter and steal, so the criminals do not usually wear gloves but rely instead on being careful in not leaving evidential traces. The second factor was that bureau staff were just scanning in marks without editing the input to help the NAFIS software match the offenders. Likewise the ten print sets were not inspected for alignment and best quality.

That said, quality examinations by experienced CSIs will find latent prints, DNA traces, shoe marks, and other evidence at some scenes. With up to 600 scenes a month examined, it was the case that quite a number of latent print submissions to the fingerprint bureau had been made. However, the results were too low and the pan-London crime squad were keen to work on some subjects of forensic identifications to start to penetrate the mainly family-based travelling criminal networks preying on the elderly.

Forensic Strategies to Make the Best Use of AFIS

On reviewing the forensic strategy inside the intelligence problem profile for the crime type, I decided to review the working practices within the fingerprint bureau and found that, on receipt of cases, fingerprint technicians were promptly scanning in the cases and searching them nationally. As part of the problem profile, I had secured from Operation Liberal the main suspect list of over 800 persons and had the list filtered with the London suspects at the beginning in order of priority and requested the following actions designed to improve the NAFIS search results:

- Starting with the suspect list, a fingerprint expert should look at the exemplar 10-print sets in Ident One in NAFIS and check all 10 digits for orientation, movement, or blurring. When possible, any digits should be replaced with better images from the fingerprint spares collection and poor orientation of digits should be corrected.
- The submitted scenes of crime cases should be inspected for quality and, in the case of poorer marks, a fingerprint expert should mark the minutiae to update NAFIS as to what and was not a characteristic within the scenes of crime latent prints for search on the system.
- The possibility of using a NAFIS internal Operational Response Database (ORD) for more precise searching of the 800+ suspects was put forward.
- After the preceding actions have been taken, research the scenes of crime marks and rerun suspects' 10 prints against scenes of crime marks.

The result from this activity was that in the first few weeks there were 28 latent print matches for distraction burglary from those cases reviewed and, in the following month, another 35 matches were made. Considering that each offender would have committed many offences, those 63 identified offenders were a gold mine of opportunities to expand casework, perform network analysis, find associates, and expand results through intelligence analysis and surveillance. Opportunities to tie in identified persons to other offences and networks around intelligence from informants were also used to good effect.

The teamwork from working on distraction burglary between investigators, field officers, crime analysts, CSIs, and latent print specialists as a strategic issue led to the poor performance figure of up to 600 reported cases a month dropping to 35 a month and a lot of offenders detected. Thirty-five cases per month can be viewed as a background residual amount of distraction burglary for a large city like London. This was a team effort linking good police tactics with quality crime analysis and gold standard forensics at the crime scene and in the processing of the forensic material submitted. The role of getting the processes right through forensic intelligence was pivotal.

Fingerprint Laboratory Support

A key issue in some police services is the availability of fingerprint sequential treatments of exhibits within a reasonable casework turnaround time. In the late 1990s, the situation in London was that all volume crime exhibits for fingerprint treatments went through the same laboratory facility as serious crime for sequential fingerprint treatments. This led to a situation where volume crime exhibits had up to an 8-month delay before they were examined, whereas serious crime cases were, of course, fast tracked. I reported on the issue and funding was obtained to install a sequential treatment laboratory. At the time, in order to have a safe facility without built-in fume cabinets in the building walls, it was necessary to design fingerprint fuming cabinets, which would be safe to use in any room with internal filtration. This was achieved in consultation with Labcaire Ltd (see Figures 4.1 and 4.2).

The laboratory offered the following facilities:

- Light search room for visible light, fluorescent examinations, and body fluids search
- CNA (Superglue) fuming cabinet
- Ninhydrin treatment cabinet
- Dye staining room
- Treatment laboratory for small particle reagent, amido black, powdering, etc.
- Humidity oven to accelerate maximum development of marks
- Digital imaging suite
- Photographic studio

The fingerprint laboratory offered fast-track examinations of street robbery, robbery, burglary, theft, vehicle crime, and other volume crime cases examined on the same day or within 90 hours, for sequential fingerprint treatment cases. This led immediately to street robbery property identifications on

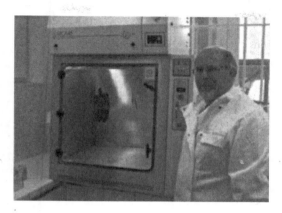

Figure 4.1 R Milne with Labcaire cabinet, Northeast London Forensic Science Support Unit (FSSU) 1996/1997.

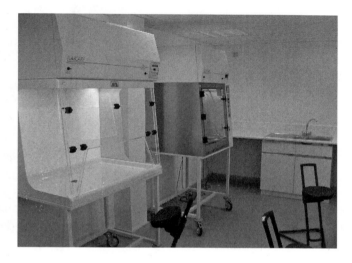

Figure 4.2 New equipment installed at the Hendon Northwest London laboratory, 2002.

discarded victims' property, resulting in real surveillance targets for crime squads. The volume crime laboratory even cleared the central laboratory's backlog of volume cases for Northeast London. Three more laboratories of the same design as part of the then new Metropolitan Police's forensic strategy were installed covering all volume crime in London with the same-day to 90-hour turnaround times. One of the functions of the volume crime fingerprint laboratories was the examination of recovered street robbery property. I examined the first item of recovered street robbery property in April 1997, resulting in the same-day latent print identification of a South African illegal overstayer. The suspect was a Caucasian with a blonde haircut with dark highlights and was picked out by the victim after arrest. He was offered a court trial for robbery and possible imprisonment or deportation back to South Africa. He selected the latter option.

The impact on forensic intelligence products was immediate. With powdered lifted latent prints being searched in the same 24-hour period as recovery, the laboratory sequential treatment cases were virtually in real time also, so most identifications received for research were from the same working week or the week before. That is not to say that identifications of older cases were not received as well. There was an immediate capacity to follow the West Yorkshire Police initiative 'Operation Converter', a process whereby every biometric identification has a forensic intelligence package for action created. However, this was resisted by Metropolitan Police management, although under the Metropolitan Police Model provision was made for cases with 10 or more potential detections under the 'corporate prisoner scheme'— a process where funding was made available for cross-divisional and cross-border cases in order to facilitate police action across divisional boundaries. Each corporate prisoner application had to have a subject or problem profile created under the Met Police Model under the UK NIM for processing in tasking and coordination. Under COMPSTAT, the removal of a subject or target is resourced under the principle of relentless follow-up.

Using DNA Matches and Crime Scene Links Effectively

In its applications, DNA has become a major tool in identification, crime linking, and detection alongside fingerprints. There have been many spectacular results achieved in serious casework and in cold-case reviews. Quite apart from the use of DNA in the single casework scenario, it has the characteristic to provide a searchable database of profiles enabling speculative searches against those in custody or already in the database, whilst at the same time providing positive links between unsolved cases.

In the forensic intelligence area, in DNA databases such as the UK NDNAD, the scene-to-scene linking of cases where the identity of the offender is not yet known is commonplace, yet the facility to link scenes in the volume area is not pursued routinely by AFIS. This is for two reasons. The first is that, with latent scenes of crime prints, usually only partial areas are disclosed, making the process less efficient in linking scene to scene, where other areas of the friction ridge structure may be disclosed. Fingerprints become really useful when 10-print sets of offenders with all friction ridge areas are disclosed as entered into the system; then, the scenes of crime latent prints with partially disclosed areas can be matched. The other way in which the AFIS process differs from operating a DNA database is that if a latent mark is missed at the time of filing and search, it will only be found if another search is launched, either mark to print or print to mark. With DNA, once a profile is entered into the database with full or good partial profiles, the database will produce the matches. Unlike fingerprints, DNA can be used to find those with familial links to offenders leaving DNA at crime scenes but who have yet to be sampled and placed on the database. This offers a forensic intelligence route into the detection of offenders.

In the UK, familial DNA has been used successfully in serious crime cases but, owing to the privatised structure of the forensic science provision in the UK, the technique is currently too expensive for volume crime use (based on price quoted to the author in 2007 for familial DNA per case). Yet the process is merely one of comparing DNA profiles on spreadsheets, which cannot be that expensive a process for the contractor laboratories but must give them a very high profit margin. Another worrying aspect of privatised laboratories was their resistance to sharing changes in techniques because of commercial in confidence issues. They worked basically to the requirements of the UK Forensic Regulator, but the Regulator's Office had a weakness in that in-depth technical assessments of the conduct of serious casework were not examined in detail.

As far as I was aware, the regulator was not in possession of detailed legacy data around cases until after problems and failures arose of a very public nature—for example, the UK Damilola Taylor and Stephen Lawrence murder cases. One of the main points in this book is that forensic services providers in police services should be able to see all their legacy data in the same detail as those who are conducting the provision of forensic science analysis and opinion. Privatised laboratories still pursue patents and seek commercial advantage, so it is possible that further problems could arise in different organisations in the future for the very same reasons.

An Inhibited DNA Casework Example

In 2006 and 2007 I researched several hundred cases, looking for a way to support a tactical assessment into getting into a number of suspected family-based criminal gangs and networks involved in a strategic crime type and subject to a rolling intelligence problem profile by the crime analysts. I found 100 cases where the confidence level was very good that we had unidentified offenders' DNA at those scenes. I enquired from the UK Forensic Science Service Gov Co. as to the cost of familial DNA products for the 100 cases and was given the figure of £5,000 per case, but as it was a bulk order they would deliver familial DNA for only £4,000 a case.

Because I did not have a £400,000 budget (approx. US$624,000 at 2011 conversion rates) to cover this approach, the work was not done, although I wonder what the real cost would have been for an in-house laboratory if we had had one at the time. There was a high probability that the work would have connected with offenders' relatives in the DNA database and given the

investigative team a very good starting point in targeting individuals, in setting up surveillance and lifestyle evaluations, and in finding possible intelligence sources relevant to the subjects under consideration.

DNA Databases and eDNA

Modern DNA databases such as the UK NDNAD produce output in the form
of eDNA reports that are electronically sent to users. The eDNA report has
details of the case(s) and persons matched, updating any existing linked series
as new cases are added. This information is fine if officers are going to act
straightaway and arrest identified offenders for the cases listed on the eDNA
report. However, there are definite inefficiencies around running such a simple
match and arrest system in that across the whole of a police business literally
hundreds to thousands of detections can be missed, leading to a self-inflicted
record of relatively poor performance, which should have been undeserved.

It is therefore definitely best practice to integrate the DNA links and
results using forensic intelligence, crime analysis, and intelligence techniques
to expand the value of the DNA results. This process has two main routes.
The first is to research other intelligence and crime analysis data around the
DNA scene to scene links. If the forensic support has healthy crime scene
intervention and recovery rates for forensic materials, there will inevitably
be other forensic material recovered from some of the DNA-linked scenes,
which will link the DNA cases into other cases by other evidential means.
Second, if forensic support has proactive offender screening in custody or in
search warrant processes for forensic material recovery from suspects, then
the area's disclosed problem in shoe and tool marks will be minimised. If
forensic support also has in place adequate processes for recording this material and screening results, then the crime analysts will be in a position to
make use of the material as forensic intelligence, improving their capabilities
and performance. Further, in the meetings and teamwork areas, forensics
will in a good business model be well placed to share examination and recovery results with the rest of the intelligence and investigative team.

Significance of DNA Forensic Crime Scene Intervention and Recovery Rates

In the Metropolitan Police, the intervention rate at burglary scenes in recent
years has been at approximately 85% of reported scenes; the target is always set
at 100%, but owing to logistical problems and the false reporting of burglaries, the target achieved is always less. The recovery rate for DNA at burglary
scenes is between 7% and 9%, with a propensity to be toward the top end of

that range. The reason that the figure is not higher is simply that the offenders have to shed blood, body fluids, biological traces, hairs, or tissue at the crime scenes for DNA to be found. Most offenders try to prevent leaving DNA as their arrest and removal from the burglary business will follow rather rapidly if their DNA is already filed on the DNA database.

The significance of this situation is that in a scenario where a DNA database produces a number of linked scenes in a series, what is the range of the total number of crime scenes in the total series? We know from the DNA recovery rate for the crime type that it is found at typically 9% of scenes, which means that it is not found at up to 91% of crime scenes. Therefore, the range of total scenes in a series with, say, five DNA-linked scenes is 5 to approximately 455 scenes (i.e., 5 × 91), although it has to be said that not all of the 9% DNA cases will have offender-submitted DNA, but it is assumed that the majority of cases (say, up to 75%) will have offenders' DNA in the case submissions.

My practical experience of dealing with many DNA-linked volume crime burglary series is that when the offenders are identified and processed, the total number of cleared-up detected scenes is nearly always at the high end of the range. The worst case I had concerned an unidentified burglar with 17 linked DNA scenes accrued over 4 years in a series before his arrest and identification. The forensic intelligence subject profile written by my team on the burglar once he had been identified during the series was that he was possibly involved in up to 1,500 burglaries with a high probability of over 1,000 detections resulting from dealing with the suspect once arrested.

In fact, when he was arrested, the offender implicated himself in 2,500 burglary cases, committed at a rate of around two per weekday over the 4-year time period. Without this research, it is likely that an officer would have processed the offender, charging him with the 17 DNA-match offences plus anything else found though recovering property, etc. In developing the concept of splitting forensic intelligence processes into hard evidence processing and forensic problem profiles for softer forms of evidence, my Forensic Intelligence Unit Territorial Policing (TP) dealt with up to 450 prolific offenders per year with multiple DNA-linked scenes prior to their arrests, resulting in many detections. The figures for 2005 and 2006 record that the Forensic Intelligence Unit TP dealt with 373 biometrically identified offenders and achieved 871 extra identifications through the creation of forensic intelligence target profiles, which were input to the crime intelligence system CRIMINT. Thus, the 373 cleared cases became 1,244 detections in that time period.

This work on hard evidence research and processing was quite apart from the other forensic intelligence problem profiles around the softer forms of evidence placed on CRIMINT, which added many more detections. This was because when police interrogated CRIMINT about a location, method, suspects' descriptions, vehicles, etc., the forensic intelligence proactive assessments would be in the responses offering quality intelligence products around crime series.

On the subject of performance, the volume crime laboratories introduced from 1997 onward, through examining recovered street robbery property, accrued 450 to 600 latent print matches per year and this, added to the DNA matches, led to identification rates of 850 to 1,300 offenders per year. These matches gave crime squads and investigators the intelligence as to who was handling the robbery property and, technically, the best intelligence they could have to expand casework and make best use of tasking police assets. The intervention rate for robbery property forensics was on the low side compared to burglary, but the percentage identification rate for much of London was in excess of 32% of submitted-marks cases per annum.

There were a few offenders, however, who nearly always managed to cut themselves breaking in, resulting in a number of detections at the lower end of the assessed range. Inhibiting factors in applying forensic intelligence with some police operational command units were always around some having poorer recovery rates for shoe and tool marks (thus compromising the overall picture), combined with poor cooperation in dealing with forensic recoveries from suspects and compounded with a resistance to dealing with any level 2 cross-border casework. In London, the Territorial Police Tasking and Coordination Group covered the level 2 crime problem by using the pan-London Crime Squad and through nominating lead divisions for level 2 casework, often supplying extra funding to get the cross-jurisdiction work done. This situation must be mirrored in other countries where, owing to parochial attitudes, cross-divisional and cross-force work is not prioritised.

In the working practices area, serious inhibitors to maximising detections are found in the attitude of police management to fingerprint and DNA identifications because many organisations view those identifications as the quick end game, whereas what they actually have is the best intelligence about who really was involved in crime as a starter toward better detection rates. The lack of forensic training given to crime analysts is just as bad, and its consequence is that often they do not communicate with forensic services departments and thus the effort around forensics as one of the best intelligence sources is underused.

Forensic Problem Profiles and the Concept of the Forensic Intelligence Report

In writing forensic intelligence problem profiles, the concept of the forensic intelligence report (FIR) was created because the forensic services department at the time wished to distinguish its work from the standard police intelligence unit's products produced under the UK NIM. A copy of an example forensic intelligence report form is included with the CD ROM. The forensic intelligence report in structure was very similar to the other standard NIM products in the range from strategic, tactical assessments to problem and subject profiles, thus fulfilling two main functions in that most forensic intelligence products are produced to support crime and intelligence analysis in the classical sense, but some forensic intelligence products are by their nature stand alone, requiring no other support, and can be submitted directly for police action.

All intelligence and analysis products must be recorded in the same systems (e.g., CRIMINT, Crime Workbench, or similar systems), and exclusion from systems just because a forensic hit is enough on its own in one case or is mistakenly viewed as just information is very bad practice (see the advice in Chapter 1 that the involvement of 'intelligence hawks'—those who think they can know in advance what intelligence and information is—in managing intelligence systems should be avoided unless management is not concerned about creating its own risk problems within its own systems).

Only quality forensics can be proven to be graded A.1 in any $5 \times 5 \times 5$ intelligence grading system. Human sources, at best, can only be graded B.1 or less owing to the possibility of error, intentional or otherwise. Senior investigating officers should have the opportunity to scan newly forensically identified offenders at any crime level to seek offenders with behaviours to match behaviour evidence found in serious crime. Such offenders can be found to emerge at any crime level. If the process relies on officers to remember to update crime report records entering biometric identifications in an ad hoc, one-to-one basis, then the possibility for failure in this area is a very real and inbuilt one.

It is worth noting that forensic intelligence reports can be generated from research and analysis of the softer forms of evidence, but this will only be possible if the forensic recoveries information can be extracted from the in-force crime report system. This crime report system is the depository for all crime investigation details, and proper use of it enables efficiency in record keeping and retrieval. Details in crime reports are the responsibility of each key player in the investigation from the original reporting officer (even if it is a telephone first report system), the investigating officer, and forensic examiner. The crime report system should be searchable and have flexible facilities to provide output in spreadsheet formats for research. It is bad practice for forensic examiners to have to create separate, manually constructed spreadsheets detailing their forensic recoveries for the following reasons:

- All stakeholders should be able to input and view relevant crime report information in as near real time as possible.
- Input to a major system such as the crime report system is an enabler of data warehousing or content management systems toward an entity-based approach.

- Creating separate manual databases causes time delay and bottlenecks in the system causing inefficiencies and, worse still, forensic misses.
- The crime report system will have industry standard protection of data and audit tools built in, enabling transparent management of the system in the interests of criminal justice.

Table 4.1 shows an example of a forensic intelligence report, which in format can be produced as a problem profile around a crime series with no clearly identified person(s) but may suggest suspects with valid reasons why they could be suspects. On the other hand, the FIR can be a subject (or target) profile around a forensically identified person(s) and may even relate in some cases to prison intelligence follow-up casework as well as for police tasking. **Like any other intelligence profile, the FIR should be copied into the police intelligence system so that any searches on relevant places, persons, methods, or other intelligence will throw up responses to enquiring or inputting officers.**

A forensic intelligence report template is included on the CD ROM.

Summary

This chapter included the following:

- The purposes and objectives of crime scene examinations
- Inhibitors to the effective uses of crime scene forensic recoveries
- Rights or otherwise to obtain or seize forensic material
- The advantages of databasing and managing forensic evidence
- A scenes of crime field force check list
- Using intervention rates and forensic recovery frequencies in crime analysis
- Issues around positive and negative management techniques
- Best practice in the main forensic evidence types
- Best use and characteristics of AFIS
- Fingerprint laboratory support
- Using DNA matches and crime scene links effectively
- DNA databases and eDNA
- Forensic problem profiles and the concept of the forensic intelligence report

Table 4.1   Forensic Intelligence Unit (FIU) Forensic Intelligence Report

Delete yes/no, etc., as appropriate

GPMS classification	Restricted/confidential/secret/top secret
FIU application type	Research

1. FIU Number and Officer Details

OCU/precinct/division (exact location)	Forensic Intelligence Desk
FIU reference no.	
Intelligence log no.	
Intelligence manager (name, rank, wt./pay no.)	
24-Hour contact number/e-mail	
Intelligence analyst (name, rank, wt./pay no.)	
24-Hour contact number/e-mail	

2. Identification of Problem

Brief summary of the problem that the FIR will be addressing	
Enter a brief précis of the problem.	

3. Intelligence Report

Summarise existing intelligence quoting existing CRIMINT intelligence ref. numbers where appropriate. Record the result of FIU research and any supporting analysis.	
Summarise all the available intelligence and supporting forensics, including named persons found during research related to forensic cases and the potential reasons why the forensics covered should be considered in the light of other intelligence with sources. *Attach mappings, graphs, etc. to the document below the document cells.*	

continued

Table 4.1 (continued)   Forensic Intelligence Unit (FIU) Forensic Intelligence Report

4. Suspect Details/Flagging/Interest Marker Request

4.1 Mark Up Info to Central Service Intelligence Unit

1. Name/company	2. Name/company
Alias	Alias
DoB	DoB
Sex	Sex
IC	IC
PNCID	PNCID
CRO	CRO
Address	Address
Vehicle(s) VRM	Vehicle(s) VRM
Telephone number(s) T	Telephone number(s) T
INFOS check folio	INFOS check folio
Date/time issued	Date/time issued
Flag at SIB? yes/no	Flag at SIB? yes/no
Interest marker at SIB? yes/no	Interest marker at SIB? yes/no
Flag at NCIS? yes/no	Flag at NCIS? yes/no
Interest marker at NCIS? yes/no	Interest marker at NCIS? yes/no
Reasons if yes at NCIS	Reasons if yes at NCIS
3. Name/company	4. Name/company
Alias	Alias
DoB	DoB
Sex	Sex
IC	IC
PNCID	PNCID
CRO	CRO
Address	Address
Vehicle(s) VRM	Vehicle(s) VRM
Telephone number(s) T	Telephone number(s) T
INFOS check folio	INFOS check folio
Date/time issued	Date/time issued
Flag at SIB? yes/no	Flag at SIB? yes/no
Interest marker at SIB? yes/no	Interest marker at SIB? yes/no
Flag at NCIS? yes/no	Flag at NCIS? yes/no
Interest marker at NCIS? yes/no	Interest marker at NCIS? yes/no
Reasons if yes at NCIS	Reasons if yes at NCIS

Table 4.1 (continued)   Forensic Intelligence Unit (FIU) Forensic Intelligence Report

5. Supervision

Forensic Intelligence Officer	
Comments	
Name (print)	Rank and wt. no.
Signature	Date

Forensic Intelligence Manager	
Comments	
Name (print)	Rank and wt. or pay no.
Signature	Date

Source: Based by the author on the Metropolitan Police Proactive Assessment Tasking Proforma (PATP).

Best Practice in Recovery of Forensic Evidence from Crime Scenes

5

Dealing with Crime Scenes

In writing this book I decided to consider that various persons involved in different disciplines within police services—ranging from experienced crime scene investigators (CSIs) with an MSc in forensic science to patrol officers who, as part of their role, from time to time must carry out crime scene examinations—may refer to the text. For this reason, this chapter is quite extensive but pitched at a level to make it of practical use to scene examiners while, at the same time, perhaps giving some forensic background to those involved in intelligence-led policing.

If work is done to this basic standard, the chances of success are good. In making best use of forensic examinations and recoveries in modern intelligence-led policing, there is more of a focus on the service provided by forensic examiners, and strategies may well be created as part of intelligence profiles requiring action and potentially positive results from forensic services. That is perhaps the main reason why this chapter was written.

Crime Scene Examinations of Serious and Volume Crimes

Those involved in criminal investigation invariably target full resources on serious crime cases employing every practical method to achieve a resolution. In serious crime examinations, police services employ their best people and screen in detailed material from suspects to match to intense and extensive recoveries from crime scene examinations. It is no surprise to note the discrepancies in results from forensic recoveries from volume crime forensics against the high returns from serious crime examinations. As previously discussed in this book, although the activity in the volume crime area cannot be expected to match the effort in serious crime casework, it should be much better in many police services than it currently is. The remedies to improving results are in the areas of intervention rates in the examination of volume crime scenes, the provision of forensic intelligence analytical products improving communication to enable the forensic screening of suspects, and the quality of the examinations of volume crime scenes:

- Properly organised processing and storage of forensic recoveries recorded in an effective crime reporting system result in the creation on demand of data for analytical purposes.
- In addition, searchable databases with digital screening systems are positive assets to police knowledge, systems, and intelligence, acting as enablers in the effective use of forensics toward the problem-solving effort in modern policing.

Perhaps one day an enterprising software writer will incorporate forensic files encompassing laboratory legacy data in the form of technical files for cross matching purposes in such crime reporting systems. However, first the working practices of forensic science providers and the formats they use would have to have some generic common standards, although in many areas this is not the case today.

In the previous chapters, the concepts of intelligence-led policing and forensic awareness of the stakeholders in intelligence-led policing were explored. In this chapter, the best practices in the main evidence types in actual search, recovery, and preservation are covered as a refresher to those whose roles involve the forensic examinations of crime scenes. With care, a higher proportion of forensic recoveries can be made better use of. This lesson was learned in the Metropolitan Police, where a programme of refresher training was given to crime scene examiners in the form of footwear evidence and DNA recovery refreshers.

The source of this advice is through many years of personal experience in evidence recovery through working with various specialists in getting to the roots of the reasons for low results with some forensic evidence types.

When a crime scene examiner is despatched to a crime scene, the organisation tasking the examiner is sending a trained person in an expensive vehicle with a considerable investment in equipment and materials. I take the view that, having despatched that forensic asset, the time taken to carry out a proper examination of the scene and recover all useful evidence will not affect the department's budget to any great degree. It will certainly cut the risk factors if events conspire to cause a serious problem around a volume crime event, which transpires later to be part of a serious crime problem. This is quite apart from the enhanced forensic intelligence and detection potential, which can accrue from producing quality forensic examination work and retrievals.

Latent print and DNA recoveries are usually effectively managed within police services for the reasons given in full in Chapter 4. It is safe to say that submissions to the Automatic Fingerprint Identification System (AFIS) and DNA laboratories are checked for quality and quantity. In many police services, this is not the case with other types of forensic marks, impressions, and samples recovered that are stored but not screened or processed to provide forensic intelligence products. The following sections deal with those different but common nonbiometric evidence types and the best practices in their recoveries.

Footwear Evidence Best Practice

This section gives practical advice in recovering quality footwear marks for the simple reason that there is nothing more demoralising than submitting marks for expert examination and achieving few conclusive results. Certainly in the UK, there have been those who, through bad techniques, have had poor results with footwear evidence and blamed the evidence type as not being useful. In practising forensic intelligence, the recovered evidence is evaluated, used, and screened against scene links and suspects. In going down that road, a refresher and focus on good practice has improved results getting the evidence type on track. It is a recorded fact by the UK National Police Improvement Agency (NPIA) in 2005 that over 25% of footwear cases submitted for expert examination result in conclusive matches but that the casework submission rate is very low compared to that for biometric evidence types.

For those wishing to explore the subject of footwear evidence further toward becoming an accredited footwear evidence examiner, *Footwear Impression Evidence,* by William J. Bodziak,[25] a former supervisory agent, Laboratory Division of the FBI, is a key publication.

Searching for footwear marks requires good forensic lighting products in the form of focussed and diffuse lighting. For dust marks, oblique lighting is required to search for marks. Even with good lighting, some dust marks will only be found by electrostatic cold searching whole floor areas with strips of electrostatic lifting (ESL) film.

Actors who portray CSIs hold a battery torch alongside their heads, but this will not do. The technique is to search low with the light rays shining across the surface at a very low angle, revealing every particle.

Footwear marks are often found in the process of using powdering techniques for searching for latent finger marks; for this reason, there is a tendency by some scene examiners to powder and lift footwear marks as a convenient means of footwear marks recovery. Footwear marks, unfortunately, are unlike latent fingerprints in that they are not made by the deposition of human sweat. In addition, the process of matching footwear marks to offenders' shoes is on pattern, wear characteristics, damage features, feathering, moulding faults, etc. Latent fingerprint identification is achieved on the coincident sequence of the ridge characteristics referred to as minutiae.

In the development of powdered latent prints, the method employed is that of building up the powder on the latent prints' ridges, thus creating the best contrast of the friction ridge structure. This is not the case in developing footwear marks, where the delicate detail required in matching the marks may be destroyed by the wrong powdering technique.

This is important: **Powdering, lifting, chemical, and casting techniques can damage footwear marks.** Do not get caught in the trap of believing that the techniques for developing latent prints are good for footwear marks, for they are examined and evaluated differently and require different recovery techniques.

Footwear marks can be in the positive or negative forms of dust marks; wet, greasy deposits; transfers of material; and three-dimensional impressions. The weather prevailing at the time can often determine the types of footwear marks left by offenders' shoes at crime scenes.

Shoe mark identifications normally come from marks, which have at least some fine detail where part of the mark is crisp and sharp. Unfortunately, the most obvious marks at a crime scene usually show the basic tread pattern, but no fine detail. Such marks tend to give rise to 'could have' or 'some support' types of comments in footwear examiners' statements when they cannot be eliminated or matched positively through lack of detail. The best marks for identification are usually made on smooth, clean surfaces by a practically clean shoe.

Marks made by a wet or dirty shoe on a relatively smooth surface at a crime scene usually look strong but have less detail in the earlier marks from the point of entry, so select the lighter marks made later as these will have the best fine detail. On a heavily textured surface (e.g., carpet), none of the marks will show fine detail, although ESL can recover marks from carpets that can be useful for elimination purposes and in indicating a route taken by an offender through a crime scene. Where papers are scattered on the floor, the papers with the strong marks will often be recovered by CSIs and the apparently blank sheets left behind at the scene. Often, however, using black gelatine adhesive lifters or ESL film on the apparently blank sheets of paper will yield marks with that fine detail required to achieve a positive evidential match. Scene examiners should experiment by standing on a sheet of paper wearing apparently clean shoes and then charging a piece of black Mylar ESL film over the paper. They will find that there is an excellent quality mark on the ESL from what appeared to be superficially a blank sheet of paper.

The best approach whenever possible is to retrieve footwear marks from the scene without any treatment. Do not mark removable items in any way. Ideally, remove the whole item, rather than cutting out individual marks, because faint marks of better quality may be missed. Always take entirety photographs with the item in situ and two measurements to record where the item was recovered so that, if necessary, the item could be placed exactly where it was found at a later date. This process improves the quality of the evidential recording. Exhibits should be labelled and properly packaged and, where appropriate, direction arrows included in the labelling.

When using adhesive lifting or photographing marks on fixed surfaces, you should use a directional arrow pointing to a reference point (e.g., the top of a door for kick marks or the direction of a window for marks on a sill at the point of entry or exit).

When dealing with removable items, always place sheets of paper and card bearing footwear marks inside a smooth card folder. Do not overdo the use of glue, tape, or labels on the actual original exhibit, but a small label can be placed on the item to ensure its future relationship with the correct packaging. Put the closed file containing the mark in an envelope on which the correct labelling, including date, address, and the item number, has been placed or written beforehand. ESL folders may be used on the odd occasion when a sheet is too large for a standard US letter- or A4-sized file. If the mark is obviously crusty or contains a lot of loose debris, place the sheet bearing the mark in the bottom of an exhibit box. **Always label, signature seal, and sign the chain of custody label and note the exhibit bag or exhibit label unique reference number in your notes.**

When packaging, do not place shoe marks directly in polythene bags or forensic exhibit bags as the marks can either be damaged or transfer to the inside of the bag in part. When packaging pieces of glass and other objects bearing marks, it is essential to fix the glass safely and securely in an exhibit box using wire or cable ties. Some exhibit boxes have insert panels made for the fixing of objects inside the box.

Examples of photographed, powdered, and gel/ESL footwear marks are in the Treadmark software on the CD ROM with this book.

Dealing with Footwear Marks Found Whilst Powdering for Latent Prints

Important notes about powdering footwear marks include the following:

- Powdering *is not the preferred method* for dealing with footwear marks.
- Brush powdering works best with dry marks on shiny surfaces that have been made by wet or slightly greasy shoes.
- Powdering *will obliterate dust marks.*
- Black powder is preferred when using black gelatine lifters to lift developed marks.

During the process of fingerprinting doors and other surfaces with powder, footwear marks will inevitably be found from time to time. Latent footwear marks found in this way can be carefully developed with **very light powdering** and then photographed and lifted. Clear adhesive lifters can be used for marks developed in Bristol black or aluminium powder, as can black gelatine lifters. In hot countries, gelatine lifters are not used because they can melt in strong heat, but where they can be used, they are superior to the clear adhesive lifters. The smooth, glossy, black lifting surface of the gelatine lifters enables quality photography even of black powder marks because there is no flaring out in imaging, which is caused when white coloured lifters are used.

Using Gelatine Lifters

As previously stated, gelatine lifters (sometimes called gelatine rubber lifters) are not commonly used in countries where the climate is hot because the lifters will melt if not kept in a cool box or refrigerator. In temperate or cold countries, they are commonly used and are a high-quality medium with which to recover footwear marks. The technique is to apply the lifter to the substrate adjacent to the mark and then, using a wide rubber roller, carefully roll the lifter onto the mark, ensuring there are no air bubbles. The lifters are supplied with a polycarbonate or acetate transparent cover and the best practice is to fix the lift in the bottom of an exhibit box for transfer to the office for photography.

In cases where storage is a problem, with large numbers of volume crime gelatine lifters, the clear cover can be carefully put back over the mark with the roller avoiding air bubbles. Lifts can be stored in this way in filing cabinets for ease of storage, but if a cover is removed for photography, then a fresh cover has to be used to re-cover the mark; otherwise, the residue of the mark will transfer back to the lifter, causing a mirror image effect, which is to be avoided at all costs. In a later section, the covering protocol is given for dealing with gelatine lifts in this way, but best practice is to package the lift without covering it and photograph the mark as soon as is practically possible.

Scanning Covered Gelatine Lifts

Often even very faint marks on covered gelatine lifters can be scanned and viewed on a scanned image even if nothing can apparently be seen visually without having to remove the cover, which is often not necessary. The Treadmark software supplied with this book has an enhancement and contrast utility built in that enables the swift scanning and processing of covered gelatine marks.

Gel lifting works on both powdered and unpowdered dust marks. Black powder is preferred as the medium if powdering has to be used. The gel lifts in three dimensions and the mark will be drawn into the gel, so allowing time for marks to absorb is required as outlined next:

- A contact time of 1 to 2 minutes is sufficient to gel lift many shoe marks, but some firmly adhering marks may require longer times of 20 to 30 minutes.
- Gelatine lifting is deceptively easy to use, but lifts can be easily ruined by careless handling, packaging, or recovering. Leave the packaging flat, as the gelatine lifts are heavy and can pull away from adhesive tape used to fix the lifts in exhibit boxes. A detached, rolled-up lift adrift in an exhibit box can be made useless for evidential purposes.
- High-quality gel lifting film is relatively costly, so use it selectively and sparingly. Always try ESL first. Indeed, ESL will often find the dust mark; the technique will not lift all of the mark, often clearing out marks and leaving a very detailed mark for gelatine lifting.
- Label the back of the gel while it is on the mark with your exhibit number, signing and dating it.
- The safest way to preserve gel lifts that are going to be photographed within 2 to 3 weeks is to place them in a proper exhibit box. If a gelatine lift is to be transported to the laboratory, secure it to the bottom of the box all the way round the edge with tape.
- Gelatine lifts may be covered with clear plastic film, but do not cover a gel lift unless you can do it without creating air bubbles. Never replace the plastic film once it has been in contact with a shoe mark.
- In dealing with serious crime marks, always attach the gelatine lifts in exhibit boxes and do not cover. Photograph the mark(s) as soon as possible in good lighting conditions.

Preservation and Packaging of Gelatine Footwear Mark Lifters

Covering Gelatine Volume Crime Lifts

In order to reduce the number of exhibits that have to be sealed in bulky cardboard exhibit boxes, the following procedure was agreed with the UK Forensic Science Service Gov Co concerning the re-covering of gelatine lifters.[4] Once the lift has been made, the mark can be re-covered with the original cover ONCE ONLY. In the event that the original cover is soiled, another sheet of acrylic can be used.

- The cover must be initialled by the finding officer at the time of covering the lift.
- The covered gelatine lift should be protected in either a shoe lift cardboard envelope or in a card document folder and then sealed in a self-seal exhibit bag. A label for photographic purposes should be included with the gelatine lift and the exhibit label section of the bag completed. Do not place paper exhibit labels inside the exhibit bag.

- Note that it is not necessary to bind the card folder with adhesive tape. All that is necessary is that the lift in its folder be placed in a self-seal exhibit bag, making use of the exhibit label on the bag itself. This point is reenforced because a number of officers have made the unpackaging of exhibits almost unmanageable with coils of adhesive tape stuck across every item.
- In cases where the lifted shoe marks are faint, it will be necessary to uncover the lift for coding and photography (See preceding note on scanning gelatine covered marks). A fresh acrylic sheet will be used to re-cover the mark. In the case of very faint marks, it is best practice not to cover the gel lift with a clear plastic cover but instead exhibit it in a box.
- Any gel lift re-covering sheets should be initialled by the person dealing with it, WHO SHOULD ALSO SIGN THE CHAIN OF CUSTODY EXHIBIT LABEL.
- The original exhibit bag should be resealed in the normal manner with the resealer's signature.

Before re-covering actual exhibits, it is a good idea to practise with a fresh blank gelatine lifter using a large, wide rubber roller, which should be a standard item in the scenes of crime kit.

Re-covering Technique for Gelatine Lifts
- Place the lift on a clean, flat, hard surface.
- Position the acrylic cover carefully on the end of the lift and place the roller on the short section of cover on the end of the lift.
- Carefully tension the acrylic cover back against the roller.
- With this light backward tension still applied, roll the cover onto the gelatine lift.

If the cover has been placed back on the lift properly, there should be no air bubbles trapped under the acrylic cover. You should practise until you get the technique right. Trapped air under the cover causes crate rings on the surface of the gelatine and can compromise the quality of lifted marks. Providing you follow these instructions carefully, it will be possible to process and store your volume crime lifts without the use of expensive, bulky exhibit boxes.

Using Transparent Adhesive Lifters
Transparent adhesive lifting sheets are only for use in lifting marks developed with fingerprint powder. The lifting of natural dirt or dust marks will result in the adhesive soaking into the particles, making them largely

invisible. This event will take place over several hours, resulting in the phenomenon of the mark disappearing overnight.

- Use adhesive lifting only on marks developed with Bristol black (the preferred powder) or aluminium powder, if the item cannot be retrieved intact. Do not use transparent adhesive lifters on unpowdered dirt or dust marks.
- Use a complete sheet of shoe mark lifting film, even if the mark only covers a small area. Do not use fingerprint tape because it usually has lower clarity with weaker adhesion properties and you risk leaving valuable parts of the mark behind.
- Write the scene details on the clear plastic-backing sheet and then cover them with the lifting film after the mark has been lifted. Attach the witness label to one end of the lift. Do not replace the lift on its paper release sheet.
- You now have a self-contained, tamper-proof item, which does not need to be packaged in a sealed bag, but should be protected from creasing. Cardboard wallets may be used to protect the lifts from damage during transit and storage.
- Do not lift marks off pieces of glass, even if you have powdered them. Package and label the whole piece of glass bearing the mark. Marks on glass give a good identification rate providing the glass is carefully packaged.

Photographing Footwear Marks

- Evidential shoe mark photographs should be taken with a good-quality single-lens reflex camera mounted on a tripod squarely over the mark. Give careful consideration to the type and direction of illumination, include in the photograph a label with the scene details, and always include a right-angled scale in the image.
- At crime scenes, always take a photograph of a visible shoe mark in situ before any treatment. These days, digital photography is very low cost, so this approach should apply to volume crime scenes as well as serious scenes.
- At volume crime scenes, you should always consider photography before attempting other techniques. If there is the possibility of loss of detail by the use of lifting techniques and if the shoe mark is of high evidential value, then photography of the mark should be your first course of action.
- Always photograph depressed marks (three-dimensional marks) before making any attempt to cast.

Electrostatic Dust Mark Lifting (ESL)[25,26]

I use a 'Pathfinder' ESL machine (Figure 5.1), which is wireless and powered by an alkaline 9-volt battery, because I devised the wireless three-electrode system used in this device in 1997, creating the first wireless ESL device. This resulted in the production of the Pathfinder, which I find is easy to use. The Pathfinder also has an earth-bonding kit supplied to enhance performance on difficult surfaces. However, there are other models on the market fulfilling a similar function.[35]

When searching for dust footwear marks, two techniques are used:

- Oblique lighting to highlight marks for photography and lifting
- A 'cold search' technique where the area in question is blanket covered with ESL film (usually directly from a roll of ESL film) to find latent footwear marks, which may not be found with the oblique lighting technique

Once located, marks can be further lifted with gel. This is a standard search and recovery technique used by the Metropolitan Police Serious Crimes Unit (SCU). It should be remembered that when dust particles are charged, only a percentage of the particles are lifted, leaving enough for gel to be used. Obviously, blanket covering of whole floor areas with lifting gel searching for marks is not viable, as the examiner would not know where

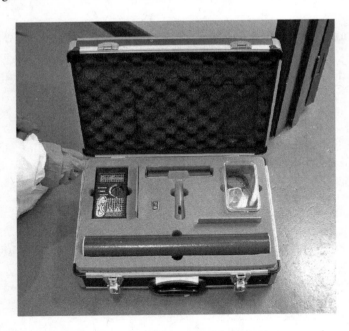

Figure 5.1 Pathfinder ESL device kit designed by R Milne.

the mark boundaries of each faint mark would be, particularly on patterned surfaces.

When lifting dust marks with an ESL device, it is best practice wherever possible to make ESLs directly from the roll of Mylar film. Although the length of a lift is determined by the conductivity of the surface, when a lift is made directly from the roll of film, the problem of trapped air under the film as it is charged is largely eliminated. Time can be saved with this technique, as lengths of film can be charged and rolled the length of an average sized room. Each strip is carefully rolled and labelled and up to five rolled lengths can be stored in an exhibit box for later examination and mounting of shoe marks in controlled conditions at the office or laboratory. Take care to make notes of the order in which the lifts are taken and the number or letter of each rolled lift so that marks found can be related to their original position on the surface. Lifts made from cut panels of Mylar should be packaged in the correct type of folder at the time the lift is made.

Mylar ESL film is best cut with a scalpel with the black side uppermost. This ensures that microscopic shards of the aluminium coating from the upper side of the film do not hang down making contact with the substrate from which the mark is being lifted. This can cause arcing at the cut edge of the film, thus reducing the lifting power. The use of scissors to cut film should definitely be avoided, as should the practice of putting a staple through the film. This will almost certainly guarantee arcing at the points where the staple perforates the film. Avoid arcing as the localised sparks cause ionisation of the film where it has vaporised around the spark, causing short circuits to the substrate below; in extreme cases, the arcing can damage the actual marks.

In the case of an ESL made from a conducting surface such as a car roof or filing cabinet top, the staple will make a short circuit. It is possible to cause burning to Mylar film by excessive charging of the film coupled with arcing caused by irregular cutting of the film.

In most cases, ESL machines will lift marks without connection to the mains or electrical earthing points in buildings, such as the main earth bonding via a socket or via a water pipe. If difficulties are experienced on surfaces with high insulation properties, then an 'earth bonding kit' should be used. These kits connect the earth plate of the ESL machine to either the earth connection of an electrical socket via a static conducting plastic cord or a water or central heating pipe. This creates many high-tension tracks through the building to the ESL film, greatly reducing the electrical resistance to the charge as the multiple high-tension tracks are in parallel. The reduced total parallel resistance from earthing points applies more lifting power to the film, thus making the process more effective.

Users can easily try out the earth bonding effect in the office before using it at scenes. Where no earthing point can be found, the earth bonding connection can be made to a metal plate attached to a nearby wall with masking tape. This technique is quite effective in many instances in enhancing the attraction of the ESL film to the substrate carrying the mark.

Dealing with Electrostatic Lifts

- Use ESL for recovering dust shoe marks, to detect marks invisible by other techniques, and to clean up marks prior to photography or gelatine lifting. Even if no footwear marks are immediately visible, ESL may reveal latent marks. Do not be afraid to try more than one lift.
- Package each ESL in a hard folder using masking tape or in the bottom of a box. Put a label with the scene details on part of the lifting film that is clear of marks. Never discard an ESL until you have examined it in darkened conditions using strong oblique lighting. Sometimes a second lift from the same area may produce better results. Any second lifts that are retained should be given a new exhibit number. Once a folder containing an ESL has been closed, it should not be reused as there is a possibility of contamination by transfer of dust from the previous mark. Note that suppliers make cardboard folders with matte black coatings on the inside surface to prevent dust particles from the cardboard being attracted to the ESL film.
- Long ESLs made straight from a roll of film can be carefully rolled up with the aluminium-coated surface outermost and stored in an exhibit box for photography back at the examination suite.
- If marks are electrostatically lifted from portable items, submit both the lift and the original item to the laboratory if expert examination is required.

Dealing with Dental Stone Casts

Although plaster of paris was traditionally used to cast footwear marks, it is better to use dental stone because of its harder, more mechanically robust features. If plaster of paris has to be used, insert a piece of hessian or cardboard into the cast when it is half full of liquid plaster to reenforce it; then, pour in the rest of the plaster.

- Do not cast a shoe mark in a soft surface until you have photographed it. Oblique lighting has to be used on three-dimensional impressed marks and the best practice is to arrange three lamps set at 120° apart, although judicial positioning of oblique lighting with a flash gun can deliver an acceptable result.
- Dental stone is easiest to mix and use from 1 kilogram bags, using one bag for each complete footwear mark. One bag may be enough for more than one partial mark but do not skimp on plaster (dental stone).

- Fill each mark completely with the mixture and cast part of the area surrounding the mark. Before the cast has completely set, engrave the scene details and exhibit number with your initials on the upper side of the cast.
- Fine detail may be destroyed by cleaning, so leave complete removal of the soil adhering to the cast to the footwear examiner. If you require a mark for local index purposes, you may remove sufficient soil with a soft, dry paintbrush to reveal the basic pattern, but leave the cast to dry for at least 48 hours before attempting this. In any event, the mark should have been photographed first, so the coding should normally be done from the photo.
- For submission to the laboratory, protect the cast suitably before it is sealed in a bag or box. Do not seal damp casts in plastic bags.

Marks in Snow

Label and photograph as soon as possible without any pretreatment. After photography, increase the contrast by spraying matte-black spray paint from one side, forming a shadow effect, and rephotograph. Allow the paint to drift on to the mark rather than spraying directly. There is no entirely satisfactory method of casting marks in snow and, in most cases, no additional evidence is obtained by casting compared with that seen in a photograph.

Dealing with Suspected Offenders' Footwear

If there is an adequate digital system such as Treadmark or SICAR (Shoeprint Image Capture and Retrieval) to scan images of the shoes, be careful to avoid contamination by using a clear plastic sheet between the shoe and the scanner glass or clean the glass after every scan. A scale must always be present in each scan; although the scanner should be calibrated once connected to Treadmark, a scale is always insurance that an accurate size image can be recovered or used at a later date. The scan will also image the forensic transfers adhering to or embedded in the shoe at the time of recording. Shoes can be scanned on a photocopier on a 1:1 ratio with a scale for screening purposes. Once scanned, the shoes should be packaged individually in paper exhibit bags and sealed awaiting a decision whether or not to retain the shoes or restore them to the suspect.

Inkless Printing of Offenders' Shoes

There are inkless print pads available for screening suspects' shoes, but these have the disadvantage that the print paper costs around £1 ($1.50) a sheet and the pads are expensive, often costing more collectively than a computer scanner! Dealing with hundreds of suspected offenders' shoes with inkless pads can become expensive and inefficient and create a low-result culture as a consequence of their use. Inkless printing of footwear by CSIs, in my view, is not an example of best practice.

The pads have the disadvantage that contacting different persons' shoes on the same pad compromises trace evidence, and the inkless print has to be scanned in order to share the image across the force. With scanners, a clean, clear polycarbonate sheet can be placed between the shoe and the scanner and the sheet packaged with the shoe. The scanned marks also show any trace evidence attached to the shoe before packaging. This is not the case with inkless print pads.

Packaging Footwear

It is essential in order to screen volume footwear marks against offenders to scan in the shoe images of offenders in custody. Using a program like Treadmark or SICAR enables prompt screening of shoes against marks, allowing informed decisions to be made concerning the retention or otherwise of suspects' shoes. This raises the issue of best practice in retaining suspects' footwear.

Shoes have to be packed in breathable brown paper bags or cardboard exhibit boxes. The chain of custody and clear labelling of the footwear packaging with signature seals must be carried out to code.

On no account should shoes be packaged in plastic bags, for within a few hours, a variety of moulds will form on the shoes, causing handling and comparison problems. There is also a possibility of health and safety difficulties with fungal and bacterial airborne material being released once the bag is opened. Laboratories will refuse to deal with mould-covered footwear and suspects will complain when their footwear is returned damaged or disposed of by police.

The handling of volume footwear evidence is best carried out with computer support recording measurable, digital images available across the police business for offender screening and scene-linking purposes. There is a complete Treadmark manual for reference highlighting the main features of the software included in Treadmark Express software and is on the CD ROM. The Treadmark software has a 30-day free evaluation licence; upgrading to the full network version is not expensive and will enable the immediate forensic intelligence use and effective management of recovered footwear evidence.

Footwear Forensic Computer Systems

Using Treadmark or SICAR, the scanning cost is minimal and using protective polycarbonate sheets on the scanner enables the use of trace evidence if required. Further, the Treadmark software has a 19,000-pattern reference library with digital measurement and comparison tools. SICAR users have access to an extensive coding library and support. Additionally, the use of computer systems enables the management of footwear evidence for quality, quantity, intelligence, and identification purposes, thus saving time and money.

Submitting Footwear Marks to the Laboratory

Most volume crime footwear submissions fall into the two categories of direct comparisons and screenings. All submissions should be accompanied by copies of the scene examiner's notes and copies of entirety photographs. Before making any shoe mark submission in a volume crime case, the scene examiner and investigating officer should discuss the following:

- The number of comparisons required
- The length of time between the offence(s) and arrest
- Compatibility of MO for the offences and the suspect
- Level of evidence required before the investigating officer will take further action (e.g., charging)

Footwear Comparisons

There are two case scenarios for footwear comparisons:

- A person is arrested for a specific offence and there may potentially be evidence other than footwear marks
- A person is arrested for an offence or brought into police custody through due cause as a suspect and a search is made to ascertain if that person can be matched to a case or series of cases

Depending on local laws, speculative searching may or may not be permitted in certain circumstances. In the UK, police have powers under the Police and Criminal Evidence Act 1984 (PACE), which was amended in 2006 to give specific powers regarding footwear searching of persons in custody:

- All the marks from the scene, properly packaged, should be submitted with the shoes from the suspect(s).
- In serious cases, consideration should be given to obtaining footwear from police officers, ambulance crew, and others who have had legitimate access to the scene around the time of the offence. If necessary, these can be examined quickly for elimination.
- **In contact trace cases, do not treat footwear with fingerprint ink, powder, or other contaminants before they are submitted to the laboratory.** The footwear examiners may use those techniques, but that activity is best preserved for their use.

- In cases where photographs have been taken at the scene, submit exhibited, actual size prints. Photographs will be considered as acceptable for comparison if the scale error is less than 1%.
- Always supply background information for the footwear examiner, such as how long after the offence elapsed before the shoes were seized and how far from the scene the offender was when arrested. Details of speculative search, time elapsed, etc. should also be given. This enables informed decisions to be made in the laboratory about carrying out further corroborative work looking at trace evidence to support the mark examination results if necessary.

Serious Crime Footwear Cases

Some serious crime cases may require a different approach and it is a good idea to ring for advice before making a submission to the laboratory. Such cases include

- Shoe marks on human skin and on clothing in 'kicking' cases
- The identification of the pattern, type, and make of footwear from crime scene shoe marks if difficulty is found in ascertaining this information from the Treadmark/SICAR footwear reference databases
- Shoe marks in blood where chemical treatments such as amido black, ninhydrin, or acid yellow dye must be used to enhance blood marks

Instrument (Tool) Marks

Basic Principles

Whenever two objects come into contact and one is harder than the other, there is the potential for the harder object to leave some form of detail. This can be some type of 'impressed mark' or striation detail, which results from movement across the surface, a 'dynamic mark'.

The Evidential Value of Instrument (Tool) Marks

In many instances it is possible for the scientist to give conclusive evidence that a particular tool was definitely responsible for the scene mark. Over 40% of cases submitted to the UK Forensic Science Service Gov Co Laboratories produce conclusive identification of the instruments submitted. The size of mark that can produce conclusive identifications can be less than 1 millimetre. The detail that can provide a conclusive result is often invisible to the naked eye. There is no need for full-width marks.

Identification at Crime Scenes

Whenever forced entry to premises is alleged or suspected that may include forcing windows or doors or cutting padlocks, or whenever property inside premises shows some signs of damage due to force, the crime scene examiner should inspect these areas closely for the presence of instrument marks. It is as well to bear in mind that more than one type or size of instrument may have been used. All marks at a scene should be considered.

Types of Instrument Marks Found at Crime Scenes

- **Impressed marks/levering marks.** These marks may show grinding detail and damage to the instrument. Where levering tools are used, as well as the impression of the tip of the tool, a second mark will often be formed at the levering point, referred to as a back mark. This should also be retrieved. Often, only very small, partial impressed marks can provide excellent evidence.
- **Striation marks.** These are mobile marks caused by the instrument moving across the surface leaving scratch marks characteristic of the tip profile or cutting edge. **Striation marks often provide conclusive matches to tools.**
- **Cut marks.** These marks are produced by instruments such as pliers, scissors, and bolt croppers and leave marks similar to striation marks. Impressed detail from the cutting blades can also give good results.
- **Boring/drilling tools.** In order to be of value, these must have a cutting edge partially turned in order that the circular striations in the swarf can be seen. Partial marks in wood and metal have the best potential for good results.
- **Saw marks.** These are only occasionally found and tend to produce corroborative evidence, but can in some instances give an indication of blade used (i.e., teeth per inch/centimetre). Consider contact trace evidence to support the tool examination.
- **Other traces.** Often paint or metal traces may be transferred from the tool used and this material can provide corroborative evidence. It has been known for paint chips to be proven to be mechanical fits to damaged paint on the examined tool(s).
- **Miscellaneous examinations.** A case may involve an item that has been damaged or thought to have been tampered with in some way. These items can be examined and assessments made of the detail present (e.g., locks and keys).

Retrieval of Instrument Marks

The following three methods of retrieving instrument marks are listed in order of preference:

1. Remove the entire item (preferred by the laboratory experts).
2. Carefully cut out the section bearing the instrument mark.
3. Cast the mark using a silicone rubber or similar moulding compound.

It should be noted that methods (1) and (2) require the consent of the victim, loser, or owner in general scenes or, in major incidents, the permission of the officer in charge of the case.

In the case of retaining small items with cash or jewellery in boxes, the valuables should be removed, ensuring that they are shown in the police property system and the items appropriately packaged with the tool-damaged surfaces protected:

- Lock plates and other door fittings can also be removed (with permission) by unscrewing, but care should be taken if striation marks cut across screw heads. These marks should be cast before removal.
- Where cutting tools are involved (e.g., wires cut with pliers, fencing cut with bolt croppers), both cut ends should be retrieved and protected. The ends cut by the scene examiner should be clearly marked.
- In dealing with tools, the levering, impact, or cutting edges should be protected.

Where the preceding methods are impractical, the third method should be employed.

Recording of Information from Instrument Marks

It is also important that comprehensive notes and measurement of the position of the marks are made in the CSI's notes. This will assist the laboratory when making test marks for comparison. All details about the position of the mark, its relationship to the surroundings, the way the door or window opens, etc. are useful to the expert examiner. All casts must be marked with indelible pen on the back with directional arrows to indicate the orientation of the mark (i.e., top and direction). Also indicate the exhibit number on the cast with indelible pen. Consider wood and paint controls.

Packaging of Exhibits

In the process of recovering the marks, contact trace evidence may also adhere to the cast. It is therefore important that the cast be sealed directly into a 'self-seal' exhibit bag and the exhibit label completed at the scene. All efforts should be made to ensure that there is no loss of any trace materials. When packaging suspect instruments, in addition to preventing the loss of contact trace evidence and relevant areas being covered with small polythene bags, the item should be protected from further damage by protection with pieces of polycarbonate sheet or, ideally, where practical, packed in an appropriate exhibit box. Exhibits can also be packaged in adjustable weapons tubes for submission to the laboratory.

Intelligence Value of Instrument Marks

Instrument marks, particularly the levering variety, have potential for assisting the scene examiner in the collation of crime scene intelligence, in addition to their evidential value. Scene examiners should measure accurately and document both the tip width of the cast and any obvious detailed damage to the tool tip. In the case of more serious crime, these marks are currently submitted to the laboratory. Any index held by a local scene examiner should in addition to the details of the marks, include information relating to time, date, type of venue, location of venue, MO, and property stolen, in order that more effective screening can be carried out.

Coding Tool Marks for Input to Police Systems

Modern crime reporting systems have facilities for creating spreadsheets from data in fields enabling filtering of data against other crime and intelligence data. Tool marks are just as useful as footwear marks in linking scenes and can reveal patterns of activity that can be missed by other means. In order to use tool mark recoveries to provide these data, the following coding system can easily be implemented with minimal training. At the crime scene, the examiner can easily use this coding and measurement system and make use of tool mark data in crime analysis. The system is simply to record the width of the tool mark in millimetres and note from tool impression marks the shape of the tool and whether or not it is single bladed.

The following descriptors enable a coding system for tool marks incorporating primary, secondary, and sometimes tertiary descriptors for input to crime report recording systems:

S: striations only
SBE: single-blade tool
DBE: double-blade tool
CUT: cutting tool
BACKMARK: tool back mark
DRILL: drilling tool
HAMMER: hammer/impact tool
SAW: cutting tool with teeth

Striations are left either because the tool is thin, such as a double glazing window removal tool, or because not enough detail has been left by a wider lever or cutter. Note that even the striations descriptor has been successfully used as a contributing scene linking factor because the marks were left at multiple scenes as a consequence of the method the perpetrator used. Back marks may be associated with striations (say, the shaft mark of an electrical screwdriver) and can be recovered and measured for width.

SBE coded single blade tool marks are perhaps the most common type of tool mark found. The code **SBE** is followed by the tip width of the mark measured in millimetres. Thus, a straight 10-millimetre wide tool mark made by a screwdriver or chisel will be coded **SBE10**. If an impressed mark is found also, this can indicate whether or not the tool narrows or widens to the tip or is just straight to the tip. Therefore, the additional descriptors **N** (narrows) or **W** (widens) can be added to the coding.

DBE coded double-bladed tool marks are made typically by case openers or builders bars. The coding technique here is to measure the blade width from left to right followed by the gap between the blades and then the width of the second blade. Thus, a coding of a double-bladed case opener with 12-millimetre wide blades and a 5-millimetre gap between them would be **DBE12,05,12**. It is not too uncommon for tools of this type to have one blade narrower than the other. Generally, from experience, I have found that the wider the blades are, then the rarer the mark is.

CUT codes are associated with wire cutters at the smaller end to bolt cutters at the top end. Often by the nature of the types of items cut with these tools, a blade width cannot normally be ascertained. The information is still useful for targeting suspects brought into custody locally and police are given some guidance for the types of tools to search for or retain from suspects. The code can be quite useful; for example, in London only 2 out of the 32 London boroughs were affected by bolt cutters being used to break locks on outbuildings, thus forming discreet geographical series resulting in police intelligence briefings to target the problems.

BACKMARK codes are applied to any part of a tool shaft leaving an impression. Back marks can have paint transfers associated with them and they can have measurable facets. An engineer's type of screwdriver, for example, has a square or hexagonal shaft and often these tools leave measurable facets. Some burglars favour this type of screwdriver to use as a lever because, unlike the round stemmed common screwdriver, it does not bend under levering pressure. If the back mark is round, then the descriptor **ROUND** can be added to the code so that the code could be **BACKMARK15 ROUND** (indicating a round back mark 15 millimetres in diameter). Likewise, the terms **HEX** (hexagonal) and **SQUARE** can be used where appropriate. If other terms are created to fit other types of tools, then all that is required is consistency in coding by the team and the creation of a reference source for guidance.

DRILL codes have simply the width in millimetres added to the code, so an 8-millimetre drill hole will code as **DRILL8**. Good results can be obtained matching drill swarf to suspects' drill bits, especially metal and plastic swarf. In the case of wood being drilled with a brace, a wood wheel or part wheel can be created from the section cut at the bottom of the drill hole and may offer opportunities to match to the cutting edge of the bit.

HAMMER codes can be measured in millimetres from indented marks. In addition, often the shape of the impact surface is revealed and can be given a descriptor (e.g., **HAMMER30 ROUND** describing a hammer with a 30-millimetre diameter impact surface).

SAW mark codes are usually described by CSIs with the single generic term, but microscopic examination of marks in a laboratory can reveal the type of cutting teeth and the number of teeth per centimetre.

When this coding structure is used, it is easy to relate the tool codes to other crime data, and these data can help resolve series within common crime types with common methods used. The data can aid managers in making informed decisions about tasking expert examiners to confirm links if necessary as well as providing police intelligence briefing products enabling officers to seek valuable potential evidence in the form of tools from suspects.

Casting Instrument Marks

The most common method of retrieving tool marks from crime scenes is to cast them. For completeness, the following section covers the finer points of casting techniques because success with forensic marks is all about taking care in finding and retrieving them.

Casting with Silcoset   Silcoset is a popular moulding material in the form of a white viscous liquid that, when mixed with a curing agent, sets to produce an exact representation of the mark. There are two common methods of application: liquid and pasting.

Liquid Method. When applied in mixed liquid form, a dam is required to prevent loss/spillage of the Silcoset. This second method of pasting a thicker mix is applicable to difficult surfaces such as the underside of top-hung casement windows

Construct a dam around the mark using plasticine or a similar medium. Measure out an appropriate quantity of the Silcoset into the issued measuring pot, ensuring that there is enough to give a thick, strong cast. Add the volume of hardener required as shown:

Silcoset	Curing Agent
12 g	Five to six drops
25 g	10 Drops

The mixture should be stirred thoroughly to ensure complete blending of the curing agent but in such a manner as to minimise the production of air bubbles in the mix. The mixture should then be poured into the prepared dam and left to set. Any excess mixture should be left in the pot with the spatula; when it can be removed from the mixing pot cleanly, this will indicate when the cast is ready for removal.

Adjustment of the quantity of hardener may be required, depending on the ambient temperature (i.e., a couple of drops more during the winter and a couple of drops less in the summer). Avoid getting Silcoset onto your clothing as it is difficult to remove such stains.

Carefully remove the cast and inspect closely to ensure that all the detail has been captured and that there are no air bubbles. If required, a second cast can be done.

When casts of deep marks in fragmented wood are removed, they are liable to tear or break, so use a scalpel or Stanley knife to cut around and behind the cast but do not cut into the Silsoset. Care should be taken when using a scalpel or knife. All casts from the mark must be retained.

Pasting Method. For this method, the Silcoset is prepared as before but with the addition of a couple of extra drops of hardener. As the mixture starts to set, it should be spread onto and into the mark, using the mixing spatula. Care should be taken not to produce casts that are too thin. Additional quantities can be added to the back of the cast whilst in situ to thicken it up. Push either a polycarbonate fingerprint lift sheet onto the Silcoset covering the mark or a small envelope. Either a polycarbonate sheet can be pressed onto the mark or an envelope will do instead if no polycarbonate sheet is available. This method is quick and useful in that a cast can be quickly made and left to set whilst the rest of the crime scene examination takes place.

A useful tip when attempting to cast marks on the underside of horizontal surfaces is to apply a slightly thicker mix of Silcoset and push it up into the mark and then push a sheet of fingerprint lift polycarbonate sheet (cobex) onto the back of the cast. Leave the cobex in place until the Silcoset has hardened. Again, be careful not to make the casts too thin. Once set, these casts are treated in the normal way.

Isomark, Microsil, and Casting Putty Materials

Isomark or Microsil is available for the recovery of tool marks from crime scenes. The material has an easily used dispensing system that automatically mixes the material during application, giving the user full control of the casting process. The system is made up of a dispensing gun, a cartridge that contains the grey casting material and curing agent, and mixing nozzles that are designed to ensure perfect air-free mix every time. It is clean, easy to use on both vertical and horizontal surfaces, and takes very fine detail extremely well. Casting materials are available in toothpaste tube type packaging with a small tube of hardener supplied. In addition, kits are available with casting putty in two halves: one as the casting medium and the other as the hardener. This form of casting putty is supplied by Crime Scene Products (Florida) Inc.

and Crime Scene Examination Equipment Ltd in the UK; it is particularly easy to use compared to the liquid types.

Other Evidence Types

In the following sections best practices around other evidence types are covered because, in effectively examining crime scenes, examiners should collect samples of any forensic material that could link a suspect or suspects to the scenes. It is acknowledged that these exhibits will normally be stored, but they represent a significant resource in providing forensic evidence that can deliver vital support toward supporting intelligence products as well as detections leading to convictions.

Ballistics

In many countries, ballistics intelligence facilities have been introduced utilising computer technologies such as IBIS (Integrated Ballistics Intelligence System) to screen and match ballistics material. The careful handling and packaging of firearms is crucial to the forensic intelligence and evidential processes. In this text, a diagram depicting the processes in dealing with ballistics intelligence within a police business is given in Chapter 7.

Manufacturing Marks

Manufacturing marks can be very useful in forensic intelligence casework in establishing a common source for materials found in different crime locations—for example, materials used by an organised crime group such as a source of bags or roll of plastic used to seal drugs or a bulk container of cutting agent with contaminants. A classic case in the UK was where bin bags were used by thieves at different scenes from the same roll of bags, with extrusion marks linking one bag to the next. Counterterrorism enquiries make use of this evidence type in sourcing materials used in explosive devices.

Items that are produced by some form of manufacturing process will, during the course of that process, acquire markings due to imperfections in the machinery used. Such markings can be of value in casework, but their interpretation requires considerable research into the specific manufacturing process.

The types of marks fall into four main categories:

1. Extrusion marks. These marks are caused during manufacturing processes that involve the material being forced through a specially designed nozzle or die, or between rollers. The marks usually consist of ridges or furrows running parallel and most commonly occur

in such items as polythene bags, adhesive tape, and electrical wire. This form of mark can be obscured by coatings or finishes and may require chemical treatment to reveal it. It is essential that all material in these cases be submitted in order to establish how quickly the marks change during production.

2. Moulding marks. These are caused when imperfections in the mould are reproduced in the item. Examples can be found in the production of coins, tablets, and jewellery.

3. Coatings. A large number of products have designs printed on them in the form of a coating—for instance, the white panels on freezer bags or company names on adhesive tape. These designs are applied very rapidly and often have imperfections that are reproduced in repeated designs. Also, in the case of adhesive tape, a coating is applied between the backing film and the adhesive layer; this often has a random appearance and, when revealed by chemical removal of the adhesive, can confirm a fit between the ends of pieces of tape.

4. Machine marks. These marks are produced by processes such as gripping, cutting, and pressing during a manufacturing process (e.g., cut marks on the edge of metal sheets, grip marks on screws being held whilst the thread is produced, or component parts being stamped out by a press).

Evidential Value of Manufacturing Marks

In order to ascertain the evidential value of particular marks, a number of factors have to be considered and the investigating officer may need to contact the original manufacturer. If this is not possible, then the maximum amount of material must be submitted. Other factors that have to be considered are the following:

- How was the product made and by what processes?
- How much of this material or these items has been produced?
- Is the detail present on all the materials/items?
- Does the detail change and how quickly?
- Are different types of detail on the same item related?

Physical Fits

Physical or mechanical fits can be obtained from a vast range of materials and items. This type of evidence can be of very high evidential value and should always be considered where anything has been broken, torn, cut, chipped, or damaged in any way. It can be used to demonstrate that two or more items were originally part of a whole.

The most common occurrences of this type of evidence come from vehicle fittings in cases of road accidents, glass in cases of burglary and assault, fabric in a wide variety of cases, and paper (e.g., a page torn out of a notebook). It is essential that, in submissions of this type to the laboratory, the exhibits be properly packaged and protected to prevent any further damage occurring after seizure.

Contact Trace Evidence

The recovery and storage of evidence from crime scenes in the forms of forensic controls and material thought to be transferred from offenders is a vital link in quality evidence chains because, through practising forensic intelligence, it is more probable that this evidential material will be used more fully in casework. Good practice in dealing with contact trace evidence is necessary.

All contact between control materials taken from crime scenes and clothing from individuals must be avoided. Take the following precautions:

- Ensure that anyone who has attended the scene or been involved with the packaging of control samples has no contact with the suspects or their clothing.
- Avoid situations where the same officer takes possession of clothing from a suspect and victim in the same case.
- Multiple suspects, the victim, and their clothing must be kept apart at all times and should not be allowed to come into contact with the same objects (e.g., police car, interview room, custody suite).
- The same officer should not search a property and then deal with a person or objects to be linked to the property.
- All exhibits should be packaged and sealed as soon as they are taken.
- DO NOT pack the control contact trace sample in the same outer container or packaging as items obtained from the suspect. Use separate sacks for control and suspect items.

Glass

General Comments

Glass particles projected from a breaking window can be acquired on the clothes or in the hair of the person involved. Some of these particles will fall off as the person moves about; the larger particles tend to fall off more quickly, and as more time passes fewer particles remain. It therefore follows that finding a number of glass particles in a person's clothing or hair shows that the person is likely to have been in recent contact with breaking or broken glass. By recovering these particles and comparing

them with a sample from the broken window, it may be possible to provide good corroborative evidence for the involvement of the person with
the crime.

If a window is kicked in, it is likely that the sharp edges of the broken
glass would cause cuts to the upper parts of the person's footwear. If so, we
might well expect to find glass particles embedded in these cuts, especially if
the offender has walked over the broken fragments.

There is the possibility that in some cases a physical fit may be obtained.
In these cases, all of the broken glass must be submitted.

Crime scene examiners should always consider the presence of footwear
marks that may be left on the glass remaining at the scene or the presence of
other forensic material such as blood. Blood may be scraped or swabbed. No
attempt should be made to lift the footwear marks from the glass. The visible
marks can be coded and the item stored securely.

Provide details of the scene including a sketch showing the size and
height of the window, size of the broken area, and the method of breaking, if
known. To enable the scientist to interpret the evidence in a case, it is important that information about the scene, such as the method by which the glass
was broken, time of offence and arrest, etc. be included in the submission
documents. The laboratory should be informed of any legitimate access to
broken glass (e.g., the suspect is a glazier).

Types of Glass
Glass evidence can be more useful than many investigators think, for even
in the case of mass-produced glass, modern forensic techniques can recover
multiple refractive indices and information from the physical makeup of
the glass.

- Plain sheet glass. Almost all modern plain sheets are made by the
  'float process'. Many windows, particularly in older houses, still contain glass made before the introduction of the float process, so there
  is some variation in the type of sheet glass that may be encountered
  at scenes.
- Patterned sheet glass. Patterned sheet glass is made by passing the
  newly made glass through rollers while it is still soft.
- Toughened sheet glass. Toughened or tempered glass is mainly found
  in vehicle windows and some windscreens. When the glass breaks,
  it does not splinter but rather breaks into small chunks which have a
  typical cuboid appearance.
- Wire-reinforced glass. Wire-reinforced glass is made by sandwich-
  ing a wire mesh between two layers of glass still soft from the production process. There may be minor differences between the glass

on either side of the wire, even though all the glass usually comes from the same batch of molten glass.

- Laminated glass. This is another type of glass 'sandwich', now commonly used in vehicle windscreens and 'bandit' on screens. Laminated glass normally consists of two or more sheets of glass on either side of a flexible plastic film, which holds the pieces together when the glass is broken. This type of glass has gained general use in products used in homes and businesses and is becoming quite common.
- Nonsheet glass. The commonest sources of other types of glass are containers such as bottles, jars, etc. and tableware drinking glasses, vases, Pyrex-type dishes and jugs, etc. These are mainly produced by moulding, although more expensive tableware may also be cut or polished; ornamental glassware can also be individually hand-blown.

How Glass Breaks

The properties of glass are such that, when it is broken, transfers to persons in the near vicinity are likely. For this reason, glass can be a most useful evidence type.

If glass breaks as a result of mechanical impact, then a large number of small glass particles will normally be generated, and these may be projected for a considerable distance from the breaking object. The projection of glass particles back toward the person or object breaking a window is known as backward fragmentation. This is the primary means by which someone breaking a window acquires glass particles on his or her clothing.

The stress built into toughened glass causes it to shatter when broken, and it is not unknown for people who have been close to this kind of glass when it is breaking to acquire full-thickness 'chunks' of glass in their pockets. When glass breaks as the result of heat (or thermal shock), the break often has an irregular pattern and may produce far fewer small particles than an impact break.

Taking Control of Glass Samples

Find out how many sources of broken glass there are. In the case of windows, this will be the total number of panes (i.e., individual pieces of glass broken at the scene). Thus, for a 'leaded light', it will be each individual square or 'diamond' of glass broken. For a double-glazed unit, it will be both the inner and outer pane. In the case of drinking vessels, it will be the number of drinking glasses broken in the immediate vicinity of an affray. It is possible that glass found on a person who was present at the scene could have been acquired from any of these sources.

Take a control sample from every individual source of broken glass. If any of these sources could be the origin of glass particles on a suspect, it follows that the laboratory must have a sample of each, in order to make a meaningful comparison.

In the case of a broken window, take several pieces, six in total if possible, from around the edge of the hole, if there is one, or remove the fragments remaining in the edges of the frame if the pane has been completely smashed. This means taking glass from the top, bottom, and sides of the hole, as there may be minor variations in the properties of the glass from one side of the pane to the other. Before removing each piece of glass from a broken window, label it ('1', '2', '3', etc.), and mark one surface with a self-adhesive label or felt-tip pen, noting whether it is an inside or outside surface.

Under normal circumstances, you should not take a control sample from the ground, as there is usually no way of proving where it has come from. Make every effort to take the control sample from the frame, even if this involves removing boarding-up. In exceptional circumstances, a sample from the ground may be taken to supplement a very small sample from a window frame or if no other sample exists, provided that

- The sample from the ground is packaged separately
- Only one window pane has been broken
- There is a reliable witness to state that there was no glass on the ground before the window was broken

In the case of other broken glass objects, such as drinking glasses, try to collect as much of the broken glass as possible, especially the full thickness pieces, making a record of how many objects were broken. Remember that half a pane of leaded light, even if it is only a few square centimetres in size, is more representative of the source than a single 30 centimetre × 30 centimetre piece from a large display window because leaded windows tend to be older products made with non-modern-industry standard glass.

Multiple Control Samples
If a suspect admits being at a scene where glass was broken and evidence is required to link him to another scene where glass was broken, then it is essential that control samples are submitted from both scenes.

From Which Side Was the Window Broken?
Some forensic science textbooks describe the process of a 'slow moving' object breaking a pane of glass. 'Slow moving' means a hand, shoe, or thrown object where radial cracks will radiate from the hole in the pane. The examination of the edge of glass from the radial cracks will reveal conchoidal stress marks, which curve away from the side of impact. In the case of a fast moving object such as a bullet or stone from a catapult, a small hole will be

made in the glass and the exit side of the hole will be larger than the entry side. In good practice, although this information is taught to CSIs, it is best for the interpretation of these features to be done by a forensic scientist. For that reason, the following advice is given.

- If it is important to find out which side of a window was attacked and then all the broken glass must be collected because, before the scientist can give any opinion on this matter, the whole window must be rebuilt. This has to be done in order to determine the primary point of impact, from which examination of the broken edges of the relevant pieces can reveal the side of the blow.
- In order to assist the scientist in reconstructing the window, a photograph of the glass remaining in the frame, with every piece marked, is very useful. The glass from the two sides on the ground should be collected and packaged separately; submit the door or window with the broken glass.

Packaging Glass Samples
Control glass samples must be packaged as soon as possible, as this will help to eliminate the risk of contamination. Each control must be packaged separately to prevent mixing of glass from different sources. State the number of broken panes on the submission form. Remember that broken glass is sharp; package the samples so that there is no chance of their puncturing the packaging, as this may lead to leakage or injury. A box of a suitable size should be used, but the box must be sealed inside a polythene bag unless it can be sealed such that there is no chance of leakage.

Dealing with Suspects
To prevent the risk of contamination of the suspect with glass from the crime scene, the following guidelines must be followed:

- The suspect must not be returned to the scene of the crime.
- The suspect must not be dealt with by an officer who has been to the scene or who has had contact with broken glass from the scene.
- The suspect's clothing should be securely packaged as soon as possible, using a separate package for each item of clothing. If more than one suspect is involved, there is a small but real risk that glass particles could be transferred between them under certain circumstances. Therefore, the suspects should be dealt with by different officers and kept as far apart as possible until after their clothing has been taken. In an ideal world, this would mean that they should be transported by separate vehicles to different police stations.

Hair Combings

Hair combings should always be taken from a person who is suspected to have been in recent close contact with breaking glass. Glass in hair combings often provides very pertinent evidence of recent proximity to breaking glass and is evidentially more significant than glass found on clothing. Always use the laboratory-prepared comb kits for taking hair combings, as they have been checked to ensure that they do not contain glass particles. A separate kit must be used for each suspect.

Please remember the health and safety instructions on handling glass. Use suitable gloves and protective goggles and be aware of falling sheet glass in large windows. Glass should be stored carefully in suitable boxes and not left open or in plastic bags on a shelf.

Paint Evidence

The term 'paint' is used by forensic scientists to describe any resin-based protective or decorative coating applied to a surface as a continuous film. Paint can provide excellent evidence, ranging from corroborative to conclusive, depending on the nature of the paint. Generally speaking, the more layers of paint that are transferred or the more unusual the chemical composition is, then the better the evidence will be.

In the case of 'liquid' paint, the evidence is only likely to be corroborative unless several types of paint are involved, although the presence of paint splashes on the suspect's hands or clothing may be significant in these cases. Paint samples of any kind should never be recovered onto adhesive tape. There is the potential for even very small fragments of paint to fit back to their original site consideration of their edge profile and surface features. Obtain the control paint sample from as near to the damaged area as possible. But in cases where there are tool marks, care must be taken not to damage the mark. For a painted object, wherever possible, submit the original item

Paint technology is constantly changing as new materials become available; many specialist paints are produced for particular applications, giving rise to a great variety of compositions. In some cases, such as in art forgeries, it may be possible to determine the age of the paint. This is normally done by knowing the date before which certain ingredients of the paint were not used in paint manufacture.

Household Paint

Household paint examined by forensic scientists usually comes from doors or window frames. Flakes of household paint often have several layers, with a minimum of a primer coat below an undercoat and topcoat. There may then be more layers of undercoat and topcoat corresponding to occasions when the property has been repainted. Different areas of the same window frame or door may show different layers of thicknesses, and some layers may be absent. The chance of having the same number, colour, and layer sequence of paint on two surfaces in different houses is very small and decreases as the number of layers increases. The exception to this is where contract painting has occurred over a number of years—for example, on an estate, where the paint at several properties may well show similar layer structures.

Vehicle Paint

Vehicles are mass produced, so it is not surprising that there are very large numbers of vehicles on the roads with identical paint layer structures. They are usually painted by spraying or dipping, and as these processes are automated, the coats of paint are of even thicknesses. Vehicles with metallic paint usually have a clear resin layer as the topcoat. In addition to solid colours and metallic paints, 'pearlescent' finishes are becoming more common.

Commercial vehicles, especially those supplied for fleet use, often leave the factory without a topcoat paint, allowing the customer to paint the vehicle as required. The paint on a van or lorry may, therefore, may be more distinctive than that found on a normal car. If there is paint left at the scene of a fail-to-stop road traffic accident, it is possible to indicate the colour and manufacturer of the vehicle. Vehicle parts such as pieces of indicator, headlamp, mirrors, trim, etc. found at the scene should always be collected. In addition to offering the potential of a physical fit, they may be the best way of identifying the type of vehicle involved.

Over a period of time, vehicles will often require repair of impact or rust damage. This often involves the application of body filler and respray paints, usually over the original paintwork. The more layers of paint put on the vehicle, the more distinctive the paint layer sequence becomes and the greater its potential evidential value will be.

Sampling Household and Vehicle Paint

Household Paint   It is important that control samples are taken from each area of damage, taking care to preserve any tool-mark impressions or cross-transferred paint. The samples should include all the layers, from the topcoat down to the metal or wood so that the complete structure of the paint is represented in the sample. A new scalpel or chisel-ended blade must be used for each painted item. It is advisable to enclose the used blade as part of the item, as this helps to demonstrate that a fresh blade has been used.

Vehicle Paint   When taking samples from vehicles, it is important to ensure that the paintwork is sampled right down to the metal, so that the total history of the painting of the vehicle is represented in the sample. Control samples of paint should be taken from as close to the damaged area as possible. If more than one area is damaged, control samples from close to each area must be taken and individually packaged. Relevant samples of the damaged areas should also be taken and packaged separately. If a damaged area includes more than one panel of a vehicle, such as a scratch running along the front offside wing and driver's door, then all damaged panels should be separately sampled.

Liquid Paint   Liquid paint may be encountered in cases of criminal damage. When aerosol cans of paint are discharged, minute droplets of paint can spray back onto the hands and clothing of the offender. These are sometimes not visible to the naked eye but may be found using a low-power microscope. Paint may also be splashed onto hands, shoes, and clothing when a brush is used. In such cases, as well as taking clothing items, it is also worth taking scraped samples from the suspect's hands using a clean, blunt metal edge; do not attempt to swab off the paint.

The following samples also need to be taken:

- Wherever possible, the original paint container should be retrieved and submitted.
- Samples of the paint deposits should also be taken and be accompanied by a separate sample of the surface on which the paint was applied.

Anticlimb Paint   Proprietary anticlimb paints are grease-based materials containing chemical markers that are often applied to drainpipes with the specific intention of deterring would-be burglars. They are designed not to harden when painted onto a surface. The paint may form a dry skin as a result of weathering, but the underlying paint should remain soft indefinitely.

The intention is that the paint will make the surface slippery and difficult to climb. In addition, anyone who does attempt to climb an object bearing this type of paint will usually acquire traces of the paint on hands, footwear, or clothing. It is important when sampling anticlimb paint that samples are taken from all the areas disturbed and that a sample of undisturbed paint is also taken.

Miscellaneous Traces

There is the potential for many different types of substances to be transferred during the commission of a crime. It is important to stress that those mentioned here are only a selection of an enormous number of possibilities. Scene examiners encountering a substance as a contact trace for the first time should therefore seek advice regarding its sampling and likely evidential value.

Cosmetics

Traces of cosmetics, such as lipstick and face powder, may be transferred from the victim's face to the clothing of an assailant during the course of a robbery or sexual attack. These traces of material may be very small, such that they are not readily visible to the naked eye but may be detected using a low-power microscope. The evidential value of such traces will usually be corroborative, but can be very good if combinations of different products are found.

Samples from the Victim   If possible, swabs of the material on the victim's face should be taken. The various areas of the face should be sampled separately, in order to keep, for example, eye makeup separate from lipstick. The samples should be taken using dry swabs as these will most accurately reflect the material transferred during the attack. As well as taking facial swabs, the original containers of cosmetics should also be submitted if at all possible, as these will give the scientist sufficient material to experiment with to find the best analytical technique, and they may be used to obtain formulation information from the manufacturer.

Oils and Greases

Oils and greases are associated with tools and machinery, but may also occur elsewhere. It is possible to analyse relatively small deposits of these materials in order to link, for example, a piece of equipment with a suspect's clothing. The evidential value depends very much on the type of oil or grease involved, but is likely to be corroborative rather than conclusive. Where only trace quantities are available, oil samples should be taken using dry swabs; thicker oils and greases should be sampled using a new scalpel blade and sealed into a glass vial.

Control samples of petrol, diesel, etc. should be submitted in a clean metal or glass container with a well-fitting screw cap. Proper metal cans should be used and not filled to the top; for safety reasons, always leave an air space before sealing to allow for expansion. It should be submitted in a sealed nylon bag.

Plastics, Rubbers, and Adhesives

Materials of this type are widely distributed and can occur in a variety of case situations. A good example from casework in recent years is the polyurethane building foam frequently used to deactivate alarm boxes. In general, unless a physical fit is found, the evidence is unlikely to be conclusive, but can often provide good corroboration.

Soil, Safe Ballast, and Building Materials

For convenience, soil and safe ballast can be considered in the same category as sand, brick, tiles, plaster, putty, cement, slate, etc. Soil evidence, which has sometimes been crucial in murder investigations, presents special problems. Thus, if the submission of soil to the laboratory is contemplated, advice should be sought on how the control samples are to be taken.

Metals

Where metal (e.g., lead roofing) has been handled during the course of a theft, it may be possible for traces of metal to be recovered from the hands of the thief by swabbing them.

Metal trace swabbing kits are available from scenes of crime supply companies. Once swabs have been taken from suspects and packaged, a sample of the metal should be obtained so that the type of metal can be confirmed by analysis and a comparison carried out. Where discrete metal fragments (e.g., swarf) have been found on a suspect's clothing, the physical form and surface detail may be important. Sampling should be undertaken using the metal traces kit or the firearm discharge residue kit. Hands should be washed before any sampling and disposable gloves used if available. If none are available, then your hands should be swabbed before swabbing of the suspect takes place. You should submit the swab from your hands to the laboratory.

Other

The following materials are occasionally involved in cases and are capable of being analysed and compared:

- Tars and bitumens
- Soaps and detergents
- Disinfectants
- Industrial chemicals
- Foodstuffs

Such a list cannot, however, be comprehensive and when in doubt the advice of a scientist should be sought.

Noxious Chemicals

Noxious chemicals are encountered in a variety of offences, including assaults, robberies, and possession of offensive and prohibited weapons. The more commonly encountered noxious chemicals are

- Ammonia
- Tear gases
- Bleach
- Acids, such as
  - Sulphuric acid
  - Hydrochloric acid

- Nitric acid
- Hydrofluoric acid
- Phosphoric acid
- Formic acid
- Alkalis such as sodium hydroxide

Submission to the Laboratory   Where a charge of possession or use of an offensive weapon is to be made, the container and liquid should be submitted to the laboratory intact. The liquid must not be decanted from the container unless there is a compelling reason to do so. The most commonly encountered containers are 'Jif' lemon-juice containers and 'Vicks Sinex' nasal-spray bottles, which are favoured for their size and their ability to squirt liquids over distances of several metres.

Packaging   If a container of liquid has its cap missing, seal a piece of polythene over the top and then keep the container upright in a sealed glass jar or in a box sealed in a nylon bag. If the container has a secure cap and you are confident that it will not leak, then the container can be sealed in a polythene self-sealing exhibit bag.

Ammonia   Ammonia solutions can easily be bought from hardware stores and chemists' shops. They are sold in a range of strengths. The main hazard associated with ammonia vapour is that it readily dissolves in the water present in the eyes and nose to form an ammonia solution. Thus, in an ammonia attack, the solution does not need to enter the eyes or nose in order to incapacitate the victim. Cases of ammonia in the eyes or nose require immediate first aid and medical attention to avoid the risk of long-term damage.

Because ammonia is so volatile, any clothing items thought to have been exposed to solutions containing ammonia must be packaged and sealed in nylon bags as soon as possible after the offence. Clothing bearing possible ammonia traces must be examined at the laboratory as soon as possible. The vapour inside the nylon bag can be tested for the presence of ammonia, but it is not possible to determine the original strength of the ammonia used.

Tear Gas Sprays   There has been a marked increase in the number of cases involving tear gas sprays over the last 10 years. Although they are referred to as gases, these compounds are solids at room temperature, but are dissolved in a solvent in aerosol sprays. The solids readily give off fumes, and it is these that cause the unpleasant effects associated with them.

Although a tear gas canister is classed as a prohibited weapon in the UK by Section 5(1)b of the 1968 Firearms Act, it is not illegal to carry or buy them in some European countries or the United States. The three most common tear gases are CS, CN or MACE, and pepper spray.

Clothing items should be sealed in nylon bags as soon as possible. The aerosol sprays should be packaged in small forensic exhibit bags.

Bleach   Household bleach is normally an alkaline solution of sodium hypochlorite, which is fairly unstable, especially once it leaves the bottle. Thus it is important to get attached items to the laboratory as soon as possible. Solutions are more stable at low temperatures, so store items in a refrigerator (not in a freezer) if there is a delay in transporting them to the laboratory.

Bleach Attacks on Clothing   When sprayed with bleach, clothing items will normally show areas of discoloration, which will be tested in the laboratory. Do not attempt to dry the garments, as this will affect the laboratory examination. If hypochlorite cannot be detected because it has broken down on the clothing, it may be possible to infer the presence of bleach on a particular area of the fabric by a combination of

- Discoloration of the fabric
- The presence of chloride (a breakdown product of hypochlorite)
- The discoloured area being more alkaline than the surrounding fabric

Items, such as clothing, that have been attacked by bleach should be packaged as soon as possible in either nylon or polythene bags.

Acids   The acids most commonly encountered in crime scenes are the following:

- Sulphuric acid is commonly found in car batteries; concentrated sulphuric acid used to be known as 'vitriol' or 'oil of vitriol' and is a highly corrosive, heavy, viscous liquid, sometimes still sold as a very powerful drain cleaner!
- Hydrochloric acid, sometimes called 'spirits of salts', is also used as a drain cleaner and as a very strong descaler. It has an acrid smell and reacts with bleach to give off chlorine, which is highly poisonous.
- Nitric acid is mainly used industrially for etching and cleaning metals.
- Hydrofluoric acid is used for etching glass and is highly corrosive. It is also found in the debris of plastics burned in vehicle fires. Do not get this acid on your skin, as it can be absorbed, causing long-term damage to bone and other tissues. Immediate treatment with an antidote is required. The fire brigade is equipped to deal with this acid and should always be called.
- Phosphoric acid is sometimes used as a descaler or in some industrial cleaners for stone work.
- Formic acid is often found in descalers for domestic kettles, irons, and coffeemakers.

On no account should acids be put into metal containers as they will react, with potentially dangerous results.

Appearance of Clothing Involved in Acid Attacks   In most cases, the clothing will show clear signs of attack by an acid as clear damage to the fabric or discoloration because the dye in the fabrics has altered. The amount and appearance of the damage, however, will depend on the fabric of the garment and the strength and type of acid used. In some cases, no apparent damage will be visible. These garments should still be submitted, since the acid splashes can be located using chemical tests, possibly together with some of the special iced lighting conditions available in the laboratory. Clothing thought to have been sprayed with acid must not be placed in paper sacks or directly into nylon bags, as the acid may attack either of these. Wherever possible, they should be placed in glass screw-top jars, but if these are not available or not large enough, the best substitute is a polythene bag. If there is any doubt as to whether the clothing has been sprayed with acid or with ammonia, then the item should be sealed in a polythene bag and then a nylon bag.

Other Substances

A variety of other substances have been encountered as possible noxious substances—some more noxious than others. Occasionally, the suspect will have created a 'cocktail' of liquids found around the house.

- For solutions of alkalis, such as caustic soda (sodium hydroxide), deal with containers of liquids as for ammonia; package clothing as for acid attacks.
- For creosote, white spirit, and disinfectants, package clothing in nylon bags as soon as possible.
- For vinegar (contains acetic acid), package clothing as soon as possible in a polythene bag followed by a nylon bag.

The miscellaneous evidence types included here may actually be used or encountered rarely. However, in dealing with crime, the methods and behaviours of offenders may result in unusual substances or devices being linking factors, so for best-practice reasons they have been included.

The Implementation of Intelligence-Led Policing

6

Introduction

In the UK, the National Intelligence Model (NIM) was adopted in 2000 in order to advance a concept called intelligence-led policing (ILP), which is currently ongoing. In 2011, the US government was looking at possibilities of bringing in the concept of intelligence-led policing. To give some background on intelligence-led policing in the United States, the US National Institute for Justice (NIJ) published a paper,[27] 'Crime Analysis in America,' written by the Centre for Public Policy, University of Alabama, in 2002, but still relevant today.

This paper cited the fact that 95% of US police services had less than 100 sworn officers and that over 50% of the total police in the United States are in those small departments. Further, there were 859 agencies fitting the criteria of having 100 or more sworn officers and 63% of those responded to the University of Alabama survey. Of those, 74% had one or more person assigned to crime analysis. The average number of analysts was 0.92 per 100 officers or less; the other 26% had no assigned analysts at all. This begs the question that, at this time, is most of America's policing effort tasked and coordinated by intelligence products derived from the identification of strategic issues and delivered by tactics derived from intelligence analysis of reported and perceived crime? The answer is that intelligence-led policing in the sense of the UK NIM is not yet practised in most US police services.

One of the major inhibitors to progress in this area cited in the 2002 report was the reluctance of sworn officers together with their unions to accept civilian analysts, and this was still a major inhibitor in 2011 as was the acceptance of civilian CSIs. The United States has at this time a hill to climb in bringing in intelligence-led policing unless restrictive working practices are dealt with. There is a desire, however, in the United States to introduce intelligence-led policing in some form under US guidelines in this decade. In a number of services, police union resistance to civilianisation prevents the recruiting of staff with specialist skills ready for work to help bring in the changes required.

One issue concerns American police unions thinking that hiring civilians is a process that takes away police jobs. Experience in the UK has proven this to be untrue. From my experience as one of the first civilian scenes of crime officers (SOCOs) recruited in the 1970s, I was dealing with volumes of forensic examinations, which my police colleagues had not been dealing with previously to the hiring of dedicated civilian forensic examiners at any form of satisfactory level, with respect to volume crime. I recall that, in 1971, my police colleagues had a celebration when they had their first forensic hits from my case submissions because, up to that time, it was unusual to solve cases routinely by means of fingerprint identifications or other forensic recoveries with respect to volume crime.

The same issue is true about recruiting crime analysts. The basic fact is that once sworn officers are placed in an analyst or forensic examiner role, *they are not expected to go out and arrest the offenders as well or patrol in a black-and-white police car.* Further, in the UK, since the introduction of the National DNA Database (DNAD), which is supported by well funded scenes of crime departments making volume and serious crime forensic examinations at a quality level the norm, DNA matches in solving and linking crime are as common as latent print matches. The advantage is that DNA, unlike fingerprints, does not have the areas disclosed problem as discussed in Chapter 4, page 103. The legal framework in the United States and the problems associated with conformity in delivering national facilities across many states are a problem the UK does not have, but these problems are not insurmountable as evidenced by previous US quality projects resulting in federal and interstate compliance.

The UK has a well developed national fingerprint system and DNA database that are still subject to a quality custody suite sampling programme to improve results under the National Police Improvement Authority (NPIA) Forensics 21 Programme, which is described in more detail later. Progress has started in improving the mass use of footwear evidence through the National Footwear Project and the coding database. The use of forensic intelligence should expand with these facilities toward delivering the promise hinted at in papers by US academics and police professionals, which are outlined later. The big issue that will follow in the wake of the technical developments is one of police business models adapting their command and control structures to encompass performance- and intelligence-led policing models with the correct levels of forensic support required for delivery.

There are sensitivities in the United States (apparent in published papers) around the issues about leadership and senior police ranks being sensitive to criticism from suggestions by lower ranks as to potential new ways ahead. I believe these views are not firmly grounded and that senior police management in the United States has broad shoulders and the imagination to take things forward. Evidence of this is the New York Police Department's success with COMPSTAT, where the idea came from William Bratton, commissioner of the NYPD, although most would admit that in modern police services many serving officers are in fact academics with considerable real work experience, which is a potentially powerful combination in bringing in change.

One problem where leadership from the US Department of Justice and the NIJ can potentially be of use is that of assisting police services to create new working business models to encompass performance- and intelligence-led policing with the required levels of forensic support. After all, police management has the problem of existing service delivery with cuts in funding, so ways have to be found to create new business models, perhaps within existing resources. There could possibly be opportunities for the United States in taking a lead in creating developments in these areas.

I was concerned to read in *Evidence Technology Magazine*[28] that in the United States, a police chief had dispensed with some of his civilian forensic evidence staff owing to budget cuts and taken 100 sworn officers off the streets to fill the gaps. The reasoning was that if things got tough on the streets, then the 100 new members of the forensics department would kit up and go out to deal with the problem. I have news for that police chief: The 100 officers will be unlikely to be helping out in real time with public order or out on the ground arresting felons because they cannot do two jobs at once. Thus, the situation in that service is really 100 operational officers removed from the streets and restricted forensic expertise in that service for some time.

A sensible balance in dealing with cuts is to balance the way ahead to maintain service across the board. Remember that it is easy to build a wreck and this applies to forensics and intelligence models.

An example of restricted working practices in the Metropolitan Police was evident over a number of years in the delivery of forensic services, which can be clearly seen as such today, but at the time the laboratory liaison system of the Met Police seemed to be effective. The working practices had been developed after World War II by the Met Police striving to make best use of its own forensic science laboratory, but by the 1990s was falling short of meeting the requirements of a modern service. In the Metropolitan Police Forensic Services, there were police detective sergeants still working as laboratory liaison officers up to the early 1990s. They were keen and dedicated partly examining serious scenes, leaving all the technical examinations to the civilian examiners and hogging the serious scenes as if they had some intrinsic ingredient that only they could dispense. The laboratory sergeants did not deal with volume crime nor were they required to make arrests because the processes involved would compromise their role in dealing with part of the examinations of serious crime scenes, so the case for not civilianising them and recruiting scientific professionals was very thin.

Their activities inhibited the casework experience progression of their civilian counterparts for years because their working practices were promulgated by senior police colleagues who had known them for a long time. They were finally disbanded in the early 1990s and in their place the serious crime units of accredited scientific professionals took over and there has been no wish to return to the old days. No one ever heard of an opportunity to finger-print a body in the lab sergeant days because it was taken away for pathologi-cal examination quite swiftly compared to the situation today.

With respect to the role of crime analysts in the UK, serious cases are administered by civilian senior analysts in some services as well as sworn officers, under the management of the officer in charge. Thus, a focus desk in an intelligence unit can, for all intents and purposes, 'run a job'—and large jobs at that—with surveillance officers calling in to impart information and all analytical factors about the case monitored and disseminated for action by investigators in the intelligence unit. That scenario is not likely to be found in areas of the United States for a while until some form of intelligence model is enabled and changes made to allow it to be implemented. The alternative method of working is to patrol hot spots tasked by COMPSTAT analysis and for police assets to self-task around their standard roles.

Common Intelligence Standards and Their Introduction: The London Experience

In 2004, together with senior members of the Metropolitan Police and senior civilian staff, we were invited to Westminster College in London to be intro-duced to the Metropolitan Police Model, the Met's version of the UK NIM, and to be workshopped in order to bring in intelligence-led policing and make it happen. The concepts covering the NIM, its three main intelligence assets, and the four main intelligence products discussed in the earlier chap-ters in this book were introduced to the Metropolitan Police team. The term 'team' is used because whether a Met employee was a civilian or a police officer did not matter; we were there to learn together and to work together to make it happen.

Senior police officers admitted that, prior to the Westminster College sessions, they ran the force according to the headlined issues in the national media—the *London Evening Standard* in particular—whilst following gov-ernment priorities. This was mixed with dealing with current serious crime issues. The Met Police was not until then really intelligence led, did not as an organisation globally use the terminology of intelligence, and was not tasked or coordinated according to strategies and tactics defined and sifted by intel-ligence analysis.

Almost every aspect of intelligence-led policing was covered in the workshops, from the confidential high-end handling of informants down to patrol officers entering logs on CRIMINT, the crime intelligence computer system. The term 'almost every aspect' refers to the fact that forensics as an intelligence source was not included or thought of at that time by the organisers. Standardised procedures such as 'QQ' intelligence codes for inputting intelligence logs were introduced because no word in the English language begins with 'QQ'. A text protocol to start a log would be, for example, QQBURGLARY. From the forensic point of view, introduced later by the forensic intelligence development team, the start of a CSI's log would be QQCSE meaning 'QQ CRIME SCENE EXAMINER' so that analysts picking up the forensic intelligence logs could filter in or out the forensic logs. It did not matter how much 'intelligence' went into CRIMINT as it is a computer and judicial use of Boolean operators and date/time parameters together with geographically defined areas can get analysts and police quickly drilling down to the material they seek.

The structure of intelligence units was covered, as well as the means by which they should be supervised and administered, and how the units identified priorities, set strategies and tactics, and followed up on casework enabled police management to task and coordinate their service.

Under the Metropolitan Police Model, any police unit running any form of operation from the bottom of the organisation to the top had to file a proactive intelligence assessment covering the details and aims of any operation(s) in the respective command unit's intelligence unit.

The reasons for the use of intelligence assessments at all levels were to cover the following issues:

- Other units would be briefed and kept clear of the operation(s).
- The operational tactics could be viewed by management and supervised.
- Intelligence could be shared with other stakeholders.
- The organisational records or memory of the results of the police activity could be kept for future reference and learning.
- Operations and manpower requirements could be assessed and cost estimated.
- The effectiveness of the forensic support in the areas of standard operating procedures and service level agreements for delivery could be monitored and reviewed.
- From the forensic intelligence development team the additional issue was introduced (i.e., to make the best use of forensic intelligence resulting from forensic examinations).
- The crime management team is enabled to make decisions as to whether to proceed, put on hold for more research, or refer the operation upward or downward for action.

At the 2004 Westminster College intelligence workshop, I noted that there was no real forensics content and that my unit was the first of its kind in the Metropolitan Police. The foresight in Met Forensic Services Directorate looking properly at the applications of forensic evidence in crime intelligence complemented the fact that, owing to the success achieved by the Forensic Services Directorate, the number of civilian crime scene examiners had been increased from about 180 staff prior to 2000 to just under 500 examiners covering the Met 24/7 following the appointment of Gary Pugh, OBE, as the first forensic scientist to be appointed as the director of Forensic Services.

As far as Forensic Services were concerned, there were problems with systems such as the crime report system designed in the 1980s and implemented in 1996, where the designers had no foresight as to the growth of forensics services and the requirements for proper information technology support it required. Neither did the Systems Intelligence Detection (SID) Team set up to improve the systems support to intelligence-led policing have any background in modern volume crime forensics. The systems had to be used as best they could, allowing for those deficiencies. However, improvements were made just after the millennium in an improved crime report system using business objects and other search tools to improve the recovery of forensic data within the context of other crime data. This was followed in 2006/2007 by an excellent data warehousing system, the Integrated Intelligence and Information System (IIP), which gave responses on any enquiry across the crime reporting system, intelligence system, custody, stops, and other databases.

Persistent old-fashioned ideas about almost any forensic hit being the end game and not being viewed as the best intelligence leads ever received were inhibitors. Proper analysis of forensic identifications really had to be a mainline objective in order to find the bulk of the offences in which perpetrators were involved. This was particularly important when cross-border casework was involved. (See mention of Operation Halifax later.)

In 2004, Met Police forensic services staff were given access to write intelligence logs in the CRIMINT crime intelligence system. A scenes of crime examiner template was designed and designated 'QQCSE' so that CSIs could input linked series or intelligence information they may have come across, developed, or been told during the course of their daily work out in the field (see Table 6.1). Likewise, CSIs could search CRIMINT by inputting Boolean searches seeking police intelligence around the crimes with which they were dealing, enabling them to contact the appropriate investigating officers and provide often useful input to investigations.

Protocols for the Use of QQCSE CRIMINT Logs

Note: These protocols were introduced in the development phase of forensic intelligence to facilitate forensic intelligence input to the required data standards required by the Metropolitan Police Model of the UK NIM.

**Table 6.1   QQCSE Template: A Suggested Format for Use in Volume Crime
Types for Intelligence Input to an Intelligence System by CSIs**

Burglary Examination Report Aide Memoire[a]				
Day	From:	Monday	To:	Tuesday
Date	From:	01/01/2003	To:	02/01/2003
Time	From:	2300Δhours	To:	0800Δhours
Nature of business:	For example, opticians, florist, pub, office, warehouse, butchers, sports centre			
Address:	All in upper case with a space between each element of the address and with no punctuation (e.g., FLAT1Δ36ΔSOUTHWARKΔDRIVEΔSE18Δ 9QL)			
CRIS no.:	As taken from the CRIS report (e.g., 1234567/03)			
Victim's name:	TitleΔForenameΔSURNAME (e.g., MrΔPaulΔSMITH)			
Victim's age/ gender/ ethnicity:	AgeΔyearsΔold MALE/FEMALE IC (e.g., 83ΔyearsΔold MALE IC3)			
Repeat offence:	Write either repeatΔvictim or repeatΔvenue			
Location details:	For example, consider the following: Is the venue detached, semidetached, a flat, etc.? Is it in a main road, cul-de-sac, or on an estate? Is it near a bus stop, a train station, a motorway, or an alleyway?			
Environmental details:	For example, consider the following: Is the area well lit? Is there CCTV or an alarm system? Is there building work in the area? Are there communal doors?			
Method of approach:	How did the suspect get to the POE? For example, down the back alley, climbed over the neighbour's fence, jumped onto dustbin in victim's back garden, and then moved it to reach rear bathroom widow			
Distraction group:	Use one of the following generic words to describe the style of distraction: Water Animal Council Request: Gas Friend Other: Note Electricity Neighbour anything that Water Social services Window does not fit into Phone Gardener cleaner the previous Toilet Police Workman categories			
Entry/ distraction method:	When describing how the suspect got into the premises, please use as many of the following key words within your free text as possible: walkedΔin levered smashed letterΔbox distracted pushed open removed slipped cut attempted bodilyΔpressure attempted drilled invited uninvited			

continued

Table 6.1 (continued)   QQCSE Template: A Suggested Format for Use in Volume Crime Types for Intelligence Input to an Intelligence System by CSIs

Significant behaviour:	When the suspect was inside the venue, did he or she do anything distinctive like close a door, put the chain on the front door, close the curtains, tidy/untidy search, cause damage, excrete/urinate/masturbate in premises, cut telephone wires, tamper with alarm, make a phone call, ask the victim to turn on the tap, ask to go into a particular room, eat/drink/smoke, etc.?
ID seen:	For example, plastic photo card, business- or council-headed paper,
Property interfered with:	Had any particular areas of the house been disturbed? The underwear rifled through, the children's toys moved, the drinks cabinet raided, food taken from the kitchen?
Property stolen:	Describe property as fully as possible including manufacturer (e.g., Sony Play Station 2) or the country of origin for passports (e.g., British, French, etc.)
Point of exit:	As POE or by other means
Vehicle seen:	Colour, make, model, registration number, etc. (e.g., Silver∆Audi∆A4∆VRM∆A123ABC)
Additional information:	Any other information that you would like to include in your report that you feel does not fit into any of the previous categories
Suspect(s) description:	Write the description in the following order: Sex, ethnic appearance, age, height, build (slim, medium, or heavy), hair, accent (e.g., cockney, Irish, Scottish, well spoken). What clothes did the suspect(s) wear? Were there any significant features about the suspect(s) (e.g., a gold tooth, a strong odour, glasses, a tattoo, or a scar)? For example: MALE IC1 18 years old F511 heavy build short brown curly hair Irish accent blue jeans dark jumper eagle tattoo on right forearm
Suspect(s) in custody:	If you know of any suspects that are in custody that were involved with the burglary you have examined, please put their details in here: Forename∆SURNAME∆dob∆CRO number∆custody number (e.g., Joe∆BLOGGS∆dob∆01/04/1960∆CRO∆12345/97A∆custody ∆number∆1234/2002MD)
Forensic retrievals:	Choose from the following list of options: fingermark∆chemical shoemark∆bigfoot code fingermark∆lift (e.g., shoemark∆R49) fingermark∆photograph toolmark∆code (e.g., palmmark∆lift toolmark∆SBE10) palmmark∆photograph forensic∆material∆ DNA∆description taken from (e.g., fibres, wood, paint, etc.) job sheet (e.g., DNA∆drinks can)

Table 6.1 (continued) QQCSE Template: A Suggested Format for Use in Volume Crime Types for Intelligence Input to an Intelligence System by CSIs

Evidence noted/not taken:	Were there glove marks at the scene, a shoemark that could not be lifted, or a toolmark that could not be cast?
Job sheet number:	The number that appears at the bottom of the job sheet (e.g., 001234)
Cont. sheet number:	The number that appears at the bottom of the continuation sheet (e.g., 001234)
Linked reference numbers:	If there are any other scenes that you feel are linked to this crime, please insert BOCU, CRIS, and/or CRIMINT reference numbers in here (e.g., MD 1234567/02 or MD L00123456/2002)
Proforma statement taken:	Enter either yes or no

Note: Symbol Δ included because CRIMINT software at the time this template was designed required a space, protocols around the nonuse of commas, etc.

^a Where Δ = a space.

The following bullet points cover the parameters to consider when writing a QQCSE CRIMINT log and the circumstances when it is expected that a QQCSE log will be required:

- All burglary artifice (i.e., distraction burglary) examinations (log to include method, etc. whether or not forensic evidence is recovered)
- All Sapphire (the Met Police operation against sex crime) examinations (log to include method, etc. whether or not forensic evidence is recovered)
- All commercial robbery examinations (log to include method, etc. whether or not forensic evidence is recovered)
- When an unusual method or type of evidence is found (e.g., an unusual device is used to gain entry or effect the crime)
- When information that has intelligence value is found or received at the crime scene (e.g., a loser or witness gives potentially useful information not previously recorded)
- CRIMINT logs to be made for every level 1 (local) and level 2 (across boroughs/forces) crime series at the time these series are being monitored in real time (i.e., not retrospectively at a much later date)

Note that QQCSE CRIMINT logs are not required just for the recording of forensic CRIS (Crime Report Information System) codes (shoe and instrument marks) or, for example, when finger marks or DNA is found because these are adequately recorded on the CRIS system as searchable data.

In creating problem and subject (target) profiles, the Met Police Forensic Intelligence Unit made use of CRIMINT intelligence system searches where the forensic teams' forensic intelligence logs would respond to searches alongside police intelligence logs, thus giving a complete picture of all the available intelligence. In drafting intelligence proactive assessments for input into police business groups for consideration with regard to the tasking and coordination processes, the Forensic Intelligence Unit would input the text of the proactive assessments into the CRIMINT intelligence system so that the intelligence was available in real time. This process contributes to the Metropolitan Police Model in ensuring compliance with the NIM. The templates were thought necessary in order to ensure compliance with the data standards required for the effective and efficient use of intelligence in the system.

As previously mentioned in this text, another 6,000 persons were arrested under Operation Halifax (Chapter 2), where biometric volume crime hits were piled up unactioned across the service and the opportunities for a massive amount of extra detection largely missed. Similar results were achieved in increasing detections by other UK police services where an effort was made to make use of forensic intelligence. One service the West Yorkshire Constabulary applied forensic intelligence through Operation Converter, where the Converter team produced forensic intelligence packages around every fingerprint and DNA match to convert the intelligence into detections at a rate of an average of 42% more detections. The Mets not running a 'Converter' operation ran at approximately 28% extra detections per forensic match, but still through developing forensic hits. The West Yorkshire Converter team had to inspect each police command unit in the force regularly to ensure that Converter staff were not purloined into other duties by ill-informed local police management; otherwise, the detection rate would have plummeted.

In the Met in 2007, a new intelligence system, CRIMINT Plus, was brought in and police officers who were not forensic practitioners implemented the system and tried to restrict what went into the new system— picking out the forensic input to be killed off for a start. Their activities led to a 60% drop in intelligence logs across the service and, in 2008, the Met Intelligence Bureau had a tasking to see if this restrictive activity was a threat to the organisation!

As a matter of record, during the forensic intelligence development project in territorial policing (TP) from 2004 to 2007, up to 80% of the thousands of linked cases (designated 'CRIS chains') in the Met CRIS were from the TP Forensic Intelligence Unit at Hendon, a small unit with an average of seven staff members. The other few thousand crime analysts in the Met provided the rest of the 'CRIS chains', for without forensics and any training in the subject, their work in scene linking was made difficult and could lack evidential support. It is interesting, in my opinion, to consider how any professional crime analyst can obtain accreditation without training in forensic intelligence, for the failure of its profession to grasp analysis of forensic recoveries as a major intelligence product from the point of view of someone who has been involved across the various disciplines is really quite staggering.

If forensics has its business applications modelled along intelligence lines, it has knowledge assets in the form of knowledge of the law, forensic science, the area worked in, due processes, etc. and can within those knowledge assets be graded secret, confidential, restricted and unrestricted, or 'open source'. Forensics also have systems assets in the forms of CRIS system applications, AFIS systems, eDNA, crime intelligence system, national criminal records, forensic case management systems, and forensic intelligence databases. Or there can be access to these system assets if the police business model provides access or even procures suitable systems or has any inkling that these systems are required to move on in meeting the best applications of the forensic technologies now at hand.

Forensics has intelligence assets, which can be graded for accuracy and reliability and can be best viewed as intelligence sources for development. The 'intelligence experts' who claim that forensic identifications are just information are misleading themselves and the organisations to which they claim to provide expertise and support. I would, for example, rather believe from a fingerprint identification, footwear link, or DNA match that an individual was really at a crime scene or associated with others than from the word of an informant selling information in a public bar.

The point being made here is that if forensic services within a policing organisation are subjected to review within the light of applying that review along the lines of support to intelligence-led policing, the following questions can be asked:

- Are the knowledge assets currently available to forensic services adequate to meet the demands of intelligence-led policing?
- Are the systems assets available to forensic services fit for purpose and in this category and is the policing organisation as a whole, including forensic services, in the loop with respect to research and planning in the systems area?
- With respect to intelligence assets, is the organisation restricting or preventing input from forensic services or even viewing forensics within the concept of intelligence-led policing?
- Are forensic science providers (laboratories and fingerprint bureaus) in the intelligence loop and are they sharing their legacy data from casework?

- Have police services been seeking advice from the right people in the first place? After all, how many leading academics have investigated any crime for real or spent a considerable part of their working lives in an investigative environment?
- In the management of public protection arrangements (MAPPAs), are other stakeholder organisations subject to limited access to relevant systems, knowledge assets, or relevant intelligence to their work?

Perhaps in looking at the modern business of intelligence-led policing, a from-the-ground-up review should be made to what are really now, in the twenty-first century, old police organisations that have developed ad hoc and been shaped by events and mishaps over long periods of time.

The Practicalities of Introducing Intelligence-Led Policing

From the experience of the introduction of intelligence-led policing in the Met Police and its functioning relationship across the UK with other police services using the NIM, it should be relatively easy to introduce a US style intelligence-led policing model based across broad principles to accommodate the various US states within their legal and administrative structures.

The reasoning behind this statement is simply that all police services use the three generic assets to function: knowledge, system, and intelligence assets. Even in COMPSTAT, its generic objectives are in line with the UK NIM. All police services plan operations around known crime problems (NIM problem profiles) and against suspected or known offenders (UK subject or target profile). They also produce strategic and tactical plans to manage the tasking of assets and the follow-up (UK NIM strategic assessments and tactical assessments; US COMPSTAT four generic products).

There is a divergence between the two systems in that the NIM is not aimed at supporting a public forum, although UK police services do strive to keep the public informed through a less dramatically staged process. With this in mind, do US police services have to make enormous changes to bring in an intelligence-led model? It is probable that intelligence-led policing with regional differences around fine-tuning on a generic model is quite possible. If it is successful, the benefits, which could possibly accrue from reduced crime and improved detections, could make the entire process fit broadly within existing budgets. It is beyond the scope of this book to suggest what forms the US model would follow, but the generic basics are outlined in this text.

William Bratton, the founder of COMPSTAT, consulted with other countries and shared the NYPD expertise, as has the UK NPIA. There is an international dialogue, which could result in a more universal intelligence-led model. Perhaps this time this will give forensics a solid place in the intelligence and crime analysis processes with forensic intelligence, in my personal view as the tenth generic analytical technique supplying truth to probability-based crime analysis.

Moving on from the anecdotal approach to describing the process of introducing intelligence-led policing in drilling down, the next practical issues are the roles of staff required and the generic structure of intelligence units required to make it happen.

Intelligence Unit Structure

In setting up a working intelligence unit, there are major practical considerations:

- Monitoring the intelligence coming in
- Ensuring that adequate analysis is carried out on received intelligence
- Ensuring that staff are updated and trained in the necessary skills
- Ensuring that intelligence field officers are tasked and that their resulting inputs are dealt with promptly
- Supervising the quality of the inputs and outputs from the unit
- Ensuring that the law concerning surveillance permissions is observed
- Having the means to access, assess, and use forensic intelligence with other analytical data
- Providing intelligence products for police tasking and coordination within an agreed time period or cycle

Intelligence Unit Roles

Intelligence Unit Manager

The manager can be either a middle-ranking police officer or a senior analyst. In small police services, a constable or sergeant might have responsibility, with one or two staff, to work on research and analysis. This role is to supervise the running of the unit and to ensure that proper authorities for surveillance are in place and that the unit delivers intelligence products in good time to meet the requirements of the service tasking and coordination processes. The manager has to be able to supervise officers dealing with confidential informants.

The Gatekeeper

The role of monitoring and receiving the intelligence coming in and out of the unit is the role of the gatekeeper. This is a defined individual who has the role of being usually the first point of contact in the unit. As part of this role, he or she should ensure that strategic material is fast tracked for action. Usually, a police officer or admin/researcher grade civilian member of staff will act as gatekeeper. Gatekeepers in adjoining police business groups and areas should become known to one another and have an ongoing working relationship.

Researcher

Researchers are tasked by the manager or analysts on behalf of the manager to find and prepare intelligence data from many sources working with the analyst(s) to deal with the higher end analytical processes efficiently. Smaller police services combine this role with the analysts who cover both functions.

Crime Analyst

In the UK, analysts are recruited into the analysts' profession and their role is to provide analytical products for use in proactive intelligence assessments for action as well as to review crime data and results as required under the current strategic assessment. Analysts are also required to prepare reports on emerging threats and to provide relevant performance data for the management of the tasking and coordination group. (See the section, 'The Daily Work of the Crime Analyst', in Chapter 3.) The analyst should provide a daily report for the daily intelligence meeting (DIM) of the police unit where the progress or otherwise of ongoing investigations is given and new intelligence introduced for management to prioritise.

Intelligence Log Supervisor

This role is usually a dual one where a police officer, researcher, or analyst member of the intelligence unit staff will also daily examine any new intelligence logs put onto the intelligence system and check them for compliance with data standards and their relevance. Each retained intelligence log has to be signed off by the intelligence log (CRIMINT) supervisor. Each intelligence unit has nominated intelligence log supervisors, but further up the business group there will usually be a higher level of supervision by a middle-ranking police officer or higher analyst checking across the whole police service for overall compliance.

Field Officers

Larger intelligence units and operational command units have field officers who are assigned by the intelligence manager to carry out surveillance. Also, lifestyle research into intelligence targets and their work is often crucial to the development of target profiles toward the possible creation of a proactive intelligence assessment for action by a police unit or asset. Smaller police services with few personnel may have to multitask skilled personnel to carry out surveillance, research, etc.

Tasking and Briefing Slide Officer

Properly structured and staffed intelligence units usually have a member of staff assigned to maintain the briefing and tasking system (usually abbreviated to BaTs). It is vital that intelligence units provide this form of output to disseminate briefings and intelligence to the working officers as they come on duty. The BaTs also enables the sharing of intelligence in the form of briefing slides across police borders and with other stakeholders as found to be appropriate.

Forensic Intelligence Researcher or Analyst

This role is included here, for many police services will not yet have someone responsible for this role. The role can be taken by a suitably trained researcher or analyst or, from experience as best practice, can be one of the forensic services team who is trained in criminalistics as an accredited forensic practitioner. Forensic intelligence is quite an extensive subject, as discussed in this book, and police services as a development issue in the UK are starting to advertise for forensic intelligence analysts or researchers. This forensic intelligence role should provide a valuable live link to the management of forensic services within the police service, ensuring that service-level agreements and standard operation procedures are in place to ensure the following:

- An ongoing dialogue feeding in the results of forensic examinations across the police business group
- Maintaining the type and quality of forensic data required by researchers and analysts derived from forensic scenes of crime examinations
- Acting on behalf of the CSI team in imaging, coding forensic marks, and performing preliminary screens against, for example, scanned suspects' footwear to add value to links for development by analysts
- Maintaining a working relationship with forensic services to ensure adequate forensic strategies are in place to service the current strategic assessment around priority crime types for the police service
- Providing forensically linked scene briefings and providing assessments of the potential detections that can accrue from linked hard evidence (latent print and DNA) matches to ensure that detections are maximised
- Providing a personal liaison with the forensic examination team both collecting new intelligence from them and at the same time cascading intelligence from the intelligence unit about ongoing casework to ensure awareness and provide better involvement between the stakeholders in the business of intelligence-led policing

- Acting as part of a cross-force forensic intelligence group meeting monthly to quarterly to discuss cross-border linked series and crime problems and involving crime analysts and police colleagues in these groups to bring their expertise to the forum
- A vital part of the role is liaison with forensic science providers (FSPs) (i.e., laboratories and fingerprint bureaus) to ensure the flow of legacy data especially important on cross-border serial crime. Often it was found to be very productive to workshop with FSPs toward improving the forensic intelligence products. Inviting key FSP team members to meetings with the intelligence team was found to be really good practice. For example, inviting the ballistics scientist to speak to the homicide and gun crime analysts gave superb quality background and gave the FSP a view of the clients' requirements.

On the topic of cross-border intelligence meetings, it was found to be good practice to invite a specialist speaker from, say, a drug squad or forensic science laboratory or a higher analyst from a specialist crime unit to attend and present casework, ideas, and new techniques to the group as part of ongoing development. This would be introduced after the main business of the cross-border meeting had been concluded. Often, from this type of forum, casework thought to be local to a police division would be found to be part of something far more extensive, leading to new research into a criminal network. For example, in dealing with Vietnamese organised crime in drug production, officers from other police areas as well as academics who understood Vietnamese culture were of great use, as was a liaison officer from the police service in Vietnam. This background was enormously useful in understanding the criminal networks and their method, which were run by family-based crime syndicates.

The forensic intelligence product my unit produced in 2007 linked 1800 (yes, eighteen hundred!) persons by fingerprints and DNA—Vietnamese nationals in association with one another and in combinations with each other over the entire UK. This enabled the sifting out of the 'movers and shakers' who could lead investigators back to the organisers involved in massive illegal human trafficking, drug production, money laundering, kidnapping, smuggling, and homicide. (See Chapter 3, Figures 3.3 and 3.4, regarding the spread of organised-crime cannabis production in the UK.) The illustration in Figure 6.1 indicates the structure of the organised-crime businesses, and the forensic links were invaluable in connecting the production sites with others higher up in the organisations including middle management and subletting criminal entrepreneurs. Note that most of the links in the maps in Chapter 3 connected across North and Southeast London.

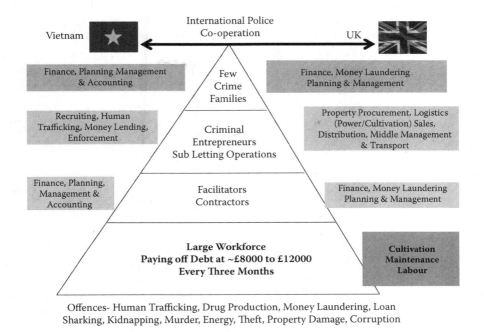

Figure 6.1 Organised-crime cannabis growers business model.

Must a Police Service Work under an Intelligence-Led Model to Benefit from Forensic Intelligence?

The short answer to this question is 'no' because forensic intelligence can be used by any investigative process or business model. However, from my experience, it is best practice to organise police within an intelligence-led concept. After all, in that scenario all the stakeholders in the police service use the language and processes of intelligence-led problem-solving policing. Earlier in this book, the inhibitors and enablers for forensic intelligence are discussed from the practical point of view of practitioners such as I who were involved in dealing with real reported crime and forensic recoveries over several years.

Forensic Intelligence: A US Academic's View

Useful research outside the UK has been published by academics looking at the problems of forensics providing useful, timely, and accurate intelligence—notably, the paper by Jordan M. Chaplinsky, University of South

Florida. In Chaplinsky's paper, the obstacles to making this happen in the United States are highlighted and discussed.[29]

In this book, practical solutions are offered to make forensic intelligence happen with evidence covering how this has been achieved thus far in the UK. Chaplinsky's paper highlights the following issues around the current status quo in the United States, covering the following topics:

- US case studies show the potential for forensic trace evidence to provide accurate and timely evidence to be used proactively.
- Widespread use of forensic intelligence in the United States has not been seen as yet.
- There are obstacles to be removed to facilitate the use of forensic trace evidence to produce intelligence:
  1. The court system must give law enforcement more authority to apply forensic science resources for intelligence purposes.
  2. Law enforcement must have a forward thinking approach to forensic trace evidence that demands that resources be utilised in investigating major and more minor crimes.
  3. With items 1 and 2 in place, this approach will increase the number of traces collected, which will increase the probability of matching offenders or linking through forensic databasing.

This is precisely what we were doing in the Metropolitan Police in developing forensic intelligence. The development of forensic intelligence in the Met predated intelligence-led policing in the UK, but the linked scenes and identifications produced were still used proactively, albeit in an ad hoc way, by investigators, for all policing has an element of intelligence use and processes for tasking. It can be argued that bringing in an intelligence-led business model formalises the processes.

Chaplinsky defines forensic intelligence as 'any intelligence produced as a result of analysing trace evidence'. I would go further to include telephone and computer evidence recovery as a branch of forensic intelligence, yet many US police services will have a business plan and budget for computer forensics but no plans for civilianisation of expansion of forensic services.

The Innocence Project

Other issues covered in Chaplinsky's paper are the work of the Innocence Project, an organisation that has spent the past 20 years proving how erroneous witness testimony and weak circumstantial evidence have wrongfully imprisoned 268 people in the United States, 17 of whom spent time on Death Row. The project secured the release of the 268 people through DNA testing and, in 117 cases, the true perpetrators were subsequently identified. This reinforces Chapter 2 in this book on the topic of forensics proving the truths required to reinforce analysis, which otherwise is based more on probability and the crime rectangle, with evidence as the fourth factor necessary to secure safe detections and convictions. Chaplinsky sums up this topic thus, 'If 75% of wrongful conviction exonerations were due to eyewitness misidentification, then how many hours are spent interrogating the wrong suspects, how many misguided leads are followed because of a faulty human account?'

Merging forensic intelligence with the principles of intelligence-led policing could help facilitate the process of using forensic intelligence for policing and security purposes. Chaplinsky goes on to emphasise that, as previously stated in this text, forensic trace evidence can serve as data to be analysed in an intelligence-led framework. Precisely the issues in dealing with forensic evidence in intelligence are exactly what has been practised in the Metropolitan Police and across the UK. His research goes on to affirm the earlier points raised in this book in the requirement to know forensic examination intervention rates, the evidence recovery rate from those scenes, the type of material recovered, the quantity of material yielding a useful profile, how much is checked against national database samples, and the number of matches.

To go further through my own experience actually using these forms of data for a number of years in real casework, often just knowing the recovery rate and how rare the evidence type is against other analytical data is enough to reinforce an intelligence assessment adequately. Further, that leads to sensible targeting of material for submission to forensic science providers toward providing that element of factual truths, which strongly support the detection processes and prosecutions. Interestingly Chaplinsky's paper mentions a 20-scene linked case in Switzerland cleared up using forensic intelligence techniques. The Met Police development project had thousands of cleared up cases.

The AutoRoute map in Figure 6.2 is of a 501 detection burglary case where the map was produced by the Forensic Intelligence Unit in order that the investigator could drive the suspect to the locations so that the suspect could pick out the premises he had burgled and confirm details about what was taken and how he had entered the premises. This gave rise to a routine problem profile being entered about the linked clusters in the CRIMINT system and the problem profile in word format with mappings being submitted to the Harrow and Edgware police intelligence unit. A single latent print match in the south cluster identified an offender who lived in the centre of the mapping used as an anchor point. Once his DNA was taken, a match was found at a burglary scene in the north cluster, so at this stage there were 32 offences involved. Using the offender's home as an anchor point, the locations of burglaries where double glazing units were removed to enter and striations were found from a double glazing removal tool cast were mapped. Only certain streets in the area had this type of offence and several properties had repeat

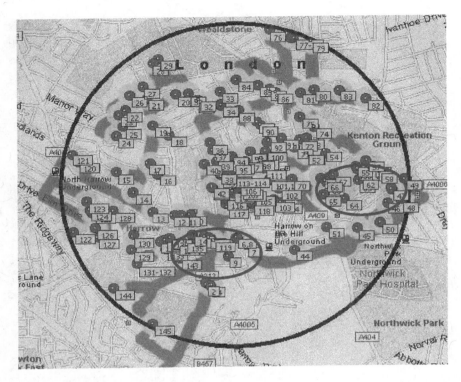

Figure 6.2 A 501 forensic intelligence detections burglary case from tool marks links Northwest London in the zone around the offender's home.

burglaries over the 2-year period. The mapping revealed a buffer zone around the identified offender's home, which is a Brantingham crime pattern.[11,30] This simple form of mapping can be a very effective and economical method and certainly helped produce a good number of detections in this case.

Is Intelligence-Led Policing Difficult to Implement?

This title question is aimed at policing professionals in countries where as yet policing is driven by traditional command-and-control structures and not intelligence led in the sense of intelligence and analysis being used as main drivers in supporting a business model based on performance management. A serving US police officer, Jon M. Shane's academic paper, 'Performance Management in Police Agencies: A Conceptual Framework',[31] was produced from the perspective of a serving police officer in the United States and covers in detail the problems associated with the current command-and-control-based management structure. Shane quotes former New York Police Commissioner Lee P. Brown, **'The command-and-control culture of the**

police department doesn't treat officers as intelligent, creative, and trustworthy people. It allows them very little discretion. It's designed to make sure that they don't get into trouble, don't embarrass the department, and don't get their supervisors into trouble'.[32]

In Shane's paper he explores the concepts involved in a police management performance model citing the advantages of working to such a model together with the benefits that would accrue were the model to be universally adopted. COMPSTAT's approach and the approach of the UK NIM are discussed together with current weaknesses leading to both models at times falling short of delivering the levels of service expected. I would recommend particularly that police managers read Shane's paper thoroughly, for his research and discussions certainly strike a chord with the thrust of this text, which is to encourage better working practices within the concepts of intelligence-led policing with respect to forensics. The suggestion that police business models should be considered in the whole with a fresh view would potentially be a means to improve many of the issues besetting modern policing.

More International Perspectives on Forensic Intelligence

In, I believe, 2003/2004 I was visited at the Met Police Forensic Intelligence Unit by Olivier Ribaux of the University of Lausanne (now Professor Olivier Ribaux). He brought with him a PowerPoint presentation showing the use of forensic intelligence in the Swiss cantons with respect to footwear evidence, whereby the evidence-finding frequencies of crime scene shoe marks were monitored and basically mapped.[3]

When there was an increase in the finding rate of a particular pattern crime, mapping was often associated with developing geographical clusters and through this process analysts could draw attention to emerging crime problems, particularly with respect to burglary crime. Working with others, Ribaux[3] produced a paper entitled 'Forensic Intelligence and Crime Analysis'. In this paper, the authors agree that forensic evidence can be scrutinised to help reveal potentially linked series of crimes and that the process is a two-step one that can be systematically applied as a crime analysis method and as an investigative tool. The paper makes reference to papers by J Birkett,[23] R Milne,[4] and T Napier's paper of 2002[16] in the *Journal of the Forensic Science Society* on evidence frequencies and databases with regard to footwear. The authors noted at the time that intelligence-led policing tempts forensic science to operate in a new context within which it has yet to find its place.

The paper by Ribaux et al.[3] concludes that at that time (2003), from their experience, forensic case data were poorly integrated into crime analysis and that with relatively small amounts of information and basic computer skills it was possible to extract interesting patterns and intelligence offering opportunities to change the research agenda by focussing on more innovative methods that combine the uses of different forensic traces.

Between 2003, when the paper was produced, and 2008, when I retired from the Met Police service, things had moved along in the UK with respect to implementing better use of different forms of forensic evidence. The UK NPIA produced its Forensics 21 Programme[33] designed to improve the use of forensics in intelligence-led policing. The NPIA also has a programme aimed at improving the application of the UK NIM. As a concept, the NPIA is, in my view, a great step forward in modern policing and its management. It represents a real attempt to move on from the old development tendencies in policing often driven by scandal before seminal changes are made.

The UK NPIA Forensics 21 Programme

In the UK, forensic services have been civilianised since the 1970s onward. Through the more centralised structure, the UK government Home Office has had control over the general direction of the development of policing and forensic services. That is not to say that the processes introduced have proven to be complete or perfect in their operations.

In order to pull together training and project development, the NPIA was created. The NPIA has various projects, of which 'Forensics 21' has a potential capacity to assist in improving issues around enabling forensic intelligence. The NPIA administers CSI training and crime analyst training but has not, as of the writing of this text, undertaken the training of crime analysts in forensic awareness and the analysis of forensic results as a distinct issue. The Forensic 21 Programme has produced work streams that are definite enabling projects with respect to providing forensic intelligence:

- The Detainee at Police Station Sampling (DAPSS) launch in 2010 aimed at improving the taking of fingerprints and DNA samples from offenders. The main four objectives of DAPSS are
  - To ensure that fingerprint and DNA samples are of the best possible quality and comply with national best practice where applicable
  - To ensure that every detainee arrested is accurately identified and appropriately sampled under the Police and Criminal Evidence Act (PACE)
  - To ensure that investigative samples are taken where necessary
  - To ensure that all pertinent data in relation to each detainee and their samples are properly obtained and recorded
- The UK National Footwear Reference Collection (NFRC) is a coding reference database of over 18,000 shoe patterns designed to assist police services to make better use of footwear evidence and

the intelligence that footwear evidence can provide. Treadmark and SICAR (Shoeprint Image Capture and Retrieval) software make use of the NFRC. SICAR, however, has two databases for users: SoleMate, a footwear coding and identification database, and TreadMate, a database of tire patterns enabling the identification of tire print designs. The SICAR approach with its database products is adaptable internationally and has the support of a multinational company, Foster & Freeman.

- Evidential Drug Identification Testing (EDIT) workshop 2010 was arranged so that practitioners were able to review current working practices and share experiences in the use of EDIT kits. EDIT kits are useful in dealing with drug possession cases; however, where larger quantities of drugs are involved in drug dealing cases, a laboratory report covering the links between larger seizures can enable upstreaming of casework as described in this book. Total use across the board of EDIT kits can compromise the ability to upstream more serious casework—an example of which is the UK Serious and Organised Crime Agency 'Operation Endorse'.

Issues covered in 2010 by the NPIA under Forensics 21 'Phase 2' were

- Citizen focus
- Forensic quality standards, process management, and consumables
- Digital kit and consumables and the National Forensics Framework Agreement (NFFA)
- Accelerated DNA technology (ADAPT) and the NFRC

Currently, the NPIA has a science and innovation strategy from 2010 to 2013. This strategy sets out the road map for the future use of science by the UK police service. It covers three main topics:

- A stronger focus on directing investment to areas that will deliver the strongest benefits to public safety and confidence
- A greater emphasis on the transfer of innovation across force borders and different aspects of policing
- Establishing stronger relationships between the research community, private sector, and policing

The Forensics 21 Custody Suite Process Work Stream toward a Better Forensic Intelligence Model

The NPIA has engaged in work to improve the processing of suspected offenders and recovery of forensic samples from suspected offenders in the custody suite. The diagram in Figure 6.3 illustrates the processes, but the image suggests a rapid process in a single-case scenario. From experience, offenders identified the same day or the next day are those who were either careless forensically or made a mistake whilst committing crimes over prolonged periods. A failure to make use of processed and stored forensic material in the analytical sense will lead to detections being missed and to intelligence gaps, so the introduction of the custody suite project, although welcome, is still only part of the picture.

The Forensics 21 Programme has created a diagram to illustrate the benefits that the programme should bring to policing. It serves to illustrate the work required to improve the use of forensics in criminal investigations. The role of forensic intelligence covers the areas between points 8 (the custody suite) and points 3 and 4; otherwise, cases are missed or links not perceived. This observation is vital to this project, providing volume forensic intelligence; otherwise, it will just deliver better processing in custody suites whilst addressing problems in fingerprint bureaus, DNA labs, and in getting more footwear from suspects into the CSI's office.

From working in a forensically efficient forensic service in that the Met Police examined burglaries within 4 hours of reporting and searched finger marks in the same 24-hour period, I can say that unless there is an improvement in the handling of footwear evidence using Treadmark, SICAR, or another system, the footwear links will be based on coded clusters with actual comparisons causing a backlog. Certainly, the crime analysts should be forensically aware or forensic researchers should be employed in order to contribute to the effective running of the Forensics 21 Programme.

Readers can browse forensics21@npia.pnn.police.uk for current updates on Forensics 21.

US National Forensic Science Technology Centre

In the United States, the National Forensic Science Technology Centre (NFTC) works with the NIJ in developing resources to evaluate the latest ideas, technologies, and training programmes to advance the use of effective forensic science in criminal investigation. The NIJ relies on the NFSTC to deliver innovative programmes to make this happen. In 2007, the NIJ awarded the NFSTC a grant to establish the Forensic Technologies Centre of Excellence. Through this organisation, the NFSTC evaluates mature and emerging technologies, providing forensic science practitioners with objective information on new tools and technologies to enable more effective investigation of crime.

The NFSTC provides many programmes that, in many ways, mirror the NPIA programs in the UK, although the issue of more centralised control

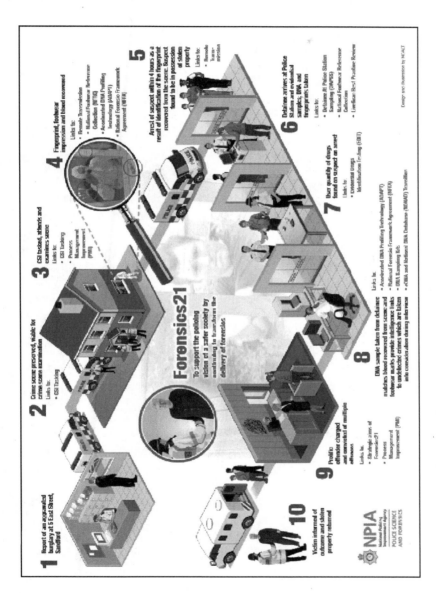

Figure 6.3 Forensics 21 end-to-end process diagram.

is not exercised in the manner in which the NPIA operates. Current programmes in 2011 are

- Field investigative drugs officer (FIDO)
- Forensic Technology Centre for Excellence
- National Missing Persons Unidentified System (Namus)
- Deployable forensic science laboratory
- Forensic information data exchange (FIDEX)
- E-crime awareness
- Lab audit CD ROM
- Michigan Public Safety
- Quality documents
- Bureau of Justice assistance projects
- Forensic DNA for law enforcement decision makers

The NFSTC also provides forensic science training and forensic technology support. Many of these issues require the attention they are being given.
However, improving working practices in different police services if they
desire to change may not have the potential to engender the change needed
to advance the issues needed to enable the best use of forensics through intelligence and crime analysis processes.

Introducing Intelligence-Led Policing: A Review

In summing up this chapter, it is proposed that, from the UK experience,
moving toward intelligence-led policing is not a vastly complex enterprise,
for all police departments universally use the same assets with whatever
name they give them. In making use of those generic assets, they produce
their own versions of processes to deal with tactics around crime problems
and in targeting individuals. Being intelligence led formalises the processes
with which police are universally familiar and ensures a corporate memory
of successes and failures.

In moving to an intelligence-led policing model, organisations will by
default have to use a performance-led business model, which by its nature
will monitor the uses of forensics and best practices in utilising forensics in
crime intelligence. The changes necessary to enable all of the processes are
more likely to accrue from moving to an intelligence-led business model. The
working practices of police, forensic professionals, and crime analysts have
to be considered in the round to make best use of stakeholder skills in creating a business model for reducing crime and improving public safety and the
criminal justice system.

Summary

This chapter included the following:

- Common intelligence standards and their introduction—the London experience
- The practicalities of introducing intelligence-led policing
- Intelligence unit structure
- Intelligence unit roles
- Forensic intelligence—a US academic's view
- International perspectives on forensic intelligence
- The UK Forensics 21 Programme
- The National Forensic Technology Centre, United States
- Introducing intelligence-led policing—a review

Forensic Intelligence Applied to Different Crime Types

7

Forensic Intelligence and Volume Crime: A Checklist

Assuming that a police service has put in place the required changes listed in the following checklist, then that service should be able to see across its entire reported crime a reasonably useful picture of forensics related in volume to the different reported crime types with which to create intelligence products for action:

- The facilities to adequately forensically examine most suitable reported crime scenes maintaining a high intervention rate
- The training and basic equipment in place to screen suspected offenders in custody
- The resources to perform some form of crime analysis capability
- Service-level agreements in place with forensic science providers to provide legacy data and a capability to support screened-in cases with cross-case forensic linking support
- Adequately trained analysts or sworn officers in the use of crime analysis and forensic intelligence
- Some information technology support to handle intelligence, forensic images, and data on the service network
- Most importantly, achievable objectives for the service to make best use of forensic recoveries within resources

If any of these items is not supported, then it is likely that the use of forensic intelligence as a routine investigative tool will be compromised even down to not making best use of latent print matches or DNA results—let alone footwear, ballistics, tool marks, or other trace evidence in the sense of the view across a complete police service where, through lack of performance management and defined responsibility in this area, the actions around biometric matches may be patchy.

In 1996 when a computerised crime report system was introduced to the Metropolitan Police through creating databases of coded shoe and tool marks, the whole picture for each evidence type was seen across the entire reported crime database. These data were collated on Microsoft Excel spreadsheets and immediately forensic marks clusters could be seen related to geographical locations and, even better, still rarer types of forensic marks could be seen against similar crime types or across crime types separated in some instances by considerable distances. The capacity to utilise these data to produce intelligence products for action was obvious, but in large organisations there are those who resist any change and have no wish to adapt.

One rather irksome feature of the CRIS system was that the forensic fields were adapted for performance management because a bespoke solution for this function had not been included by those planning the system and the original CRIS system restricted the characters to 10 in number in the searchable forensic features fields. This was eventually partially corrected when a new CRIS system was introduced with business objects search facility. Those involved in forensic intelligence research and analysis had to put up with the forensic fields being populated with management performance codes and references.

The Importance of Service Champions in Delivering Intelligence-Led Procedures including Forensics

For this important reason, each service should seek a champion to oversee the process of being intelligence led. This role should cover policy, standard operating procedures, role changes, proposals for legislative change if required, plus an ability to seek finance and resources. These activities will require time to work through but will improve the performance of police services and minimise public criticism, especially with reference to the 'CSI effect', where taxpayers expect a modern, scientific, intelligence-led police service using the best processes that modern management, technology, and science can deliver.

In 2003 I caused the setting up of the 'Operation Bigfoot' shoe mark coding utility on the Met Police intranet, a set of web pages supporting a database of identified manufacturers' shoe patterns. This was an example of the Met Police installing a forensic intelligence enabling facility, with information technology support and forensic service provider assistance from the Forensic Science Service (FSS) Agency Gov Co combined with a properly trained and equipped forensic CSI field force, with high scenes of crime intervention rates. For reported burglary across London, the intervention rate was over 85% (i.e., 85% of reported burglaries were forensically examined by a CSI).

The improvement through part computerisation at the time in Operation Bigfoot was a step forward from the previous facility I had set up in 1986 (as described in Chapter 1), where the coding database was on microfiche and supported with paper publications listing the most common shoe patterns and their FSS 'Chorley' shoe codes. The Bigfoot intranet facility enabled the ease of updating the reference and drew attention to the CSI field force of footwear evidence, and the evidence type could, at least for quantity, be performance managed. My office received any scenes of crime shoe marks that could not be found on the Bigfoot Database and submitted these to the FSS Gov Co laboratory for identification and coding; then, the updates were published by my staff in the Bigfoot intranet reference. On the same day as the footwear marks were found, CSIs entered the codes for the marks or descriptors if the marks were not yet an identified pattern in the crime reports. These data were then available in real time to be extracted on spreadsheets for research and analysis.

In 2010 the Bigfoot utility was replaced by the UK National Police Improvement Authority (NPIA) National Footwear Reference Collection (NFRC), which was available online to all police services in the UK at no cost. International users can access the NFRC via Treadmark software. See the sections in Chapter 8 covering Treadmark and SICAR (Shoeprint Image Capture and Retrieval) software.

The Importance of the Effective Use of Digital Technology

From development work in forensic intelligence in the Metropolitan Police, one of the inhibitors was the lack of digital images caused by the photographic department using chemical film and being slow to adopt digital imaging (finally stopping the use of film in 2007!). The lack of a bespoke network software system such as Treadmark or SICAR resulted in the forensic intelligence desks adopting Bayesian probability methods aligned to other information and intelligence to produce forensic intelligence reports.

To be frank, what should have been easy issues to deal with were made difficult by restrictive practices and information technology inertia to change. There was no problem, however, using Microsoft Office applications and there were advances in data warehousing a more entity-based records approach. Thus, having the right information technology support available is a major enabling factor in dealing with the linkage between offenders being processed and crime scene material.

A good example of correct dealings in an evidence type is the use of the Integrated Ballistics Intelligence System (IBIS). Here, crime scene ballistics exhibits and ballistics exhibits from suspects are evaluated, recorded digitally, screened, and searched. The areas-disclosed problem is solved with bringing the suspects and the scenes exhibits through a quality process, which benefits from expert manual confirmation of links. Footwear marks and tool marks also have systems that can be used, but most police services have little in place to deal with volume casework. It is wondered why lots of positive results occur when a single-case suspect and scene case are handled but not in many volume cases. The fact is that, without Treadmark, SICAR, or another system in place, the opportunities to find many more single-match cases out of the volume database is compromised and will not happen. Thus, investment in this area and 'biting the bullet' are the key if a service is to get volume crime forensics out of the cottage industry stage.

In recent years, through the use of IBIS technology, ballistics intelligence services have been created in a number of countries. Ballistics intelligence units embrace the principles of forensic intelligence covering the following points:

- Digital processes are used to handle the screening of all recovered ballistic material.
- Suspect firearms are test fired to ensure that the forensic mark areas' disclosed problem is covered.
- The system enables direct comparisons and cold-search facilities.
- The concept of the unknown gun is covered in a similar way to linked series with other evidence types indicating a serial but unknown offender at the onset.
- Forensic intelligence products are routinely produced through the effort to deal with an evidence type in a quality manner.
- The inputs are recorded in police submissions and the outputs from the ballistics intelligence unit are used to update police records, including intelligence systems and products.
- Like other forms of forensic evidence, ballistics matches can be used to create stand-alone products for action.

The modern ballistics intelligence approach using digital technology is a positive example of what can be achieved if the major components enabling forensic intelligence are put into place. The diagram in Figure 7.1 shows the processes involved by a policing organisation dealing with ballistics intelligence service inputs and the routes for the police service to update its own systems and that of the ballistics intelligence service. Note how large the processes section is for forensic intelligence.

The upper area indicated as 'IBIS & sequential forensic/fingerprint treatments', relates to the NaBIS processes and sequential treatments of exhibits at

Figure 7.1 *(See facing page)* Forensic intelligence processes dealing with National Ballistics Intelligence Service (NaBIS) data in the Met Police Intelligence Bureau (MIB). (R Milne edited diagram, 2008.) MIB: Met Intelligence Bureau; NaBIS: National Ballistics Intelligence Service; NaBID: National Ballistics Intelligence Database; Ident 1: the UK National Automatic Fingerprint Identification System; OIC: officer in case; PNC: police national computer; CRIS: Crime Report Information System; CRIMINT (Plus): Crime Intelligence System (SAS Company, Memex); QQCSE: crime scene examiner intelligence logs.

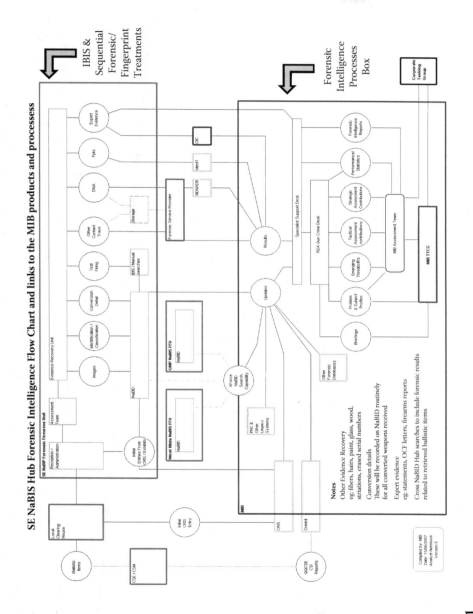

SE NaBIS Hub Forensic Intelligence Flow Chart and links to the MIB products and processes

Figure 7.1

the NaBIS hub. The lower area indicated 'Forensic intelligence processes box' is the forensic intelligence processes area. Note how large this area is and how the processes from the specialist support desk (Forensic Intelligence Desk) connect to the inputs and outputs of the police service in the form of crime records and intelligence back to the NaBIS hub for dissemination. Through these processes intelligence from the NaBIS hub is processed, researched, and analysed; then the resulting intelligence products are updated on the hub so that intelligence is shared and disseminated.

In earlier sections of this book, it is stressed that in producing forensic intelligence processes, policing organisations can just adapt what they already have. However, for well resourced organisations such as the Metropolitan Police in good economic times, a more structured approach was trialled with some success. In the previous chapter, there was an anecdotal account of the introduction of intelligence-led policing to the Metropolitan Police. The following box section includes notes made by the author at the time after the first year of managing the Met's Territorial Police Forensic Intelligence Unit (TP FIU), a part of the development section of the Met's Directorate of Forensic services.

These notes cover the roles and processes in setting up the TP FIU 2002/2003. It was agreed to set up the unit in 2001, equipment was procured, and staff selected, but it was into 2002 before the unit began to function. It suffered later in 2007 from moving into the Met main intelligence unit from what I shall call the 'Minderman effect' (see Chapter 1 regarding advice from John Minderman and Chapter 3 regarding the placing of analysts in the 'AI' and 'AI3' positions), whereby the unit was only focussed on certain priorities compounded by staff being 'borrowed' to support staff shortages of researchers and analysts covering routine, nonforensic research and analysis in other sections of the main intelligence unit. **However, the objectives of forensic intelligence data collection were already created, so intelligence products were created and the data are still available today in the Met's systems for any investigator, researcher, or analyst to make use of in the creation of intelligence products if the analysts are aware of what to do with the data. Certainly, under the Forensics 21 Programme, the forensic intelligence data are available for use on demand.**

The following briefing notes cover initial setup problems and describe the information technology problems; it is possible that many police services will find similar problems, for some systems and processes are not always created with forensic services viewed as a primary user. In 2011 Met Police footwear evidence was processed by the Met's Operation Scarlet Team using the NPIA Footwear Reference Database providing footwear links and matches for analysts and investigators. The CSI team intelligence researcher project 2007/2008 at Enfield Borough was successful and highlighted the way ahead in the best practice of where to place a forensic intelligence capability. (If readers study the Forensics 21 'end to end' diagram in Chapter 6, they will note that is exactly where the NPIA has placed the forensic intelligence researcher.)

The briefing notes in the following section are included as a reference for those who wish possibly to create or adapt their own business model for using forensic intelligence.

Forensic Intelligence Briefing Paper 2003—Volume Crime

R Milne, Manager

PROGRESS MADE 2002/2003 IN SETTING UP THE FORENSIC INTELLIGENCE UNITS

In April 2002, the North and South Forensic Intelligence Units commenced operating, with one forensic intelligence manager and one forensic intelligence officer (FIO) analyst in each unit. By June/July 2002, each unit had a complement of two FIOs with a data in-putter and researcher, assisted by two, temporary research/data input staff from an agency.

During the above period, staff were sent on a series of training courses covering IT and intelligence processes. The development managers underwent intelligence manager training under the Met Model and National Intelligence Model.

Both units produced a good level of proactive assessments tasking proforma (PATPs) (i.e., problem and target profiles) hampered by large IT changes leading into 2003 (i.e., a new Crime Report Information System (CRIS) release 10, CRIMINT level 2 server for level 2 cross-divisional crime). Changes from the OTIS to the AWARE system (the Met's new intranet network at the time), which made CRIS screen scrape technology used from 1996 to 2002 for recovering bulk volume crime forensic data for analysis redundant, to be replaced with search tools, which locked large databases because of multiple address fields in single data cells. This has only been resolved after 5 weeks when business objects training became available so that staff could overcome the problems with data fields. The CRIS changeover made data access impossible for whole sections of London throughout the summer of 2003. Hendon, in particular, where TP FIU was located, was the last site to be upgraded to CRIS release 10.

To add to the above, on 1 June 2003, the two FIUs covering North and South London respectively were split between territorial policing (TP) command and specialist crime (SC) command. This resulted in the two FIOs for North London having to cover all of London. The consequence of this was that the researcher and data-inputter had to be used as temporary FIOs, leaving one Blue Arrow temp as the data-inputter.

By November 2003, the two temporary FIOs had passed their boards, creating a situation where the same number of staff, now confirmed in different roles, were operating in the same unit. The only gain was a part-timer going full time as a data-inputter. The complement now is four FIOs and two data in-putters. In addition to the above, the FIU TP now also has an Operation Sapphire (sex crime) focus desk, which technically leaves the unit one FIO short.

THE FORENSIC INTELLIGENCE UNIT TP (FIU TP) IN THE NIM STRUCTURE

The Territorial Police (TP) FIU is a level 2 crime cross-border and cross-force intelligence unit covering TP forensic intelligence with respect to all volume crime in Metropolitan London.

The TP FIU links directly to the pan-London Territorial Police level 2 tasking and co-ordination group. This activity in intelligence-led tasking of the whole of TP fits into a 2-week cycle under the NIM and Metropolitan Police Policing Model.

Output from the unit in the form of PATPs is directed to the TP core desk for dissemination being put forward under the forensic escalator as defined in the NIM. In this activity, forensic services at this forum is represented by the Forensic Intelligence Unit manager.

With regard to the FIOs, they relate to intelligence link groups, which meet monthly in each quarter of London, where representatives from the Service Intelligence Unit (SCD10), the 32 London boroughs, British Transport Police (BTP), and adjoining county forces attend to receive and cascade intelligence. In addition, the FIOs attend monthly meetings with crime scene examiners from the boroughs of North and South London together with other specialist representatives from SCD4 (Fingerprint Bureau) and FSS (Forensic Science Service). These meetings are required under the NIM and Metropolitan Police Policing Model and provide useful intelligence about emerging problems as well as the opportunity to cascade intelligence research back to the field force for awareness in developing cases where appropriate.

FORENSIC INTELLIGENCE (FI) DEVELOPMENT ISSUES

TP FIU staff are actively engaged with all of Forensic Services in improving forensic intelligence techniques and products from the crime scene to custody suite to the courtroom. Forensic intelligence products resulting from liaison with Forensic Services include:

- New electronic Bigfoot shoe mark coding manual on the force intranet
- Improvements in forensic data handling and processing including the reformatting of extracted forensic data to make best use of CRIS release 10 data; the introduction of improved techniques

to merge data from multiple sources to enable the efficient integration of forensic data using a modern search engine

- Improved crime mapping techniques linked to the 'mathematics of scene linking' coupled with standard descriptors as universally used in forensic science reports and statements (i.e., 'highly significant, strongly supports, moderate support,' etc.) relating to assessments of the significance of evidence types found in clusters
- Quality assurance of and cleaning up of data to make it more useable and the reporting to line management of problems with individuals or groups involved

EMERGING DEVELOPMENT ISSUES 2003/2004

- National Automatic Fingerprint Identification System (NAFIS) developments—populating fingerprint databases resulting from intelligence information to enable:
  - Use of NAFIS modules for specific crime types or operations (starting with burglary artifice) as led by strategic/tactical assessments under the NIM
  - Use of remote fingerprint readers to support intelligence-led operations
  - The targeting of exhibits from defined method or crime types as led by intelligence to mini labs for fast tracking
- Training and development of CSIs around the input and use of intelligence with reference to the NIM and data standards through workshops, knowledge products, and practical assessments of the usefulness of forensic intelligence supplied by police personnel and police staff
- For forensic practitioners (level 3) attachments to the FIU (hands on) so that officers can appreciate in a practical sense the operation of the FIU and evaluate their own contribution
- The linkage with the FSD Footwear Development Project in supporting the project with real-time intelligence data
- Products and input to the Met model of the NIM covering the following:
  - NIM knowledge products
  - Intelligence data products
  - Knowledge products regarding best practice and data standards
- The expansion of the MPS forensic intelligence model to other forces, leading to national standards in forensic intelligence—the prize being a completely joined up national forensic intelligence database. (*This was not the case in 2003 and has only started to happen in 2010 with the introduction of the National Police*

Improvement Agency's National Footwear Reference Collection (NFRC), although DNA and fingerprint searching were already on a national basis in the UK.)

- The publishing in early 2004 of a paper on terminology in forensic intelligence to enable greater flexibility in data extraction for analytical purposes; gun crime, arson, sex offences, and serious crime are particularly bad in standardisation of terminology, where often different expressions are used to mean the same thing (e.g., 'fire started by unknown means, by unknown persons, setting fire to unknown material', etc.—should read, 'entered communal stairwell and set fire to rubbish bag against front door')
- Providing the forensic learning curve in the support of NIM objectives in the following areas:
  - The ability to quote the forensic probabilities around evidence types pertaining to an individual problem profile or suspect
  - The development of the abilities of the FIU TP to support the new intelligence-led tactical and co-ordination of level 2 crime in territorial policing
  - The ability of Forensic Services through intelligence to appreciate the availability of TP resources on a large scale to make best use of Forensic Services Directorate (FSD) products—for example, the burglary artifice project utilising the following strands:
    - The use of an NAFIS module to house the artifice suspects' database (*The facility, known as an Operational Response Database (ORD), was available but not taken up at the time by the Met Bureau, although the national operation 'Operation Liberal' against distraction burglary defined the use of ORDs as best practice in maximising the potential for identifying crime scene latent prints and some other UK police services used ORDs.*)
    - The use of remote fingerprint readers for screening persons stopped during operations against the artifice database created (*relatively new technology at the time but found in common use by many police services in 2011*)
    - The creation of Automatic Number Plate Reader (ANPR) data to populate that system with the details of artifice suspects' vehicles (*relatively new technology in 2003 but now used routinely by all UK police services*)
    - The use of the FIU TP artifice database to support police operations in real time
    - The use of TP resources (i.e., TP Core Desk, Territorial Support Group (TSG), and TP Crime Squad)

- The creation of special schemes on the computer aided despatch (CAD) system to target resources in real time and notify the FIU TP for immediate research against up-to-date intelligence data
- The link with borough forensic managers (BFMs) for CSI examinations in the golden hour to support operations
- The use of volume crime sequential fingerprint treatment and evidence recovery laboratories to fast-track exhibits recovered during operations

The important message is that the modern approach to distraction burglary artifice operations is only possible after the research and development of many strands of activity by Met Forensic Services and the FIU TP over the past 18 months. This project would have not have been conceived at this time were it not for the FIU input.

PERFORMANCE

Figures are for financial years April to March.

	Totals 2002 to end 2003	
2002/2003	789 linked scenes	260 Judicial disposals (JDs)
DNA	524 linked scenes	234 JDs
Totals	1,313 linked scenes	494 JDs
2003	1,072 linked scenes	242 JDs (April–November 2003)
DNA	520 linked scenes	100 JDs (April–November 2003)
Totals	1,592 linked scenes	342 JDs (April–November 2003)
	Totals since FIU North FIU TP started in April 2002 to end 2003	
Totals	2,905 linked scenes	836 Judicial disposals (JDs)

In addition, the TP FIU unit has provided:

- Linked scene DNA data for the force
- Bigfoot footwear scene data (cleaned up)
- Instrument-mark scene data
- Best advice knowledge products
- Online shoe mark coding (Bigfoot) manual
- Bespoke complete databases of priority crime types
- We have also conducted in 2002/2003 visits to every Operational Command Unit (OCU) regarding forensic intelligence awareness. During 2003 we are hosting visits from borough (divisional or precinct in other forces) teams and outside forces on a regular basis.

R Milne, 1 December 2003

A Case Study: The Barkingside
Jewellery Burglar, 2002–2006

On extracting the Met Police Bigfoot crime report shoe mark data covering 2002 to 2003, it was noticed that Reebok 49 (R49) shoe marks were present across a distinct geographical distribution in Barkingside Division in Redbridge Borough in Northeast London. In addition, the type of property stolen was high-value jewellery and the offender was committing offences on weekend days and bank holidays only, entering via the rear of properties by removing double glazed windows or using levers to force windows. The local crime analysts at the time had completely missed this series because their focus was on hot spots in a weekly cycle and they did not consider forensics other than latent print or DNA matches, which told them who was identified or positively linked unsolved scenes, so no real effort on their part was required. The cases in the series were lost to the analysts in the general volume of daily reported crime. This burglar was active only 6 months of every year and the temporal separation of the scenes led to this intelligence miss.

The original burglary series started in October 2002 and ceased in April 2003. My office created an intelligence problem profile in the form of an intelligence proactive assessment and input the profile into the force intelligence system CRIMINT. The series had ended in April 2003, so the intelligence assessment was intended at the outset to be of use if intelligence was received on a case in the series or if a biometric match was made so that investigators could make inroads into achieving more detections at a future interview stage with a suspect. However, in October 2004, the series started again.

In response, my unit updated the problem profile and updated the intelligence system and crime report links (called CRIS chains), and the case was evidenced via the CRIS chains and other records. The problem profile was acted on by Redbridge Borough Police, who increased high-visibility uniform patrols at weekends and bank holidays in an attempt to divert the offender away from the area. On a Sunday in November, which was a very cold day, the high-visibility patrols met on the corner of a street to receive sandwiches and coffee from a catering van arranged by the police management; whilst they stood eating their lunch, the burglar entered a house across the street from the rear and removed thousands of pounds worth of jewellery—so the high-visibility approach was a failure. The offender continued to leave Reebok 49 shoe marks and my unit thought that perhaps a plainclothes crime squad approach would have been a better tactic to stop suspects subtly and find the person with the shoes or in the act of committing an offence. I caused a geographical profile to be made using the now 2002 to 2004 data, for the burglar, as in the previous years, had commenced offending in October and ceased in April each following year.

The geographical profile showed a centre or node in Beehive Lane Redbridge to the west of the series, which revealed a distribution along a mile-long stretch of the Eastern Avenue always north of the main road, probably because of the better quality housing there. The offences thinned out the further east the series went. In Beehive Lane there is Redbridge underground tube station. What the geographical profile indicated was that this was likely to be a travelling offender, whose insertion point into the area was Redbridge underground tube station and the person was possibly not a neighbourhood marauder in that the suspect may not reside in the area.

In this case, what could be learned about the profile of this burglar in the area of the facets of the person's abilities, lifestyle, and general behaviours? In Chapter 3 (Figure 3.2), the concept of the Radex was outlined and mention made of the range of behaviours and methods that can be explored analytically with the technique of smallest space analysis. Here, the behaviour terms used to describe this burglar are 'conservative, tragedy, and adaptive' in that the offender exhibits facets of his behavioural makeup in that he has professional skills in breaking into dwellings and takes care to avoid leaving biometric evidence.

These skills enable another facet of the person's behaviour in that he is targeting high-value property of a monetary and personal value to the victims. The offender has regard for his victims only in that he considers their lifestyle in that he is maximising profit with little or no regard for them as persons. The offences are committed starting at the weekend when the Diwali 'Festival of Lights' is celebrated by people of Asian background between mid-October and November annually; the victims would be likely to remove high-value items from the bank or secure storage particularly over the weekend. The offender was unlikely to be alcohol or drug dependent as the temporal data indicated that offending was targeted at profit maximisation and not randomly—on the need, for example, to feed a drug habit. The fact that the offences ceased each April and restarted each October also indicated an offender's lifestyle arranged around personal lifestyle preferences.

In this case the offences continued into 2006, ending when the offender was arrested at his home in Southeast London in Croydon. When his property was searched, he had £50,000 in cash in his premises; the shoes were found and his activities supported a lifestyle whereby he had purchased a villa in the Caribbean, spending April to early October there every year supported on the proceeds of burglaries. He commuted by train to Redbridge, where there was a wealthy Asian population and targeted gold jewellery items. Forensic intelligence techniques can unravel this type of criminality, which day-to-day police tasking based on a weekly cycle may not perceive.

On the topic of where forensic intelligence best sits within policing, had there been a forensically aware analyst at Redbridge at the time of the Reebok

49 burglaries, the series would likely have been spotted. The use of my level 2 crime, forensic intelligence development unit, looking across borders, had the problem of introducing intelligence packages across different police business groups, who may or may not have acted upon them. The forensic intelligence unit was producing problem profiles daily and inputting them into the force intelligence system and, collectively, eventually thousands of cases were involved in a high number of packages. I had to task a researcher daily to check for detections on the crime report system against the proactive intelligence assessments on the CRIMINT system, for often officers would routinely use the research but not update my unit on results.

Thus, best advice is that forensic intelligence is best collected and disseminated directly from crime scenes at all crime levels at a divisional level rather than remotely at level 2. Those involved in sensitive enquiries can always locate forensic intelligence material across the whole of the police business group and still make use of it within a confidential environment. John Minderman's advice in Chapter 1 about forensics being like behaviours in that they are found at all levels in criminal investigation is key to getting forensic intelligence to work effectively.

Setting Up a Forensic Intelligence Capability

The key stages are to organise either through extra resources or by making use of existing resources and manpower-adequate facilities to enable the examination of most if not all suitable crime scenes. Once set up, the process of forensic intelligence needs managing, so even if existing officers or civilian staff are given role changes, management has to maintain an overview of the following issues:

- Forensic intervention rates
- Evidence recovery rates by crime type
- Number of forensic identifications accrued
- Number of forensic intelligence problem and target profiles
- Number of forensic strategies created in support of the policing organisation's strategic and tactical assessments
- Number of forensic intelligence logs on the police service intelligence system
- Monitoring of the use of the police service briefing and tasking system
- Forensic sampling rates from persons in police custody
- Provision of forensic science laboratory legacy data and the sharing of same

- Monitoring across all forensic submissions of the quality of laboratory reporting scientists' statements in the categories 'conclusive', 'strongly supports', 'moderately supports', 'weakly supports', and 'not matched'
- Number of detections accruing from the use of forensic intelligence
- Amount of cross-divisional and cross-force take-up of forensic intelligence packages

On the topic of managing forensic intelligence of importance is the issue of the perceptions of opinion-forming senior police about forensics. Those with extensive police service experience will note that often, in times of austerity budgets or national emergency, the forensic department can be depleted of its budget and resources by other business groups with respect to routine crime levels 1 and 2 casework and their budgets spent on patrolling officers' overtime, etc. In 2001 I had an allocation of funds for a content management system to enable the maintenance of the preceding bulleted points with ease. The budget was reallocated for police overtime following the 9/11 attack on the Twin Towers in New York. The words of John Minderman are worth noting at this point, for forensics, like behaviours, can occur at any crime level, thus restricting forensic examination services development and, in this case, preventing a facility to meet requirements that had to wait several years before data warehousing was introduced. However, in my view, content management would have provided the platform for a casework management system (see the Memex casework management system in Chapter 8).

The content management system was never purchased, although some years later development work was done on a forensic casework management system, which had still not yet been delivered to the Met Police in 2011. An issue I encountered in the Met Police experience was the lack of appreciation by rank-and-file officers of the volume of the contribution of forensic trace evidence (not latent prints and DNA) to casework. Between 2002 and 2004, the Northeast London forensic laboratory submissions were researched for volume crime case results for Northeast London; there were many glass, tool mark, shoe mark, and other trace evidence cases. In presenting forensic awareness lectures, I would project the 'Forident' spreadsheet covering literally hundreds of volume crime forensic cases filtered by evidence type and let the glass, shoe, and tool cases scroll round the screen whilst delivering the presentation. This usually caused looks of surprise in the audience and even more so when the data were filtered by offenders' names, where prolific offenders would have lists of cases with different evidence types matched to them across police divisions. It was common for the crime types and premises types to be similar types of targets against each prolific offender.

The casework in the spreadsheet consisted mainly of cases where offenders were avoiding leaving biometric evidence, thus causing investigators to resort to the extra effort of using trace evidence analysis to provide the evidence to advance the cases. The important issue is awareness, for part of the problems inhibiting the use of forensic intelligence possibly rests with ill-informed decision makers embedded in traditional restrictive working practices, although they may actually be unaware of the full potential of forensics and consequently do not champion change.

There was effort involved in producing the 'Forident' spreadsheet in that a person had to read copies of all of the laboratory statements to tabulate the results, which actually showed very well what was being paid for. The content management system or a casework management system—had they been purchased—would have enabled the access of these data without using an employee's time to do it. The case for information technology support in this area is self-explanatory. In Chapter 8, some technology products are covered that are capable of performing these functions and it is suggested that employing suitable systems actually saves more than their costs; they are definite enablers of forensic intelligence.

Forensic Intelligence in Arson Investigation

The inclusion of a section of arson crime is potentially a useful exercise, for amongst types of crime, arson is often the most difficult with which to deal; yet, compared to serial burglars, for example, the population of serial arsonists is quite small. Unlike burglaries, however, arson scenes are often scenes of severe damage with few clean surfaces to find latent prints, and fire makes the recovery of other trace evidence challenging, to say the least. Probably more importantly from the point of view of this text, the outline of the approach used in the development project to look at arson can be mirrored in any crime type, providing that the forensic intelligence enabling features are in place.

The Directorate of Forensic Services in the Met Police spent a considerable amount of time and money on fire investigation training to try to increase the then low 3% detection rate for the crime type in the first few years of this century. In response to the effort by the Forensic Services Directorate, I worked in partnership with Peter Mansi, the head of fire investigation, London Fire Brigade (LFB). Gary Pugh, the Met Police Forensic Services director, had funded the staff (continual professional development; CPD) training and introduced Peter Mansi and his team to my forensic intelligence desk in the Met Intelligence Bureau (MIB). At the time, the MIB had not declared arson crime as a strategic issue and did not task my desk to look at the crime type.

As the forensic intelligence manager working for the MIB but also involved in the Forensic Services Directorate's development of forensic intelligence,

I had access to all of the Met's arson crime data and global sets of forensic recoveries across all crime types up to the categories 'confidential' but not 'secret'. This capability was enabled by the forensic examination field force having a high intervention rate and recording their findings on the Met crime report system as well as recording intelligence logs on the CRIMINT system where appropriate. Through Peter Mansi, I now had access to the London Fire Brigade's Real Fire Database. To set these data sets in a concise setting, the Met Police recorded allegations of arson where, under the UK Home Office recording rules, there was a defined victim or loser. The London Fire Brigade Real Fire Database recorded deliberate fire setting, where there may or may not have been a defined loser or victim (e.g., a rubbish fire in the street or setting fire to an abandoned motor vehicle with no registered owner).

When both data sets were compared in 2004, the Met recorded about 3,000 arson crimes a year and, at its peak at the same time, the LFB Real Fire Database was recording 26,000 deliberate fire settings. As part of a national arson reduction project, under the Office of the Deputy Prime Minister, the LFB was involved in the programme with arson control officers assigned to each quarter of London to work with suspected, mainly young fire setters, to make them aware of the possible consequences of their actions. The merging of both organisations' data sets did not take a lot of effort and was accomplished by one person as a part of daily duties, so the cost to have these data available for research and analysis was minimal. The data structure is shown in Figure 7.2.

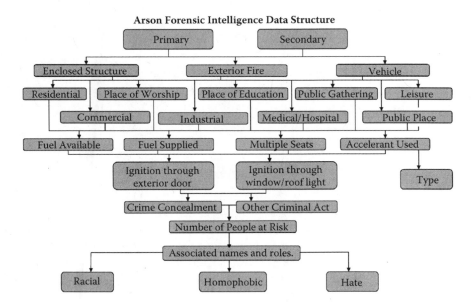

Figure 7.2 An arson crime partnership data structure.

The Arson Crime Partnership Data Structure Outline

The first two main categories covering primary and secondary fires are taken from the UK Home Office classification:

- **Primary fires** are fires in dwellings and commercial properties, and high-value fires.
- **Secondary fires** are viewed as rubbish fires in the street, etc., although perhaps setting fire to a public walkway over a main road would be classified as secondary, but the value lost could be over half a million pounds.

These primary classifications were used by the LFB Real Fire Database. Following on from the two main categories there are three main types of generic fire locations:

- **Enclosed structures** are fires in any form of building.
- **Exterior fires** are fires in the open (e.g., wheelie bin fires, fires set to vegetation, etc.).
- **Vehicle fires** include road vehicles, boats, aircraft, or any form of transport.

The data are then divided into the types of enclosed structures, open exterior areas, and vehicles. These data are crime report and real fire database data and serve to filter large data sets down when looking for patterns of deliberate fire setting.

The next level of data is defined by the results of the examinations of the fire scenes by fire investigators (CSIs), for it is only by recording the forensic findings of these examinations that further filtering of research can take place. The forensic examinations can ascertain whether or not the offender brought his or her own fuel to start the fire (fuel supplied) or just used materials lying around at the scene (fuel available) as fuel to start the fire in the categories:

- **Fuel available**
- **Fuel supplied**
- **Single or multiple fire seats**
- **Accelerant(s) used and type(s)**
- **Other forensic evidence found** (e.g., DNA, latent prints, forensic marks (shoes/tools), contact trace such as fibres, wick material, unusual flammable liquid mixes, etc.)

The next set of categories is defined by the examinations of the fire scenes ascertaining the methods by which the fire was introduced. Here, there is some flexibility, for offenders will innovate on how they start fires, sometimes revealing their signature—for example,

- **Via door (e.g., letterbox or breaking glass)**
- **Via a window—forced or glass broken or via an open window**

The next level to consider is there another motivation for the fire to have been started, which is normally elucidated from the details of the police and forensic investigation where an attempt to conceal another crime using fire may be revealed—for example,

- **Crime concealment**
- **Other criminal act, etc.**

The next level is to record the number of people at risk, for terrorists would perhaps attack targets where the number of casualties could be high:

- **Number of people at risk**
- **The roles of the people at risk**
- **Other motivations (i.e., racial, homophobic, or hate crime)**

Some Arson Casework Examples

At the onset of the partnership with the London Fire Brigade, I met with Peter Mansi and agreed to open a partnership desk in the Forensic Intelligence Unit. Peter and other external stakeholders could actually work at the desk and benefit directly by having research, analytical, and intelligence products in the forms of problem profiles and target profiles created—instead of the traditional civil service method of conducting meetings with minutes where resulting action may or may not have taken place and issues left unresolved. Some examples of casework are included next.

Exterior and Vehicle Fire Setting by Youths in North London

An arson reduction officer, Claire Purton (later to become Mrs Mansi), called the Forensic Intelligence Desk to raise the issue of a 'Crime Stoppers' intelligence item sent in by residents on a housing estate in North London. It appeared that a group of children led by one particular individual were suspected of setting fire to bins and vehicles in the street around the estate. Upon analysis of the combined Met/LFB exterior fires and vehicle data in the area, a rectangular shaped mapping of exterior fire scenes was revealed. Each leg of the rectangular mapping went by the months; for example, the January fire setting was at 2 o'clock on the map, the February fire setting at 11 o'clock, and so on.

In addition, each fire scene was adjacent to a dead end of a street where the scene as an escape route could be left by a public footpath with no vehicular access. This was evidentially not a random distribution of fire scenes; further, although most of the exterior fires were not in the Met's crime report system, the vehicle fires on the system showed flammable liquid (gasoline)-assisted fires in the vehicles' passenger compartments—not accidental engine or electrical fires. An intelligence problem profile in support of the Crime Stoppers data was produced and Claire, with local police officers, interviewed the young suspects under the arson control scheme remit and the series stopped.

The Islington Traveller—'Fuel Available'—Arsonist

The Met Forensic Intelligence Desk received an e-mail from a London Fire Brigade fire investigator with anecdotal evidence to the effect that in the north part of Islington Borough there had been an increase of deliberate fire setting whereby bin bags of refuse had been piled up against dwelling walls and under vehicles and then set alight. Because a high proportion of the fires were not in the Met Police crime report system (owing to these being exterior fires in the street outside), the police data had not shown the series. The combined data sets showed a dispersed cluster of fires fitting the 'exterior fire', 'vehicle fire', and 'fuel available' categories—ranging from exterior fires with no defined loser or victim recorded on the crime report system up to police-investigated fires in the category of 'being reckless as to endanger life'.

One of the larger fire scenes consisted of four sequentially parked vehicles being set alight by means of naked flames applied to plastic sacks full of refuse placed under the vehicles. To compound the problem, the vehicles were parked adjacent to a filling station, causing operational problems for fire fighters attending the scene and the evacuation of residents at risk. The fires fitting the profile were mainly started in the late evening after dark. As the fires were increasing in frequency and size with definite risk to life, an intelligence problem profile was created with a forensic strategy to ensure that police scenes of crime personnel attended to examine the scenes even if the cases were not suitable for recording on the police crime report system (i.e., exterior fires with no defined victim, which were normally just recorded on the LFB Real Fire Database). This activity could produce a forensic intelligence hit to upgrade the problem profile to a target or subject profile with named suspects for investigation and/or surveillance.

A briefing slide was placed on the Met Police MetBats briefing and tasking system to improve awareness of the series, which also had an intelligence log placed on the CRIMINT intelligence system. A few days after the posting of the problem profile, a crime scene examiner attended the scene of a 'being reckless to endanger life' fire, recorded in the Met CRIS system, outside a ground floor apartment in the geographical cluster area, where plastic refuse sacks had been placed under the victim's bedroom window and then set alight. The victim awoke to the sound of her windows cracking; because the fanlight had been open, the plume of flame from the burning sacks had been able to enter her bedroom and set fire to the curtains. On making her escape, she saw a man in his late teens outside the window. The man ran away and got into a small black hatchback car and sped away from the scene.

Fire fighters attended with a crime scene examiner. On examining the scene, a disposable gas cigarette lighter was found directly adjacent to the pile of burned sacks. The lighter was exhibited and submitted to the forensic science laboratory and a full DNA profile was found on the lighter's flint wheel. The profile was matched to a 19-year-old man who lived some miles away in East London. Unfortunately, because the lighter was a moveable exhibit, the Crown Prosecution Service did not wish to proceed with a prosecution, but we had our intelligence hit. The case was referred to the borough intelligence unit where the suspect lived, which tasked a field officer to establish the suspect's lifestyle and to carry out discrete enquiries and some directed surveillance. The suspect did indeed have a small black hatchback car and purchased illicit drugs in a nearby High Street where there were reported refuse sacks, fuel available, and fires behind the shops in the same location.

The details of the suspect's car were entered into the intelligence system and another briefing slide created indicating the car to be of interest to police and its details uploaded onto the Automatic Number Plate Reader (ANPR) System so that, upon this vehicle appearing in front of Met patrol cars, the ANPR system would alert police. The consequence of this activity was that the vehicle was stopped by police some 10 miles away from the suspect's home address with other passengers, who were found to be in possession of street robbery property from a robbery offence committed only minutes before; they were successfully prosecuted, receiving custodial sentences. The fire series stopped and it was discovered that the suspect went to Islington regularly in the evenings to visit a girlfriend and it is believed that on his way home, for kicks, he set fires. The disparate nature of the mapped series it was believed was a result of the offender not being on foot but selecting his opportunities to indulge in fire setting whilst cruising in the locality.

The forensic intelligence arson database gave a view of potential developing risks across Metropolitan London and made it relatively easy to relate hard evidence biometric and other forensic recoveries, including mobile phone data, to potentially linked fire series. Data from the LFB Real Fire Database set the police arson data within the context of the whole distribution of deliberate fire setting scenes across the city.

The Broadlove Lane Neighbourhood Arsonist

Another case referred by arson reduction officers was the Broadlove Lane series of deliberate fires and hoax emergency services calls that, up to 2007, were plaguing this location. Indeed, the Mayor of London's office was aware of the problems on this estate. In the police arson case data, there were only a few recorded arson cases, but one address in particular had had two arson attacks where flammable liquid had been poured through the letter box and the premises set alight. By sheer luck, the victim had not been injured or killed on each occasion, but a mobile phone call had been made to emergency services at each arson attack.

There were many exterior fires to rubbish bins on the estate and hoax emergency calls in the LFB data. To the residents of the estate, there was a constant feeling of fear because fires would be seen outside from time to time and frequently fire engines would arrive in response to the hoax calls. The LFB real fire data had records of the mobile phone numbers used in the hoax calls. An analyst was tasked to research those telephone numbers and the IMEI numbers of the mobile phones and the various sim cards used in two telephones. This led to a crime report system search to see if any of these telephone numbers were in the crime records data. It transpired that, in 2002, a person was recorded on an assault crime report in central London who gave one of those telephone numbers, claiming to be a victim at the time. The address given in the 2002 report did not exist, but if it had been real it would have been next door to the most arson-attacked apartment on the estate. The individual did in fact live elsewhere on the estate and a warrant was secured to search his apartment. In the apartment the two mobile phones used in the hoax calls and in some of the emergency calls reporting arson attacks were found in the suspect's possession and the cases were solved.

The Oxford Street Department Store Arsonist

In mid-May 2007, Peter Mansi, the officer in charge of London Fire Brigade's Fire Investigation Team, called to use the partnership desk in the MIB Forensic Intelligence Desk. We routinely searched the forensic intelligence joint fire and arson data for links, clusters, and possible emerging threats. Using the 'commercial premises' and 'number of people potentially at risk' search parameters, it was noted that in some years there was normally one fire in a central London department store of an accidental nature, and, in some years, none at all. From April into May 2007 there had been seven arson attacks in department stores in the Oxford Street area committed whilst the stores were open and full of customers. To have this many arsons against the low background arson crime rate was in my view significant enough; however, the arsons being committed whilst the stores were full of customers was quite worrying. Most arsonists attack premises after closing when they are empty of people and quiet, so these arsons were viewed by my desk as a high-risk item.

An intelligence package was sent to the affected police boroughs but it was rejected as a series because different methods had been used to set the fires. However, the analysts with no scenes of crime forensics experience had not appreciated the fact that all of the methods were designed to create a time delay, indicating that an offender of some experience and possessing an element of planning was at work. Collectively, from the statistical point of view, the rareness of each factor in combination resulted in a probability calculation indicating that it was most improbable that this was just a random coincidental collection of offences. Thus, whilst the borough staff should have been scanning CCTV to look for the suspect, the case was instead brought back to the Forensic Intelligence Desk.

The methods used at the arsons were by using cotton wool and super-glue to create spontaneous combustion (time delay) to set fire to fire lighters placed in clothing on racks or on other fuel. The arsonist used batteries and steel wool (short time delay) and then lighter fuel as a flammable liquid to spread the fire rapidly onto other suitably flammable surfaces. The series continued into June 2007, when, on 15 June, the arsonist set fire to the dress circle curtains in the National Theatre on London's South Bank of the Thames. He then proceeded across the Thames to the Embankment, where he entered the Savoy Hotel to case the ninth floor bedding store. We know this because he was filmed on CCTV furtively walking back to the corridor a few times before entering the store and then leaving quickly. Within seconds, the bedding store was on fire. Fortunately, security staff discovered the blaze and tried to put it out, but had to call the London Fire Brigade.

On replaying the video, security staff discovered the actions of the arsonist. He left the Savoy Hotel and proceeded to Evans Clothing Store of Oxford Street where, using cotton wool and superglue as a time delay, he placed fire barbecue lighters in the pockets of a row of hanging acrylic garments and started a rapidly developing fire. Fortunately, the store sprinkler system put out the fire. All these attacks took place whilst the attacked premises were full of hundreds of people.

I visited the London Forensic Science Service laboratory Fire Investigation Unit and compared notes with the fire scientists. They had remains of fire lighters from some of the scenes, which had traces of a resin in them as a physical linking factor. With some urgency, the Forensic Intelligence Desk posted images of the arsonist on the MetBats briefing system so that all police coming on duty could view the pictures. A woman police officer in Wimbledon called in to say she believed the person was a man called Maccini, whom she had arrested the week before for shoplifting cans of lighter fuel from a shop. Police from Marylebone Division went immediately with a warrant to Maccini's home and he was found coming out of the front door with a backpack containing all the items required to set all the fires found at the arson series. Further, he had a digital camera with images of the attacked premises in it.

The officer in the case was contacted and advised about the National Theatre arson, which unlike the other fires, was not in his jurisdiction. He went to the theatre and recovered a high-definition video showing the same individual entering and leaving the theatre just before the fire broke out. The lesson here is that repeat occurrences of evidence types and methods in defined geographical areas can be significant and at least indicate that further work in researching an apparent problem should be done. This applies to coded and/or measured forensic evidence types as well as methods, even if those factors may seem common. It is only through research that these factors can be seen to be common, for the most common feature in one area can be rare elsewhere and, if found in a cluster, why is the 'common factor' not spread uniformly elsewhere?

This simple concept from personal experience can possibly not be understood by some crime analysts who have never been exposed to real crime examination, forensic, or investigative work. The danger is that major links can be missed if assumptions are made and the facts not properly checked. This was the case with the department store arsonist, for his actions were not perceived at all by the borough intelligence units, who were in denial. The issue of the IA3 position of the analysts (see Chapter 3, Figure 3.6) in the intelligence bureau raised its head with this arson series, for arson crime was not a strategic crime type in the then current strategic intelligence assessment, so questions were raised as to why the Forensic Intelligence Desk was looking at the problem as the focus was to look only at strategic tasked research. I argued that attempted murder by arson and endangering life fell within the concept of emerging threats, for which the UK NIM has a catchall feature to cover activity in this area. However, it all depends how strong the researchers are in standing up to performance managers; otherwise, the research would possibly not be done until after a tragic event.

A further spin-off of the LFB Met forensic intelligence partnership was the creation of the 'eFIT One' electronic means of notification of deliberate fire setting. This project was funded and delivered in time but stalled because no CAD desk could agree to receive the eFIT Ones. eFIT was designed to replace carbonated paper forms, which had suffered from a high percentage of the forms never making it to any investigator's desk.

Because the London Fire Brigade Fire Investigation Team members were stakeholders in the arson intelligence partnership, they introduced Met CSIs and forensic intelligence staff to the International Association of Arson Investigators (IAAI). The Met Directorate of Forensic Services bought a corporate membership for the directorate's staff so that they could benefit from the CPD provided by the IAAI-UK chapter.

The 10-Point Plan for Arson Investigation

As a contribution to the partnership, in 2005, Peter Mansi, an IAAI-certified fire investigator, produced a 10-point plan for the investigation of arson. In my opinion, the plan was a significant advance in methodology in dealing with arson crime and embraces forensic intelligence as a concept.

1. Identify the geographical area and time frame to be covered.
2. Obtain and select appropriate fire service incident recording information.
3. Obtain and select the police crime report and intelligence system information.
4. Plot all data (police service blue dots and fire service data red dots— both data coincident locations as green dots) on a map.
5. Visit incident locations, make sketches, take photographs (gather copies of existing scene photographs, notes, etc.) and obtain local intelligence.
6. Identify telephone numbers (especially first callers).
7. Conduct case conference(s)—internal/external.
8. Develop or adjust action plan; set timeframe; set 'milestones'.
9. Assess action plan at milestone dates.
10. Close case or revert back to stage 3 for updates and stage 8 to reassess the action plan.

The IAAI is unique in giving aspiring individuals access to training all the way from basic evidence technician through to fire investigation technician through to a US standard recognised accreditation of certified fire investigator. On retirement from the Met Police in 2008, I became the IAAI regional representative for London, for in 30 years of my service I routinely examined fire scenes and wished to give time to improve my own expertise and that of other members.

Forensic Intelligence Possibilities in Dealing with Illicit Drug Marketing

Reproduced later is a paper written following a drugs forensic intelligence workshop in 2006 called 'Tell Us Something We Do Not Know Already'. Julian King, who managed the Specialised Crime Forensic Intelligence Unit, Met Police, and I jointly produced the workshop. A forensic intelligence analysis was carried out on the test purchases of class A (hard) drugs in Southwest London over a period of several months. Dean Ames, a forensic scientist at the UK FSS Gov Co specialising in comparing drug batches for impurities, packaging, and other factors, compared the test purchase drug batches. The resulting data gave forensic intelligence links with batches of linked substances being traded by different dealers. The journey to crime for these individuals was mapped and dealing clusters analysed. The police culture at the time was to make test purchases, intercept 'fast parcels', and focus on single case-by-case prosecutions. There was a perception by police (not shared by me) that all forensic results were reactive after the fact and therefore 'information' rather than 'intelligence'.

My view was that the big picture was being missed at the time and forensic opportunities compromised by the current working practices of both the police and Customs (HMRC). The Customs focus was on performance management; instead of routine forensic sequential treatments being carried out, in many instances the packaging and drugs were destroyed. I sought a budget to fund the FSS Gov Co drugs intelligence linking products in order to link larger police and Customs cases and to seek the search internationally of cross-border AFIS and DNA databases. Further, I wanted to cover this approach nationally to unravel the links between criminal networks. Two problems were evident at the time:

- Police working practices focussing just on test purchases and parcel intercepts as single cases in the main
- A fascination with evidential drug testing (EDIT) kits in order to save money

The postal sources of the drug 'fast' parcels were of extreme interest and I wished to treat the packaging materials fully sequentially and have the FSS Gov Co carry out comparative analysis of the recovered drugs. Likewise, I desired the comparative analysis of the test purchase drugs. I further needed to relate Customs seizures from the same sources outside the UK subjected to comparative forensic intelligence analysis by the FSS Gov Co and then make use of the resulting information and intelligence.

It should be pointed out that EDIT kits are extremely useful in screening suspected drug substances found with suspected persons but their exclusive use, unless the suspect challenges the kit result, compromises the work on upstreaming forensic intelligence casework. Further, there was a perception amongst some Forensic Services Directorate colleagues that the drug linking work was not so much science but rather more of an art, so there was resistance to funding the laboratory work. Intelligence forensics is unlike that required for absolute proof in a court of law, but its prudent use can point investigations in the right direction, where it can significantly increase the likelihood that hard evidence will be found. Forensic intelligence can inject the elements of truth into the casework, enabling detection, prosecution, and the shutting down of networks even thousands of miles away.

Indeed, prior to my retirement in 2008 from the Met Police, the FSS Gov Co kindly worked on two cases for my unit. The first case linked heroin seizures from harmful London gangs to an ethnic criminal network importing the drug into the UK. The links were between the gangs in two UK cities and led to a UK export link to a European criminal network. The second case linked two fast parcel cases to two Customs concealment seizures at UK airports. SOCA carried out an operation in the source country, shutting down the drugs laboratory, and the forensics identified a person who was actually a British subject with DNA and fingerprints in the UK systems. He had travelled to that country to set up the drug production and trafficking routes, using all of the techniques of fast parcels, concealments, drug mules, etc. to get the product from the laboratory to the dealers. The forensic treatments were key to providing evidence; the other result would have been arrests of just a few drug smugglers and some unmarried mother receiving parcels.

Another inhibiting factor to this work was the different descriptors and terminology used by the two main UK forensic science providers (FSPs)— although they were most helpful and agreed to populate a common spreadsheet to record the data that the Forensic Intelligence Unit required. A version of the spreadsheet is provided on the CD ROM with this book. In my last case—alas, unfinished before retirement—I collected reference samples from one FSP to compare with casework submitted to another FSP for casework upsteaming purposes.

I wrote the following paper in 2007. It explores these issues and is included as background. The original research used Professor David Canter's interactive offender profiling software and the technique of a form of cluster analysis called 'smallest space analysis' and was used to visualise the links between locations of linked substances with the journeys to crime of individuals dealing linked substances. I thought that it surprised senior Met officers, who intimated that they would champion the approach but did not actually follow through with support at that time or later.

A Paper Aimed at Exploring the Role of Forensic Intelligence in Dealing with Illicit Drug Production and Marketing

THE AIMS OF THE PAPER

The aim of this paper is to outline the means by which analysis of impurities in and comparison of drug batches, combined with data around packaging, concealments, and importation source data, can be used to 'upstream' casework by forensic intelligence research and analysis. The concept of standardising the terminology and core processes of different forensic science laboratories in different countries as an enabling factor for forensic intelligence applications is discussed.

Objectives of the paper are

- To identify that which we do not already know using forensic data/information as a catalyst
- To identify the higher levels of networks involved in the supply/distribution of illicit drugs through the mapping, analysis, development, and investigation of forensic data/information across national and international borders
- To explore a forensic and intelligence-led model for processing such intelligence at a strategic level
- To develop a forensic tactical option to disrupt organised criminal networks involved in the supply/distribution of illicit drugs
- To extend operations nationally and internationally by forensic means with our partners in law enforcement, Customs, SOCA, and Interpol to produce prevention strategies in identifying and disrupting criminal networks in other countries through the use of forensic-linked drug casework

Drug organised-crime network identifiers using practical observation and recording methods allied with forensic examinations can accomplish

- Fingerprint identifications and links
- DNA matches and links
- Drug type
- Drug purity
- Drug profile
- Weights
- Method of concealment
- Type(s) of concealment, packaging, markings, logos, and imprints
- Fingerprints
- DNA
- Prisoner debriefs
- Covert human information sources (CHIS)
- Field intelligence officers (FIOs)
- Test purchase operations
- Controlled deliveries
- Financial investigation
- Telecommunications and computer analysis

PRACTICAL WAYS AHEAD TO UTILISE ILLICIT DRUG FORENSIC DATA TO TAKE CASEWORK UP TO HIGHER LEVELS IN THE DRUG DISTRIBUTION CHAIN

In general terms, because of the toxic nature of drugs, users require small amounts, so generally depending on the drug type, literally thousands of deals can be sold from a kilogram of a drug in bulk. The heroin distribution model, as an example, has far fewer bulk wholesale dealers trading in very large amounts than street dealers, so one person or criminal network with a few kilograms can be supplying literally hundreds of dealers and thousands of user deals. The model is therefore pyramidal in style.

Clearly, for each kilogram distributed there are a limited number of dealers with 100 grams or more, although at the bottom of the supply chain there can be thousands of users with small amounts. Clearly, in this scenario some progress can be made if effort is concentrated on the limited number of persons found to be in possession of larger quantities of drugs, which have some physical and scientific link between them. Here, correlation between the scientific, physical links and various intelligence sources available can offer opportunities to take casework up to the next level and for international law enforcement agencies to produce useful packages for operational tasking. A further facility potentially offered is to use this approach to try and identify and close down criminal networks who are exporting drugs in bulk by forensic examination of the materials used in the forensically linked cases, the recovery of finger marks, DNA, and the use of the properties of the physical materials mixed in the drugs and wrappings themselves.

Further, through the use of modern geographical information system (GIS) techniques, it is possible to use GIS techniques to monitor and track patterns of dealing to street level, up through linked casework to larger distribution areas extending nationally to internationally if required and, at the same time, to identify the journey to crime of both dealers and users to identify clusters of activity. With GIS techniques, we can relate the closeness of dealer arrests to scientific links and their journey to crime and distil, from a vast amount of data, manageable numbers of persons for further research in the telecommunications, financial, surveillance, or other areas. Spin-offs from this approach offer suspects for fingerprint comparisons or DNA swabbing or the opposite opportunities of expanding forensic identifications to achieve sanctioned detections.

Here, by viewing the drug problem from the commodities viewpoint, we can see the big picture wherein single operations sit. Single ownership of the problem carries the risk of not seeing where research sits in the big picture and, here, teamwork with law enforcement agencies working on local issues can, for example, feed into the EU intelligence resources to give us a picture from the street level upward. The ability for each forensic science laboratory to feed and receive from an EU central drug trafficking database would be a real, live process (Figure 7.3).

GEOGRAPHICAL INFORMATION SYSTEMS AS A FORENSIC INTELLIGENCE RESEARCH TOOL

Modern police radio networks give law enforcement agencies access to accurate GIS location data for each drug recovery event and locations covering the home locations and activity areas of offenders linked to those drug recovery events. As an industry standard GIS system, the facility can zoom out from street level to nodes outside the starting country and zoom in to another location in another country, but only if there are compatible data rather like 'Google Earth'.

Further, through the use of GIS with the Metropolitan Police Service (MPS)/Liverpool University 'Interactive Offender Profiling System' (IOPs), the system exists to relate the times, locations, drug type, forensic profile, wrappings type, etc. to reveal the extent and development of drug dealing and to study the whole drug problem as a commodity market with relative ease. IOPs has built into its programming a geocode loader, which accepts most standard geocoding formats. Further, the technique called smallest space analysis is built in, enabling multivectored correlation between geographic, temporal, and other facts data at the click of a button. The correlated data can then be put back as geographical data with the case facts attached from the data.

Maps were made using Prof David Canter's Interactive Offender Profiling System (IOPs) in 2006 for a forensic intelligence drugs workshop. Here, several weeks of class 'A' drug data were mapped around arrests of possessors and dealers together with their journey to crime from home, and the locations of prolific persistent offenders (PPOs) and bail hostels were related to the class 'A' drug recovery clusters revealed in the mappings covering *all* of Southwest London. Mappings of subjects

---

Figure 7.3 *(See facing page)* Diagram showing inputs and outputs in linked drug cases from the Forensic Intelligence Desk to the MIB Drugs Desk. (R Milne, 2007.) SOCA: UK Serious and Organised Crime Agency; SCD7: Specialist Crime Directorate drugs (flying squad); BOCU: borough operational command units; HMRC: Her Majesty's Revenue and Customs; C/deliveries: controlled drug deliveries (fast parcels, etc.); CHIS: covert human information supplier (informant); Forensic provider: forensic science laboratories; CRIMINT: Crime Intelligence System; STOPS: police 'stops' database of stopped persons; TIMS: telecoms data; FIU: Financial Intelligence Unit; SCD3: Specialist Crime Directorate Middle Market Drugs.

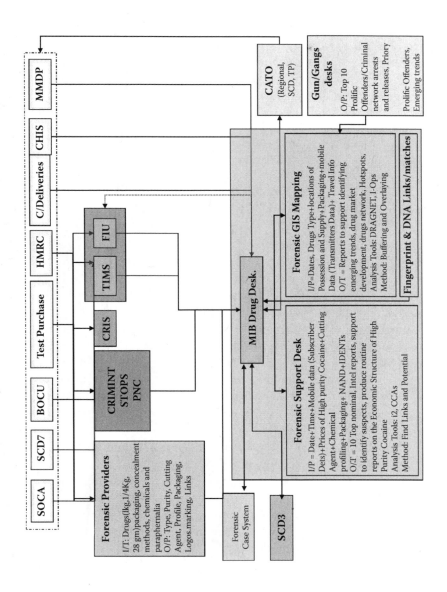

Figure 7.3

dealing linked substances across the MPS were made and the GIS system, like Google earth, can zoom in to individual property level in the street

A case was covered where four suspects were selling class A drugs on the same estate and met under a row of trees at the end of a street. The drugs being dealt were linked to a larger batch in South London, which in turn was linked to a seizure in Dover and a large seizure in Birmingham, England. The questions raised were about the relationships between these individuals and, if telephone/computer analysis were done, could this lead us to third parties who may not even have Criminal Record Office (CRO) records?

On a larger scale, linked substances were shown in mappings with the journey to crime of the arrested persons. By applying 500 metre buffer zones around clusters, the locations of PPOs can be related to the dealing clusters and, likewise, the journey to crime to these clusters together with telephone data, etc.

RISK ASSESSMENT COVERING THE CONSEQUENCES OF NOT STANDARDISING FORENSIC ANALYSIS DESCRIPTORS IN ILLICIT DRUG CASEWORK

A forensic intelligence strategy based on covering drug dealing as a large international commodity market will only succeed if there is a standard approach to data inputs from the forensic service provider (FSP) laboratories. Currently, this is not the case. From the current Metropolitan Police experience, half of London is serviced for drug analysis by the LGC laboratory and the other half by the FSS laboratory. Further, both FSPs provide spreadsheet data covering cutting agents and wrappings data with physical appearance notes. Both spreadsheets are different and two separate data sets have to be examined with difficulty in establishing crossovers between the two FSP casework sets. An example of a spreadsheet designed to accommodate input from different laboratories' legacy data is included on the CD ROM.

The introduction of low-cost evidential drug identification test (EDIT) procedure street kits may lose us the wrappings and appearance of tablets, data, etc., unless steps are taken to recover this information. Nevertheless, at least the kit reaction identifying the basic class of drug can be recorded and the arrest location and other data still can give us cluster information to relate to larger seizures in the possession of dealers. In this area, the MPS policy in using EDIT would not be affected by the changes being sought by implementing a forensic strategy for utilising forensic drug links to advance casework up the distribution chains set up by criminal networks.

In a multinational effort to combat illicit drug criminality, the plain risk is that, without standardisation of forensic services, attempts to link casework are and will be restricted across the EU. This situation is not conducive to the current attempts at EU teamwork in this area to combat the illegal drugs problem.

Items that have to be in place to enable forensic intelligence in tracking drugs across Police and national borders include:

- Standardisation of accredited forensic laboratory procedures (i.e., same descriptors and similar operating procedures)
- The nomination of one scientific organisation to referee the processes
- Standardisation of documentation and database products so that they are immediately recognisable as such
- The development and mentoring of the setting up of forensic intelligence facilities in law enforcement agencies to interface and convert the forensic information into intelligence products for action
- The setting up of one forensic science provider to receive reference samples of larger seizures dealt with by accredited laboratories

CONCLUSION

Countries are being targeted by criminal networks illegally importing and distributing literally tons of illicit drugs. The approach of being able to visualise the illicit drugs market combined with forensic intelligence within the current investigative effort in a more joined up and aggressive approach is required to track criminal networks back to sources. Funding this proposal will give us links between persons caught with larger amounts of illicit drugs to follow further investigation and forensic examinations of wrapping materials to enable the identification of offenders internationally at the sources of the drug distribution chains. The present situation in dealing with the problem plainly does not readily offer these options.

R Milne, 2007

This report, with a PowerPoint presentation, was discussed with the UK Serious and Organised Crime Agency (SOCA) emerging developments officer visiting my office in 2007. The visit was in response to a desire by SOCA management to reintroduce forensic intelligence because it had been sidelined by the organisation that had preceded the setting up of SOCA. The emerging developments officer took the concept to SOCA, who produced their own version of an operation to upsteam casework using forensic intelligence as 'Operation Endorse'—which, through SOCA's efforts—had a considerable effect on the UK's cocaine trade.

Summary

This chapter included the following:

- Examples of forensic intelligence applied to different crime types
- The importance of 'service champions' in delivering forensic intelligence
- The effective use of digital technology
- A forensic intelligence briefing paper from 2003—setting up forensic intelligence units
- The forensic intelligence unit in the NIM structure
- Forensic intelligence development issues
- A case study—burglary
- Setting up a forensic intelligence capability
- Forensic intelligence arson case studies
- A 10-point plan for arson investigation
- Forensic intelligence possibilities in dealing with illicit drugs markets
- A 2007 paper exploring the role of forensic intelligence in dealing with illicit drug production and marketing
- Practical ways to utilise illicit drugs forensic data
- Geographical information systems as a forensic intelligence research tool
- Items that have to be in place to enable forensic intelligence in tackling drug cases across national and international boundaries

The Need for Investment in Information Technology

8

Introduction

Throughout the experience of exploring possibilities in providing effective forensic intelligence, the most frustrating issue from my point has been the funding and procurement of bespoke information technology products to deal with footwear and tool mark evidence. The processing of latent prints and DNA is already at an excellent standard but, as previously discussed, without the recovery of other forms of forensic evidence, detections are lost and, worse still, skilled offenders are allowed to become prolific nuisances. If there is a main message this book conveys, however, it is that unless the actual skill base and quality methods are used by the forensic field force in the search for and recovery of forensic evidence, the investment in any digital system will not be realised to its full potential. Indeed, the new system may merely highlight deficiencies in the working practices areas. To compound matters, if those managing crime analysis have no real understanding of forensic intelligence, then their work will also be weakened and to some extent compromised.

That said, included in this chapter are some examples of useful systems where the manufacturers did openly provide material for publication. These are easily available and, with the proper business and working practices, can support and transform the results with respect to linking softer forms of trace evidence. With respect to footwear evidence, the systems covered are Foster & Freeman Ltd Shoeprint Image Capture and Retrieval (SICAR), a well established system used in many countries.

The system Treadmark is produced and marketed by Crime Scene Examination Products (Florida) Inc. and Crime Scene Investigation Equipment Ltd. UK. Treadmark is a shoe mark coding, identification, measurement, and searching system. Both these systems are described and casework examples are given.

It is worth noting that the only reason for many police services achieving little with footwear evidence is entirely because of their reluctance to invest in one of these systems. By putting nothing in place, the entire process of screening offenders and linking crime scenes is made difficult and compromised with manual processing backlogs or no activity in this area at all.

In addition, the Memex 'Law Enforcement Solution: Case' casework system is covered in this chapter. This system, produced by SAS Ltd, has the ability to deal with entities within records under the concept of **'people, objects, location, events'** (POLE). This approach to handling casework can save time and money within policing organisations, which are faced with the other options of trying to link together disparate systems and then copying and pasting intelligence and information into spreadsheets. It could be argued that the costs in time and money can outweigh the cost of purchasing a bespoke system to deal effectively with casework. Perhaps police services should compare their performances with similar services and seek out the best methods in seeking better performance with forensics. It is of interest to note that there is an extensive body of research in various disciplines to point the way ahead but that, frustratingly, old ways and resistance to change are still rife.

There is one major piece of advice from experience that I can offer and that is that police businesses should invest to maintain the expertise and quality working processes of their forensic services, for by this means they will gain most benefit from systems like SICAR and Treadmark. This does not mean bogging those services down in a bureaucratic 'tick the box' accreditation nightmare where staff can only function in a work-to-rule environment rather than by quality training, performance management, and running ongoing continued professional development (CPD).

The model used by the International Association of Arson Investigators (IAAI) is an excellent example. At the introductory levels students and new employees can take 'evidence technician' and then progress to 'fire investigation technician', and finally, once established in the actual work of a fire investigator, can study for 'certified fire investigator' (CFI). Those with the CFI qualification have to attend training events and maintain their expertise and must renew their CFI certification every 5 years. None of this process is designed to bury the fire investigators in a bureaucratic morass that bogs a field force down and causes poor performance.

The process with regard to CSIs is a similar one and the National Institute of Justice (NIJ) in the United States has sponsored the IAAI 'evidence technician' online study and qualification. There are over 30,000 persons logged in taking this course, which is a far larger number of students than there are IAAI members, so this facility is being well used. 'Evidence Technician' can easily become the introductory course for aspiring CSIs as well as fire investigators, for it covers the essential skills and processes for dealing with and packaging forensic exhibits, giving organisations a standard training package that is recognised.

One of the major advantages for forensic management is that, by using SICAR or Treadmark, management can effectively manage footwear evidence retrievals and results.

General Information on Foster & Freeman Shoeprint, Image, Capture, and Retrieval System (SICAR)

This section is reproduced by permission of Foster & Freeman Ltd, as is the casework example of the Coventry murder, where footwear evidence and the use of SICAR were pivotal in solving the case.

There are many computerised systems available for footwear and tyre track analysis, of which the most comprehensive and most widely used is SICAR. SICAR enables footwear marks and tyre tracks from a crime scene to be identified and linked with footwear marks and tyre tracks found at other crime scenes or in the possession of a suspect. It is used by law-enforcement and forensic agencies throughout the world from the United States and Australia to Europe and the Middle East. It stores footwear sole unit and tyre tread patterns in the form of images and associated text and is simple to use yet powerful in action, combining the skill of the human being in recognising the components of a complex design with the speed of computer searching and data retrieval.

SICAR 6 works on Windows 7, XP, and Vista.

SICAR is available as either a stand-alone system or as part of a network, which can be tailored to the individual user's needs. A SICAR network allows each installation on the network to access the other SICAR databases distributed across that network, aiding the task of crime solving across arbitrary police borders.

Versions of SICAR may be

- **Full SICAR installation**
- **Data entry terminal** that will allow users to create records and enter information that can be analysed by users with a full SICAR installation (particularly useful at remote sites)
- **Database viewer,** allowing monitoring of records submitted for identification and matching
- **Library viewer,** which will allow users to search and view SoleMate and/or TreadMate (see below) and also to create their own reference database collection for use alongside

SICAR Reference Databases

SICAR has two reference databases associated with it: **SoleMate** for footwear and TreadMate for tyres.

- **SoleMate** is the most extensive footwear database in use in the world and comprises records of footwear showing both a print and a photograph of the sole unit and photographs of the footwear uppers along with brand, model, and availability information. This is updated quarterly in line with the footwear industry's seasonal changes of footwear.

- **TreadMate** shows images of tyre treads and is updated annually. Both SoleMate and TreadMate link together sole units or tyres using similar patterns, such as when a brand uses the same sole unit with a new logo or when a sole unit pattern is used by a different brand. This means that if the investigating officer finds a pattern similar to his questioned one, he immediately has a group of very comparable prints to examine without having to continue to work through the entire set of search results.

SoleMate

SoleMate, the SICAR-compatible reference shoe print database, is arguably the most comprehensive and up-to-date footwear mark database currently available (Figure 8.1). Over the past 12 years, Foster & Freeman have developed a considerable number of important contacts, including with major brand names, in the footwear industry. This allows them to collect new footwear marks prior to their release to the retail market, ensuring that users receive timely information with updates quarterly. Approximately 1,000 brand names are represented by approximately 28,000 footwear records from the UK, United States, China, and Europe. SoleMate footwear mark records are multi-image and comprise a print of the sole, a photograph of the sole, and composite image of four views of the upper plus brand, model, and availability information (where available). These records comprise mainly sportswear, work wear, and casual wear and include many well known brands such as Nike, Adidas, Reebok, Puma, Skechers, Ellesse, Fila, Ben Sherman, DC Shoes, Etnies, ES, Vans, Caterpillar, Merrell, and Dr. Martens. SoleMate uses the same footwear reference system as the suppliers so that it is easy to trace further information when required.

Figure 8.1 Examples of SICAR SoleMate images.

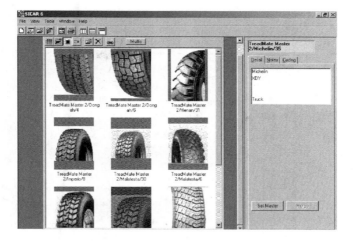

Figure 8.2 Examples of TreadMate images.

TreadMate

TreadMate is an extensive international tyre database comprising approximately 8,000 records (Figure 8.2). As with SoleMate, each record is provided with brand and model information plus, where possible, notes on the tyre's availability.

Both SoleMate and TreadMate group together records of different brands that use the same sole or tread pattern or from the same brand where there is a minor difference such as the introduction of a new logo. These marks groups allow the user to take into consideration the range of possible footwear or tyres that could have made the print and to allow some indication of how common the pattern is. All records are fully precoded using the standard SICAR coding scheme to allow searching against shapes, brand logos, and text found on the footwear or tyre.

SICAR is provided with a free footwear and tyre samples database of approximately 500 records taken from SoleMate and TreadMate.

Operating Outline of System

There are three database types:

- **Scene of crime database**
- **Suspect database**
- **Reference database**

Users may set these up to suit their own needs and, depending on the configuration of their systems, can have as many of each as required. If these databases represent geographical areas, then they can be configured to be neighbours of each other so that users can start searching their own local areas, easily expand the search to neighbouring databases (areas), and gradually expand the area searched depending on the search results.

The user selects which database he wants to create a record in. All records comprise text and images. The text fields are fully configurable. Images can be entered directly from a camera, scanner, or preexisting image file. Each record can have multiple images showing different views of the same shoe or tyre. The record is then coded with shapes from one of 10 footwear shape families, with the option of allocating the shape to a selected area of the footwear sole unit, brand logos, and text found on the footwear or shapes from one of the nine families of tyre shapes (Figure 8.3).

The user specifies which database(s) he wants to search and looks for records matching the one created. Searches on shapes, logos, and text may also be carried out without creating a record in advance. Whilst the user can search in any available database, the recommended methodology is to first search in the reference library, comprising all reference databases whether SoleMate, TreadMate, or user-generated ones, where a full image, and hence full coding, of the footwear or tyre is available. Imagine trying to search a partial crime scene print showing the toe area of a shoe against a scene-of-crime database. The same shoe might already exist in the scene-of-crime databases but, again, only as a partial print, maybe of the heel area. There is absolutely no possibility that these two prints would ever be matched.

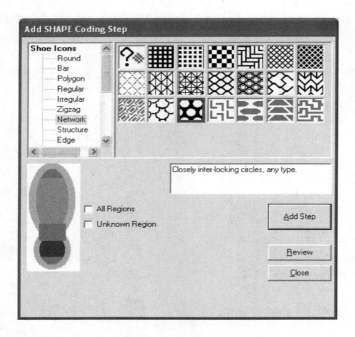

Figure 8.3 Coding shapes, brand logos, text selector features, and tyre coding shapes. (Reproduced by permission of Foster & Freeman Ltd.)

However, if each is searched and matched in a reference library, then each of the two scene-of-crime prints can be matched to the relevant reference prints and hence to each other. If no match is found in the reference library, then the next option is to search all the crime and suspect databases, bearing in mind the previous problems. In this case, the user has the option of starting to search locally and expanding the search as described before.

Alternatively, searches can be carried out on any text criteria such as dates, addresses, names, sizes, MO, operator, manufacturer, etc. depending on the fields configured.

Search results are produced in order of best match for shape searching and in alpha-numeric order for text searches. They can be displayed as multiple thumbnails or single, larger images as the user wishes.

Search results reveal individual large images or thumbnails with several images on a page.

Regardless of the search specified or the databases searched, once a matching record is found, a link can be made from the query record to the matching record. The user can then examine the Links Tree for his query record, which will, as a minimum, show the matching record plus any other links made to the matching record and the reason for the links (Figure 8.4). These other records will all have similar shape, text, or logo coding and may be from

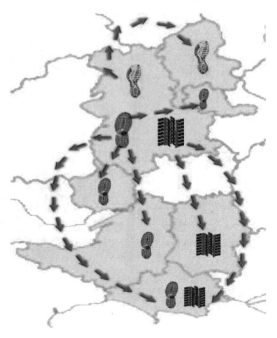

Figure 8.4 Example of information extracted from a Links Tree showing related footwear marks and tyre track information in different regions. (Reproduced by permission of Foster & Freeman Ltd.)

scenes of crime, suspects, or marks groups. Additionally, they may be records which have been explicitly linked for some other reason, such as two crimes being committed in the same area or two offenders being known to each other. The user will be able to examine and analyse the Links Tree to extract additional intelligence for crime solving.

SICAR also provides information about how common a particular pattern is in specified geographical areas between certain dates and a variety of statistical reports. It interfaces with scene-of-crime management systems for more efficient data input and crime scene analysis.

A SICAR Casework Example: Incident No. 20410— The Coventry Murder

At the end of October 2004, a woman was violently beaten to death in her home in Coventry in the English Midlands. West Midlands Police very quickly apprehended a male suspect, who was found to have blood on his socks but not on his shoes. Footwear marks in blood were discovered in the kitchen of the victim and photographed as evidence. The identification of the shoe brand and model, along with other evidence, would be vital to the investigation.

Partial Identification of the Footwear Mark

The crime scene footwear mark image was sent to the UK Forensic Science Service in Birmingham, where staff identified the shoe as one retailed under the brand name of 'Mountain Ridge'. They could offer no further details, providing the West Midland Police with the limited information they possessed in the form of a photocopy of an inked reference footwear mark sample on a sheet of paper.

The investigating officers took a lucky guess that this was a walking shoe and visited retailers of 'outdoor pursuit' equipment to try to find the source of the Mountain Ridge footwear. Eventually they discovered that this brand was unique to 'JJB Sports', a large chain of shoe retailers in the UK.

Unfortunately, there was no footwear with this sole pattern in stock at the time of the officer's visit. Furthermore, on contacting the company's head office, the investigators thought that they had reached a dead end when the JJB Sports Company staff were unable to recognise the sole pattern as matching any of their shoes.

The Footwear Mark Is Referred to Foster & Freeman

Within minutes of contacting Foster & Freeman Ltd, investigators had confirmed that the footwear mark found at the crime scene had been produced by a shoe from the Mountain Ridge-branded range and that there were two models using soles with that particular pattern: a shoe called 'College Low' and an ankle boot called 'College Mid', which had the same design but was

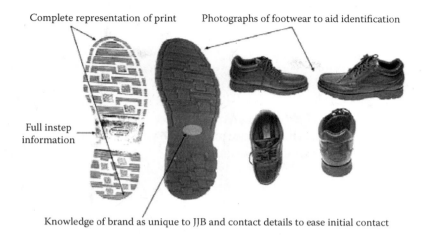

Complete representation of print   Photographs of footwear to aid identification

Full instep information

Knowledge of brand as unique to JJB and contact details to ease initial contact

Figure 8.5 Shoe images supplied in the Coventry murder case. (Reproduced by permission of Foster & Freeman Ltd.)

slightly higher. Foster & Freeman were also able to say the footwear was available in-store from mid-2002, as well as providing complete images of the sole, showing information in the instep area and photographs of the uppers of the shoes (Figure 8.5). Also, importantly, the company was able to say that no other brand was known to have used this sole.

This information provided investigating officers with sufficient information to go back to JJB Sports and not only locate the store but also trace the shop's copy of the actual receipt issued to the suspect when purchasing the footwear.

Court Case Results in a Successful Conviction

The case went to court in the spring of 2005, with the suspect being convicted of murder in October 2005. The information provided by Foster & Freeman using SoleMate was acknowledged by the West Midland Police as being 'most helpful as the identification of the shoe brand and model was vital to the investigation and together with other evidence, had assisted the police in presenting the prosecution's case'. See http://fosterfreeman.com for further information on SICAR.

General Information on Treadmark Footwear Evidence Storage, Screening, and Comparison Software

This section is reproduced by permission of Crime Scene Examination Equipment Ltd UK and Crime Scene Products (Florida) Inc. The outline of how Treadmark is used operationally is supplied by the Leicestershire Constabulary UK with permission to publish, as is the linked burglary case example.

Treadmark has proved to be a valuable tool in managing footwear evidence. Making use of an organisation's own internal computer network, or in the stand-alone 'Express' version, it provides a database of footmarks found at crime scenes and images of footwear taken from suspects and persons in custody. In either the network or stand-alone versions, Treadmark provides for users anywhere in the world the UK National Police Improvement Authority's National Footwear Reference Collection (NFRC) of over 19,000 coded shoe patterns, which is constantly updated on Internet servers. In addition, users can add new patterns found in their own jurisdiction and share the data with the NFRC, if they wish, for all users to benefit.

The NFRC database in the Express version is accessible to all those who have an interest in footwear evidence—for example, forensic science students or small police services with limited resources. To cater to small police services, a Treadmark Express licence covers five stand-alone computers under the same licence and the software enables Treadmark Express users to send casework *by agreement* to one another. This facility enables smaller organisations using Treadmark Express to send or receive casework with other small services across a state, or to a Treadmark networked in, say, a large police service or a state laboratory.

Calibrated images of footmarks can easily be input to Treadmark by crime scene investigators. Custody officers have an easy means of taking images of the soles of the shoes taken from suspects. Footwear expert examiners can process the images—identifying the pattern code, marking up damage features, and searching the database to make scene-to-scene and scene-to-suspect links. Using the Treadmark software, these links are added to a 'crime series' that in turn forms the basis of valuable intelligence reports.

Treadmark models the processes used generically by footwear specialist examiners in that once a search is made, responses can be checked side by side, measured for comparison, and overlaid to enable users to screen cases effectively for intelligence linking as well as sorting suitable cases for submission for expert examination and matching for court.

Treadmark has a report-writing facility, saving valuable time once set up to user requirements, and can generate performance data, enabling forensics management to monitor casework and respond to staff needs.

In addition to providing codes for identified shoe patterns from the database, Treadmark has a defined set of easy-to-use descriptors to file marks not found in the reference database, so searching is enabled in either the coded or uncoded scenarios. Once a reference code is received, the descriptor filed cases are easily edited with the correct codes. In addition, the software gives the pattern frequency for each coded case, enabling estimations of how rare or otherwise the pattern is for use by analysts.

In dealing with suspects' shoes, these are scanned using a standard computer scanner. Crime Scene Investigation Equipment Ltd UK and Crime

Scene Products (Florida) Inc. can provide clear, polycarbonate sheets to protect the scanner from contamination, and best advice is to pack the clear protective sheet with each shoe. The advantage of scanning is that it minimises the possibility of contamination and provides a good quality colour image of the shoe sole together with any other trace evidence attaching to or staining the sole at the time of securely packaging the footwear. The use of ink, WD40, or veggie print pads to 'print' offenders' footwear is to be discouraged because of potential contamination issues. In any event, a computer scanner is not intrusive and actually cheaper to use.

Thus, with Treadmark, the lockups or police charging stations should be equipped with scanners to capture footwear images from those in custody, as should the scenes of crime examination lab. The scenes of crime department can then easily deal with screening the casework and providing links for the crime analysts. The advantage of links enabled to the forensic science laboratory expert reporting scientists for peer review is obvious (Figure 8.6).

Treadmark enables measurements in all images for comparison purposes to be accurate to 1/10 of a millimetre, no matter what magnification the viewed image is set at. The overlay facility makes one of the marks semitransparent for making comparisons if a match is found to appear as a mechanical fit for screening purposes, easily revealing damage features and wear patterns in level 2 detail marks and thus making screening for reference to footwear by police and CSIs relatively easy.

One advantage of the Treadmark system is that it only takes about a couple of hours to train a user to start using the system. Once a scanner is installed,

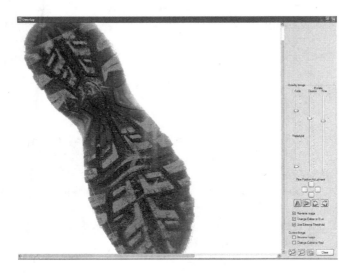

Figure 8.6 Treadmark main screen showing how simple it is to make overlay comparisons from search responses. (Reproduced by permission of Crime Scene Investigation Equipment Ltd.)

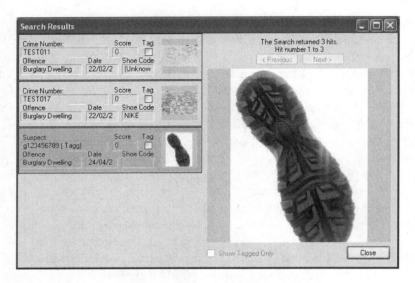

Figure 8.7 Treadmark search response from which responses are selected for measurement, mark up of overlay. (Reproduced by permission of Crime Scene Investigation Equipment Ltd.)

the software enables the user to calibrate it, making every scanned image available for accurate measurement from then on. In the case of importing photographs of marks, the software is easily updated from the scale in the photograph, enabling accurate measurement. Measurements are accurate at any screen magnification. The original images are not altered in any way as the system works from copies and every action is monitored with a complete audit trail for court if required.

Like SICAR, Treadmark enables the imaging, capture of scenes of crime shoe mark images, their identification for coding, and search against the scanned footwear of potential suspects (Figures 8.7 and 8.8).

Treadmark in the Leicestershire Constabulary: An Outline

The following section was supplied by the Leicestershire Constabulary and is included with their permission. The Leicester PowerPoint presentation is included with the CD ROM.

Within the Leicestershire Constabulary, Treadmark is networked, enabling the following facilities:

- **Computerised intelligence database**
- **Footwear images from detainees stored**
- **Footwear images found at crime scenes stored**

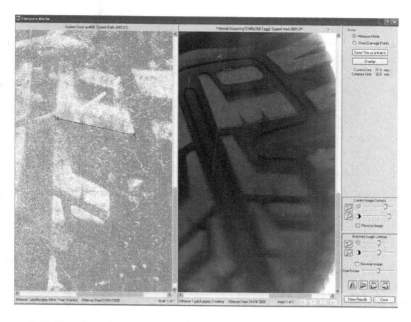

Figure 8.8 Treadmark measurement screen. Measurements between points are accurate to 1/10 of a millimetre. (Reproduced by permission of Crime Scene Investigation Equipment Ltd.)

- **Has the ability to link scene-to-scene and scene-to-suspect with footwear**
- **Provides valuable intelligence**

The Legal Aspects of Using Treadmark in the UK

In January 2006 the law changed with the introduction of Serious and Organised Crime and Police Act 2005, Section 118. This amended the powers contained within the Police and Criminal Evidence Act 1984 (PACE) so that an officer or designated person (e.g., a detention officer) **'can take footwear impressions from any person arrested for a recordable offence'**. This can be done with or without consent. An impression may only be taken without consent where a person has been arrested for, charged with, or informed that he will be reported for a recordable offence and he has not previously had an impression of his footwear taken in the course of the investigation for the offence.

- Taken with consent, Section 118(2): **'The consent must be in writing and recorded in the custody record'**.
- Taken without consent, Section 118(3): **'Footwear can be taken without consent'**.

- Section 118(5): The officer **'will inform the detained person that footwear may be subject of a speculative search'.** Although the powers apply to a person arrested, charged, or reported for **any** recordable offence, *in Leicestershire, footwear will be scanned into Treadmark for specific crimes.*

(Note that in the Leicester business model and in its working practices, Treadmark is used in such a way as to fit in with the service's resources.)

Thus, footwear scans are only taken in Leicestershire under the following scenarios: All detainees brought into custody who

- Have a history of burglary
- Have been arrested for burglary
- Are suspected of burglary of any type
- Are distraction burglars (even if in custody for another offence)
- Have been arrested for taking vehicles without consent
- Have been arrested for theft from a motor vehicle
- Have been arrested for robbery

The Police Officer's Role

- To establish whether footwear impressions are required, either due to the suspect's arrest for a qualifying offence, or if not actually arrested (etc.) for burglary/taking a vehicle without consent or robbery on that occasion or for some other recordable offence
- To check the appropriate records of the detainee to determine if he or she has a previous record for burglary of any type and to advise the custody sergeant and detention officer that the detainee's footwear needs to be scanned onto Treadmark

Procedure in Preserving Footwear Evidence

If an officer needs to seize and preserve footwear for forensic evidence:

- Package in medium size windowed paper exhibit bag with sole facing outward and scan through bag

If an officer is seizing footwear for a specific reason, the officer should ensure that

- Footwear is still scanned onto Treadmark and that relevant notes are entered in the Treadmark comments box to this effect to enable speculative search against other crime scenes and sharing with bordering police services

The Internal Processes by Footwear Examiners

Footwear examiners at Forensic HQ examine all the scanned footwear against crime marks and report to the area analyst on any links they find. If officers believe they have a detainee who may have been involved in crime, they should ask for an urgent search. To aid in this process, information on processes and procedures is near to every Treadmark scanner in the force. Area briefings also advise on patterns of footwear being left at scenes for intelligence purposes.

A Typical Leicestershire Volume Crime Linked Case Example

From October 2007 to February 2008, a division ('CW LPU') experienced an increase in burglary of dwellings, particularly on Beat 49. There were no evidential leads to link the crimes to possible suspects. There was, however, limited intelligence to indicate who was responsible.

On 12 February 2008, officers were called to a burglary in progress at a premise in Leicester. Suspect 1 was arrested inside the property and was charged with this offence.

It was strongly suspected that suspect 1 was responsible for other crimes in the area; however, officers needed something to reinforce these suspicions.

Footwear marks had been recovered by scenes of crime officers (SOCOs) from burglary scenes on Beat 49 (Figure 8.9). Despite several of the footwear

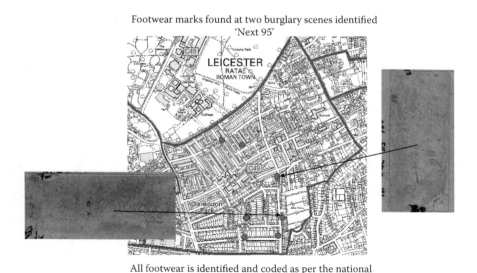

Footwear marks found at two burglary scenes identified 'Next 95'

All footwear is identified and coded as per the national coding system i.e. Next 95

Figure 8.9 Footwear recoveries mapping from Beat 49, Leicester. (Reproduced with permission of the Leicestershire Constabulary.)

marks being classed as 'poor' quality and not of value evidentially, the following example shows how valuable the marks were for intelligence purposes.

The seven burglary offences where footwear marks were found by SOCOs were put to suspect 1 and he admitted committing these offences. Suspect 1 also admitted to a further 10 offences; coupled with the offence where suspect 1 was found at the crime scene, this totals 18 burglary of dwelling offences detected.

Without the intelligence link provided by Treadmark on scene links, suspect 1 may not have admitted any further offences.

Advice from Leicestershire Constabulary Regarding Treadmark

Treadmark is a valuable intelligence source, which can be fed into analytical products by the area analysts, but scene marks need to be preserved and scanned onto Treadmark and footwear from detainees needs to be scanned onto Treadmark TO MAKE IT WORK.

The preceding example is typical of casework regularly produced daily by the Leicester forensic services team, placing them amongst the highest achievers in the UK in 2011 for results with footwear evidence. The model they have in place also enables the expansion of DNA matches and latent print identifications into the areas of 'softer' forms of forensic evidence, thus increasing detections significantly, as was the experience in the Metropolitan Police.

Intelligence Software Solutions

Modern police services invest in information technology solutions in order to search for and share knowledge in two main forms in the intelligence area, which, depending on the application at the time, are deemed to be either 'information' or 'intelligence'. In previous chapters, the three generic intelligence assets were discussed (i.e., knowledge, systems, and intelligence assets). Included next is an example of a modern software network solution to case management. **Memex Law Enforcement Solution: Case** is a system that offers the flexibility to make use of 'information' and turn it where appropriate into the other two system asset forms. The Memex product is produced by an international company, SAS, that offers performance management solutions to governments, industry, and businesses.

In my role as the Met's forensic intelligence manager, with my staff I had access to a Memex system for crime intelligence storage and search called CRIMINT and its updated version in 2007 CRIMINT Plus. CRIMINT operated mainly at crime levels 1 and 2 under the UK National Intelligence Model (NIM); a separate level 2 server catered to cover cross-divisional intelligence. Each level 1 server was dedicated to a single division, so searches would have to be across selected divisions, but the level 2 server covered the entire police business groups in single searches. The Met Police solved, to some extent, the cross searching of disparate systems by producing its own in-house data warehousing system: the Integrated Information Platform (IIP).

The following section describes a modern system that integrates police case data, saving time and money. In addition, because crime reports, intelligence, custody, and statement forms are searchable (unless confidential or restricted to view by users), it provides a potentially useful facility for forensic services to employ for forensic intelligence purposes. The Memex casework system is a remarkable facility that is flexible enough to cater to most requirements of modern police services. In addition, Memex produces 'Law Enforcement: Custody' network software fully supporting records in the custody environment and Memex (SAS) provides consultancy for police services.

Memex Law Enforcement: Case Software—A Police Casework Solution

This section has been reproduced by permission of SAS (Memex).

Overview: Case Formation

Memex Case can build any kind of file type required and is entirely determined and configurable by the customer. The provided case file builder allows the user to select the case file type he or she wants to compile.

The case file builder can be launched from within a crime investigation or can be launched by clicking the case file builder menu option from within the Memex Enterprise Solution.

When building a case, the user may elect to create a new file or open a previously created one. However, Memex Case only displays previously created case files that the user has permission to view, which is itself dependent on the access permissions set within the case file record. The user permissions for viewing case files are controlled by the system administrator.

For new case files, the process is configurable by the customer, but as a default is set by Memex to prompt the user to select a file type from the mandatory file type field.

Again, this field can be configured by the customer to offer a default value, but initially is set to pre-arrest advice. The field selection is then interpreted by the file builder wizard and used to populate the list of appropriate manual of guidance (MG) forms. **Management guidance, or 'MG', forms** in the UK cover the range of forms used by police in recording written evidence and other aspects of dealing with police casework. These documents are stored in the police service systems and provide with permissions a searchable resource alongside other main police network systems. In the case of forensic intelligence, the notes and statements of CSIs, investigators, forensic scientists, etc. are available to search against crime forensic data for use by analysts.

MG forms list:

MG1	File front sheet
MG2	Initial witness assessment
MG3	Report to Crown Prosecutor for charging decision
MG3A	Further report to Crown Prosecutor for charging decision
MG4	Charge sheet
MG4A	Conditional bail—grant/variation
MG4B	Request to vary conditional bail
MG4C	Surety/security
MG5	Case summary
MG6	Case file information
MG6B	Police officer's disciplinary record
MG6C	Police schedule of nonsensitive unused material
MG6D	Police schedule of sensitive material
MG6E	Disclosure officer's report
MG7	Remand application
MG8	Breach of bail conditions
MG9	Witness list
MG10	Witness nonavailability
MG11	Witness statement
MG12	Exhibit list
MG13	Application for order on conviction
MG15	Record of interview
MG18	Other offences (TIC)
MG19	Compensation claim
MG20	Further evidence/information report
MG(c)	Continuation sheet
MGFSP	Submission of case for scientific examination
MGNFA	'No further action' letter template

A configuration file, which is editable by a system administrator, allows case file types to be associated with any number of mandatory and optional MG forms and/or other documents. This provides flexibility in meeting future potential changes.

In the management of the content of all forensic services documents from electronic scene notes to reporting scientists and court statements, the potential of Memex Law Enforcement Solution: Case is a tempting proposition for organisations seeking to make best use of their investment in forensics.

Lifetime Case Information

Memex Case allows the user to start an automated search of the underlying database for any relevant records that should be in the case file. The user can reject any or all identified individual records or accept the search findings. The actual records themselves are not copied or moved in the process of associating them with the case file, but rather a link is created between the case and the original record. These links determine which records belong to which case file.

Memex Case also provides the ability to add any existing records to the case file from within the system, such as but not restricted to crime reports, single person records, vehicle reports, and so on. The records can be viewed at any point from within the case file by clicking the case records button, which displays a list of all accessible records held in the case. Any covert records that the user does not have permission to access are hidden from view.

Any additional material not already captured within the system, such as but not restricted to Microsoft Word documents, scanned images, and so on, may be attached to the case file at any time.

Case Linking

Memex has a case file building wizard that prepares all documents input into the system. This enables the cross search and correlation—in the case of the topics in this book, the notes and records of all forensic examinations, evidence statements, and legacy data—to enable analysts to make use of the information to turn it, with other intelligence, into forensic intelligence products for police tasking and coordination in a modern intelligence-led environment.

The case file preparation wizard manages the preparation of the appropriate MG forms and their content. Where possible, the wizard autopopulates the MG form fields from the records and information attached to the case file builder, such as but not limited to the single person record, custody record, and offence.

The user can add any internal or external documents and forms relevant to the case. The document types can be any file type and are not restricted to Microsoft Word files. The system has the ability to select any existing record and add or link it to the case file (e.g., a single person record for any person involved in any capacity, a vehicle record, property, intelligence report, forensic findings, forensic results statements, CSI notes). Offences are linked automatically to the case file, as part of the wizard creation process.

Any records added to the case are not physically copied or moved to the case file, but rather a link is created to the original record, which remains in its own database area. As such, any changes to the original record can be viewed when the record is accessed from the case file. Memex Case used constrained value lists published by the UK National Police Improvement Agency (NPIA) via a code list management service.

As with all casework and intelligence systems, permissions to access case files are set by administrators and intelligence assessments are graded in the $5 \times 5 \times 5$ system described in Chapter 1.

Protected Records in Memex Case

Case files and their associated records can have two levels of security applied to them that are referred to as 'protected' and 'covert'. In the case of protected records, if the user is not on the access list, he or she can see that there is a record, but if he or she tries to open it, a message is triggered to contact the relevant administrator to obtain permission to view. In the case of covert records, their existence will not show in search responses so the user will not be aware of their existence.

Forensic Intelligence: A Summary

Intelligence-led policing benefits from modern casework handling systems and the focus in forensic intelligence is in linking cases, linking offenders to cases, supporting crime analysis, and targeting resources to find the evidence that results in detections and prosecutions. Thus, forensic intelligence is enabled by having access to systems like Memex Case, which is a complete police casework solution from the crime to the courtroom. (See www.sas.com for further information on Memex Case.)

In developing forensic intelligence inputs to the Met Police's CRIMINT system, a template called QQCSE for CSIs was produced to cover details of crime scene examinations; the protocol was to create an intelligence log in cases where CSIs had discovered potentially useful intelligence in the course of their work. The QQCSE form was created to assist the CSIs in adhering to the data standards required by the Metropolitan Police, and it had customised fields covering most of the commonly found evidence types and other data required to complete a quality intelligence log. In addition, intelligence logs were created where coded forensic marks were found or where forensic crime scene links had been established. Intelligence logs were also required for strategic crime types where it was agreed in the forensic strategy for the crime type that CRIMINT logs would be created.

The reason for CRIMINT input was that although the details of forensic examinations were recorded in the crime report system, there are areas of research and information not recorded on crime reports because they are to do with various forms of intelligence sources. The inclusion of forensic intelligence logs covered the risk of missing vital links by researchers and analysts. Keep in mind John Minderman's advice (Chapter 1) that forensics-like behaviours can occur at any crime level, so intelligence must be available so that those involved in producing intelligence products for police tasking can find it. In police working practices, however, some individuals regard the intelligence system as a specially reserved place for what they decree is intelligence, and they restrict access to stakeholders such as crime scene examiners. The point of view put forward in this book is that information can become useful intelligence in light of other information and that what seems to be intelligence can, in other circumstances, become just useful background information; therefore, it is best to err on the side of caution.

Intelligence applications of forensic recoveries are developing in many police services and I believe that, from the forensic intelligence development exercise in the Metropolitan Police, many useful ideas and processes were developed. I hope that those who read this book can use or further develop them.

Did we succeed? Yes, we did and the following is a matter of record in the Met's systems:

- Over 10,000 crime scenes were linked in the early territorial police (TP) development.
- From the linked scenes in the TP development, 3,000 extra detections accrued.
- Over 6,000 persons were arrested in Operations Halifax 1 to Halifax 8 and some 10,000 eliminated from enquiries.
- Biometrically identified and linked/associated with cannabis cultivation sites linked to organised crime were 1,800 foreign nationals.
- Large databases covering each major evidence type were maintained and researched daily.
- Every latent print match and DNA link or match was looked at daily for further development if possible.
- After a slow start in 2004, the Forensic Intelligence Unit increased production of problem and target intelligence profiles (input in the CRIMINT level 2 server) following the reorganisation of the unit into Hard Evidence Research & Processing and Forensic Problem Profiles. These were input to the Met Intelligence Model for police action at the rate of approximately one a day. Nearly 1,000 assessments were made between 2004 and 2007. Most of the target profiles were around biometric matches, so charges and detections resulted.
- As part of the TP intelligence team with the pan-London Crime Squad, dozens of forensic identifications were achieved in support of distraction burglary operations. The TP team cut the offences from 300 a month down to 35 a month.
- A converter of illegal firearms produced in Lithuania and smuggled into the UK, resulting in a number of deaths of youths, was closed

down following an intelligence assessment covering the batches of gas guns converted. This was in 2006/2007 just prior to setting up the UK National Ballistics Intelligence Service (NaBIS).

- Work was carried out on a number of high-profile cases in the Met Intelligence Bureau, some of which were covered as major news items.
- The Oxford Street department store serial arsonist was arrested before any deaths or injuries occurred, following the input of a linked scene problem profile and MetBats briefing slide with CCTV photographs.
- A Partnership Desk was created with links to external organisations and academia, resulting in a number of solved cases—particularly arson cases.
- A number of prolific career criminals who engaged in working practices to attempt to defeat divisional policing by travelling across forces were convicted.
- Organised crime commercial burglaries were solved. One case, in particular, in 2005, involved the stealing of hi-tech video equipment from companies supporting major movie productions in the UK. Footwear evidence provided the links and intelligence from a forensic linked scene branched off to point officers in the right direction to deal with a professional criminal network.
- Work on hard evidence links revealed the activities of offenders leaving trails of linked DNA cases. These often revealed the activities of 'prolific and persistent offenders' (PPOs). Not only were we able to use forensic intelligence to find and define PPOs, but also each of the larger linked series resulted in massive amounts of judicial disposals (or detections) once the offender was known and processed. The maximum number of detections for *one* such person in 2006 was 2,500 detections accruing from a 17-linked DNA series. There were many more and it is possible that, with no management of the forensic intelligence, the 2,500 case offenders would have been dealt with for just the 17 linked cases. The Forensic Intelligence Unit produced problem and target profiles around linked cases literally daily.
- An organised crime team of confidence tricksters was identified and problem/target profiles created. Some arrests were made in 2007, but I believe the individuals were still committing offences into 2012! It is all about the tasking of police and there are still problems with the UK NIM, which the UK NPIA is working on.

Is forensic intelligence worth the effort? My opinion is that it is worth the effort and that not to develop processes within policing organisations to deal with it is inefficient and wasteful. I look forward to hearing about the experiences of readers, for, with some ingenuity, forensic intelligence can be implemented at little cost using facilities already available in most police services.

The UK Forensic 21 Programme is embracing forensic intelligence and at this time, at least in the UK, it is becoming mainstream. Users are starting to use forensic science in new directions and it is my belief that forensic intelligence will become one of the leading facets of twenty-first century forensic science.

Forensic intelligence is already there in every policing organisation. It just needs a slightly different view on forensics to see it.

References

1. http://oxforddictionaries.com/definition/forensic
2. http://oxforddictionaries.com/definition/intelligence
3. Ribaux, O., A. Girod, S. J. Walsh, P. Margot, S. Mizahi, and V. Clivaz. 2003. Forensic intelligence and crime analysis. *Law Probability and Risk* 2:47–60.
4. Milne, R. 2001. Operation Bigfoot—A volume crime data project. *Science and Justice: Journal of the Forensic Science Society* 41 (3): 215–217.
5. Lambourne, G. 1984. *The fingerprint story.* London: Harrap, p. 171. ISBN 0245-53963-8.
6. Cherrill, F. 1954. *The fingerprint system at Scotland Yard.* London: Her Majesty's Stationery Office.
7. Henry, E. 1900. Report to the Belper Committee.
8. Inman, K., and N. Rudin. 2000. *Principles and practice of criminalistics.* Boca Raton, FL: CRC Press, p. 32. ISBN 0-8493-8127-4.
9. Canter, D. 1995. *Criminal shadows.* New York: HarperCollins. ISBN 10:0006383947.
10. Metropolitan Police website http://www.met.police.uk/crimefigures/
11. Canter, D., and D. Youngs. 2009. *Investigative psychology.* Chichester, W. Sussex, UK: Wiley. ISBN 978-0-470-02397-6. (Chapter 1 discusses the propensity for police and CSIs to do the work necessary to attain conviction rather than to fuel systematic research. ROC curve, pp. 409–410; the Radex and SSA, pp. 111–113; bridging policing and psychology, pp. 15–19; decay function, p. 75; geographical profiling, pp. 404–406.)
12. The International Association of Crime Analysts website: http://www.iaca.net/about.asp
13. New York Police department website: http://www.nyc.gov/html/nypd/html/crime_prevention/crime_statistics.shtml
14. Moses, K. R., P. Higgins, M. McCabe, S. Probhalkar, and S. Swann. Automated fingerprint ID system (AFIS). NIJ website (Chapter 6, Figure 6-2, pp. 6–9).
15. Crime in England and Wales 2009/2010. UK Home Office Parliamentary reply. *Hansard Reference* vol. 497 col. 836–840 2008/2009.
16. Napier, T., and F. Pearson. 2002. Scene linking: Using footwear mark databases. *Journal of the Forensic Science Society* (39): 42.
17. From NPIA UK National Footwear Reference Collection November 2011, which the Treadmark software with this book accesses online.
18. Link for download from Microsoft: http://research.microsoft.com/en-us/projects/nodexl/
19. Ratcliffe, J. 2008. *Intelligence-led policing.* Cullompton, Devon, UK: Willan. ISBN 978-1-84392-339-8. (Audit Commission Report 1993 findings, pp. 36–37; COMPSTAT, pp. 76–79.)
20. International Association of Intelligence Analysts. Copyright notice: Source Intelligence Analysis Net: http://www.intelligenceanalysis.net/index.htm

21. Link to website National Institute of Justice USA: http://www.nij.gov/
22. Canter, D., and D. R. Youngs. 2009. Presentation IA-IP Conference.
23. John Birkett, J. 1989. Scientific scene linking. *Science and Justice: Journal of the Forensic Science Society* 29 (4): 271–284.
24. The use of forensic science in volume crime investigations: A review of the research literature. Home Office report 43/05. Source: Home Office UK website: http://webarchive.nationalarchives.gov.uk/20110220105210/rds.homeoffice.gov.uk/rds/pdfs05/rdsolr4305.pdf
25. Bodziak, W. J. 1999. *Footwear impression evidence.* Boca Raton, FL: CRC Press. ISBN 0-8493-1045-8.
26. Milne, R. 1997. The electrostatic lifting of shoe, tyre and finger marks at crime scenes. *International Journal of the Fingerprint Society, Fingerprint Whorld* 23 (88): 53–64.
27. O'Shea, T., K. Nicholls, J. Archer, E. Hughes, and J. Tatum. 2002. Crime analysis in America. Centre for Public Policy, University of South Alabama.
28. *Evidence Technology Magazine* (US publication). 2011. Vol. 9 (May–June).
29. Chaplinsky, J. M. Can forensic trace evidence provide useful, timely and accurate intelligence? University of South Florida. http://www.sarasota.usf.edu/Academics/CAS/Capstone/2010-2011/Criminology/CHAPLINSKI-Forensic%20Intelligence.pdf
30. Clarke, R., and J. Eck. 2003. *Become a problem-solving crime analyst.* London: Jill Dando Institute of Crime Science, University College London WC1H 9QU. ISBN 0-9545607-0-1. (Brantingham crime patter theory, pp. 17–18)
31. Shane, J. M. 2010. *Performance management in police agencies: A conceptual framework.* New York: John Jay College of Criminal Justice, p. 21.
32. Webber, A. M. 1991. Crime and management: An interview with New York Police Commissioner Lee P. Brown. *Harvard Business Review* May/June: 111–126.
33. NPIA Forensics 21. February /March 2010. Source open Internet UK Home Office. Update forensics21@npia.pnn.police.uk
34. Receiver operator characteristics (ROC). Wikipedia http://en.wikipedia.org/wiki/Receiver_operating_characteristic
35. Milne, R. 1997. The Pathfinder wireless mark lifter and electrostatic dust mark lifting. *Journal of the Fingerprint Society.*

Index